THE
FAMILY
TREE

AUTHOR'S FAMILY CHART

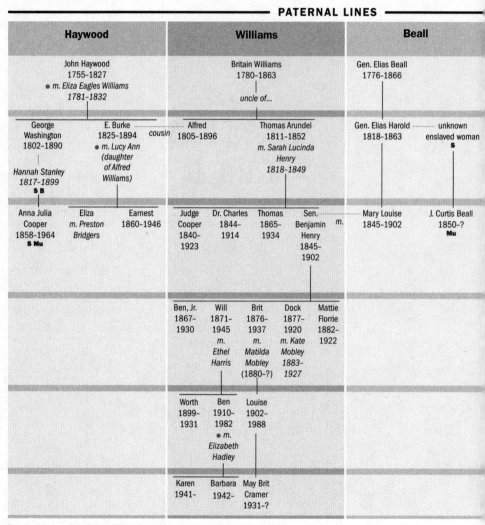

PATERNAL LINES

Haywood		Williams		Beall	
John Haywood 1755–1827 ● m. Eliza Eagles Williams 1781–1832		Britain Williams 1780–1863 *uncle of...*		Gen. Elias Beall 1776–1866	
George Washington 1802–1890 | Hannah Stanley 1817–1899 **S B**	E. Burke 1825–1894 ● m. Lucy Ann (daughter of Alfred Williams) *cousin*	Alfred 1805–1896	Thomas Arundel 1811–1852 m. Sarah Lucinda Henry 1818–1849	Gen. Elias Harold 1818–1863	unknown enslaved woman **S**
Anna Julia Cooper 1858–1964 **S Mu**	Eliza m. Preston Bridgers / Earnest 1860–1946	Judge Cooper 1840–1923 / Dr. Charles 1844–1914 / Thomas 1865–1934	Sen. Benjamin Henry 1845–1902 *m.*	Mary Louise 1845–1902	J. Curtis Beall 1850–? **Mu**
		Ben, Jr. 1867–1930 / Will 1871–1945 m. Ethel Harris / Brit 1876–1937 m. Matilda Mobley (1880–?) / Dock 1877–1920 m. Kate Mobley 1883–1927 / Mattie Florrie 1882–1922			
		Worth 1899–1931 / Ben 1910–1982 ● m. Elizabeth Hadley / Louise 1902–1988			
		Karen 1941– / Barbara 1942– / May Brit Cramer 1931–?			

People not noted as **B**lack, **Mu**latto, or **S**lave were considered to be White.

Mobley	**Hadley-Moore**				

| | Thomas H. Moore
1804–1881 | James B. Moore
1814–1870 | | Jane Moore
1840–c.1920
S B | |

| James Monroe Mobley
1823–1903
m. Matilda Keziah Henry
1829–1879 | Sarah Ann Moore
1826–1895
m. William Henry Hadley
1826–1895 | Milford
1861–
1920
S Mu | Sog
1865–
1900
S Mu | Louis
1862–
1901
S Mu | *1st*
cousin | Lula Moore
1875–?
S Mu |

| Reuben
1847–1904 | Lula
1859–1954 | Frank
Hadley
1849–
1924 | Charley
Hadley
1850–
1876
m. Josie
Gordon | Joe
Hadley
1854–
1942 | Marion
Madison
"Buddie"
Hadley
1857–1931
m. Emma
Smith | Johnie Moore
1887–1912
Mu |

1st cousins of
Williams brothers

| John Ivey
1883–1958 | Kate
1883–1927
m. Dock
Williams | Henry
1856–
1935 | Norman
1874–1912 | Douglas
1890–
1957
m. Berta
Alverson | Bessie
1894–
1918 | Annie
Laura
Murrah
1887–
1982 | Clifford
1884–
1978 |

| John B.
"Bud"
1880–
1929 | Elizabeth
1912–2002
● m. Ben
Williams | Evelyn
1917–2001 | Lillian
1918–2010 | Louise Teel
1910–2002 |

Only family members who appear in the book are included in this chart.

THE
FAMILY
TREE

A Lynching in Georgia,
A Legacy of Secrets, and
My Search for the Truth

Karen Branan

ATRIA BOOKS

NEW YORK   LONDON   TORONTO   SYDNEY   NEW DELHI

ATRIA BOOKS
An Imprint of Simon & Schuster, Inc.
1230 Avenue of the Americas
New York, NY 10020

First Atria Books hardcover edition January 2016

ATRIA B O O K S and colophon are trademarks of Simon & Schuster, Inc.

For information about special discounts for bulk purchases, please contact Simon & Schuster Special Sales at 1-866-506-1949 or business@simonandschuster.com.

The Simon & Schuster Speakers Bureau can bring authors to your live event. For more information or to book an event contact the Simon & Schuster Speakers Bureau at 1-866-248-3049 or visit our website at www.simonspeakers.com.

Interior design by Kyoko Watanabe

Manufactured in the United States of America

10 9 8 7 6 5 4 3 2 1

Library of Congress Cataloging-in-Publication Data has been applied for.

ISBN: 978-1-4767-1718-0
ISBN: 978-1-4767-1720-3 (ebook)

This book is dedicated to
Edna and the "Ancient Mariners"

"O Man God, I beg that this that I ask for my enemies shall come to pass: That the South wind shall scorch their bodies and make them wither and shall not be tempered to them. That the North wind shall freeze their blood and numb their muscles and that it shall not be tempered to them. That the West wind shall blow away their life's breath and will not leave their hair to grow, and that their fingernails shall fall off and their bones shall crumble. That the East wind shall make their minds grow dark, their sight shall fail and their seed dry up so that they shall not multiply."

—An ancient Negro folk curse recorded
by Zora Neale Hurston

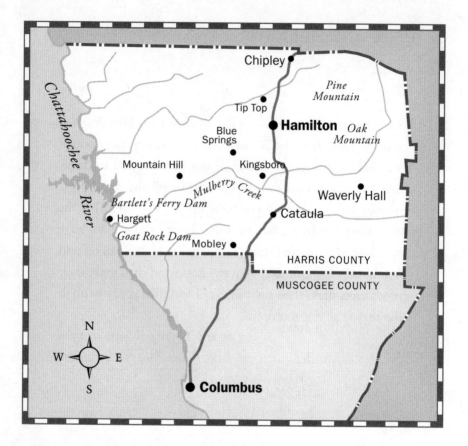

Chattahoochee River

Chipley

Pine Mountain

Tip Top

Blue Springs

Hamilton Oak Mountain

Mountain Hill

Kingsboro

Mulberry Creek

Waverly Hall

Bartlett's Ferry Dam

Hargett

Cataula

Goat Rock Dam

Mobley

HARRIS COUNTY

MUSCOGEE COUNTY

N

W E

S

Columbus

CONTENTS

CONTENTS

PROLOGUE

In 1984, G'mamma was ninety and I was a middle-aged journalist sitting on the edge of her magnificent antique sleigh bed, atop her hand-crocheted ecru coverlet littered with orange peels, gazing at those perfectly manicured, fire-engine-red nails I'd known since childhood. We were in her house in Hamilton, Georgia, the house I had known since childhood. The ever-present Salem cigarette teetered precariously between her long white fingers. She'd smoked three packs a day for as long as I could remember. Now she was little more than bones and wrinkles and a cloud-wisp of hair, but the life-force was as fierce as ever.

I had come to hear her stories and preserve them for my children and future generations. Placing my tape recorder gently beside her, I, someone who had unflinchingly interviewed murderers, corrupt officials, and gang leaders, eased timidly into an oral history with this frail woman. Any fears of intimidating her with equipment and interrogations vanished as she slipped into Tallulah Bankhead mode, spinning stories of girlhood crushes on male schoolteachers, her love of handwork, her pride in her antiques and other "pretty things." There were few needlecrafts she had not mastered.

Above the mantelpiece, next to her bed, hung a large tinted photograph, *Miss Berta as a Young Belle,* brown eyes flirtatious beneath an elegant straw bonnet proudly perched atop careful curls. The hat was a gift from Mr. Bob, her father. She was his only child, an adored, spoiled, quick-tempered, high-strung girl.

G'mamma had clearly relished our conversation, but I could see that both she and the tape were running out, so I decided to end with a simple question. "And what is your most unforgettable memory?" I asked.

"The hanging," she replied without pause, a faint, nervous smile playing at her thin lips. "They hanged a woman and some men right downtown in Hamilton when I was young. I was told to stay home, but everyone else was going, so I sneaked out."

As I look back on that moment, in which I was exposed to the first whiff of knowledge about a huge and terrible event, I realize that a combination of ignorance, inexperience, a lack of readiness, and a certain training in southern behavior made me hold my tongue.

In the adjoining parlor, my mother eavesdropped. "You can't believe some things she says," she warned me as I left. "She embroiders, you know." I could not know then that eleven years later I'd embark on a full-scale excavation of this piece of family history, and that my mother, who learned early to revere her sheriff patriarchs, would continue the embroidery of memory.

My experience with memory embroidery began early, though I would not see it that way until I began my research for this book. When I was eleven and my sister ten, we learned that my father was keeping a huge secret from us. Although he was still a well-loved and successful physician at the time, he was drunk, as he often was back then, when he told us this story. As usual we'd been begging him to stop drinking, and so he told us this story as a way of explaining why he drank and could not stop. When he was a very young man living in Hamilton, he had accidentally killed a young black woman. She "sassed" him, he explained; she had refused to step aside to let him pass.

"I backhanded her and her head hit one of those iron poles outside Cook's Store. I didn't mean to kill her." His patent-leather hair glistened in the late-afternoon gloom of our living room. I thought he looked like Clark Gable. "Nothing was ever done," he continued in a voice softened by alcohol. "They just took her home, told some lie, and nothing was ever said about it again." Then he added, "If you ever want to punish someone for a crime, do nothing. They'll do a much better job on themselves than you could ever do." I took that knowledge, made more potent by the warm bourbon of his breath, and tucked it away on a shelf reserved for things that scared me. In that way, I never really forgot them; I simply deflated their power, turned them into "stories."

❧

In 1993, on a rainy night in April, that story G'mamma told came looking for me in another bedroom, my own on Capitol Hill in Washington, D.C. Outside, a gentle April rain fell; my husband was away in South Africa, filming a documentary. This time the story came in the form of a hypnogogic vision, a scene appearing in the mind's eye at the threshold of sleep. I saw a large, dead black woman laid out at the end of my bed, a burn across one of her temples. She spoke without words, but the message was clear: Go home. Find out what happened. I had always sensed that a day would come when my career as a reporter and my complicated family history would collide in some crucial way, and I was certain this was that long-expected assignment. I accepted it without question.

I was not alone in my new preoccupation. The nation, indeed the world, was being drawn to acknowledge past wrongs. While racial violence flared with the ruthless beating of Rodney King by Los Angeles police, followed by race riots and the burning of African American churches throughout the South by white skinheads, old racial crimes were being revived and some actually prosecuted.

At the time that I experienced this vision at my home on Capitol Hill, I'd been thinking and writing about the young woman whom my father, now dead, told me long ago he'd accidentally killed; I'd been doing so as a way to ease her into my consciousness. I thought that she might be the one I saw in my vision, and thus went home to learn more about what happened between this nameless young black woman and the surly teenager who would become my father.

I returned to Hamilton, a small town no longer peopled with my grandparents, aunts, and uncles, but still home to cousins and elderly men and women, black and white, with strong memories and ties to my kinfolk. It was no longer a thriving village of cotton gins and overflowing mercantiles; a train depot; large, ambitious white families; and longtime black servants. Now it was a town of antique shops and thrift stores, a tanning parlor, a drugstore, and several low-end restaurants. Still standing were the Confederate statue and the antebellum houses of Mobleys, Williamses, Hudsons, and Bealls, one inhabited by Little Sister Hudson Garrett, the last descendant of one of the ruling families, and still living on the square.

"Your father never killed that woman," my aunt Evelyn told me. She would know. Only twelve years old at the time, she was with him when whatever happened took place. Indeed, he'd told me it was Evelyn whose "honor" he was defending by smacking a black girl who refused to step off their path. "He backhanded her, sure. That sassy little Pearly Lee. But she didn't even fall down, much less die. Where'd he get that crazy idea? Why, Pearly Lee died just recently." I checked; she was right. Others, black and white, men and women, confirmed her version. "Ben Williams never killed a soul," they'd say, shaking their heads in wonder that he could hold such a misconception for so long, could drink on it, drug on it, die and carry it to his grave never realizing it wasn't true.

Nevertheless, as I asked my questions, other stories of violence, racial and otherwise, emerged. "Surely you know about Tip Top?" someone would ask, then proceed to tell me about my great-uncle Dock Williams, a rough-and-tumble, red-faced old son of a gun, who murdered and was murdered atop Pine Mountain in 1920, and about Louis "Sugar Bear" Murray, a black man who was hanged in the jailhouse for the crimes of the rich men's sons who were really responsible. In addition to the Tip Top murders, I was treated to more tales of white-on-white murders—the Mobley brothers who killed the Truett man, the Truett man who killed the Robinson man, and on it went. In the courthouse I found a "Parties Unknown" box of coroners' reports detailing more grisly murders, bodies of black men and women dumped in the river, weighted with rocks. On that one visit, I heard so many violent tales that, as I drove home, I envisioned the waters of the serpentine Mulberry Creek and the once-magnificent Chattahoochee River red with blood, not clay, their beds pebbled with teeth and bones.

Back in Evelyn's tiny dining room, I asked her about "the hanging" of G'mamma's memory. "Oh, that," she half-scoffed. "That was a bunch of men fightin' over some colored woman." She took a drag off her cigarette, curled her lip, and added, rolling her eyes, "They did that back then, you know."

The next day, at my sister's house in Atlanta, I picked up a book she'd just received for her birthday. There, in a sentence, I found all I needed: "Three men and a woman were lynched in Hamilton, Georgia, on January 22, 1912." Back home on Capitol Hill, adrenaline rushing, I sprinted the seven blocks from home to the Periodical Reading Room at the Library of Congress. At best I'd thought I'd find a paragraph or two buried deeply within a newspaper. Wrongly, I'd assumed southern newspaper editors were not proud of mob justice and often let such events escape notice.

I had not expected bold headlines, a major front-page story in the *Atlanta Constitution*: *FOUR NEGROES LYNCHED BY HAMILTON AVENGERS; WOMAN ONE OF VICTIMS. Avengers,* my brain tabulated: Avenging what?

And then I saw it coming like headlights gleaming out of the fog, the third boldfaced headline: *Negroes were accused of murdering Hadley.* Hadley. My mother's maiden name. Which Hadley? Murdered? This I'd never heard. The next headline and some further probing provided the answer: *Hadley, Who Was a Well-to-do Planter Was Shot Sunday Afternoon While Sitting in His Home— Negroes Held on Suspicion—About Hundred Men in Mob.* By now I had stopped breathing, but not reading. Suddenly the microfilm machine lost focus and, while I fiddled frantically, an intercom announced that the library was closing and lights began to blink. I would have to wait until tomorrow.

I turned the machine off and for a moment sat drawn into myself, barely breathing, eyes closed, scalp drawing tight the way it does just before a virus settles in. Well, here it was, the thing I sought. "Be careful when you go shaking those family trees," Evelyn had warned. "You never know what you'll find." She was sure as hell right about that.

Norman Hadley, the murder victim, was my cousin. My great-grandfather, Marion Madison Hadley, the newly elected sheriff, was his uncle. A sickening shock coursed through me. A cousin I'd never heard of had been shot through the head and killed. It never occurred to me that a kinsman had ever been murdered. Both sides of my family—sheriffs, deputies, a judge, legislators, a senator—seemed so well defended, especially against black people.

A woman and three men, one of them a preacher, two of them farmers, all of them black, had been hanged by a mob of men, many surely related to Norman Hadley. Beside the baptismal pool, outside the Friendship Baptist Church, a short walk from where the sheriff lived. Hanged and shot more than three hundred times on a wintry January night. And as I sat there growing numb, I intuitively knew that many more of my kinfolk had been caught up in that madness, on one side or the other.

I desperately hoped the sheriff had tried to stop it. In that moment I experienced an odd sense that I had known all these people, the murderers, the silent ones, the murdered ones, the powerless ones. I felt myself there with each man, woman, and child snared in that net and I hungered for every detail of their lives. Who were they? How did they live, think, vote, love, laugh, write, speak, work, live, raise children, treat their neighbors? What did they know of one another, the murderers and the murdered? What long road had they traveled together? I was not willing to accept that this was simply the way white southerners dealt with "racial matters." This was, to my knowledge, the only public lynching ever carried out in Harris County. There was something I and perhaps others could learn from this tragic affair. Perhaps we could understand what turns mild-mannered, churchgoing family men into cold-blooded killers, how something so shameful happens in the heart of a simple village and virtually disappears and where, if anywhere, it goes; whether it ripples down through generations, finding new forms in the future; and where, indeed, I might find its residue in my own life. I determined to learn all I could.

CHAPTER ONE

My Sweet Village

When I was a child, the nation was freshly out of World War II and recovering from the Great Depression. Farm folks were scraping the manure off their shoes, getting educations and entering professions, buying ranch houses in the city and not looking back. While my father's family, the Williamses, had more than most, they had still suffered during the Depression. My mother's people, Hadleys and Moores, never had much of anything. Mamma remembered hunger and her excitement when "any ol' piece of meat" came their way. She talked about the women's—her grandmother's, her mother's, her own—fears of having to go to work in the cotton mills.

My father's mother scrimped and struggled in her chicken business to send her smartest son to medical school. Being a doctor spared my father from war, an escape he did not appreciate, but it provided him a job with the military as medical inspector for the brothels of Phenix City, Alabama, across the Chattahoochee. My parents, a dazzling couple, dressed fashionably and belonged to the country club, while my father moved from one beautiful woman to the next, one glittering new automobile to another over the course of my childhood, adolescence, and early adulthood.

For five short years, from 1941 to 1946, we lived more or less as a family in a brand-new, white-brick ranch house on a manicured half-acre lawn in a neighborhood inhabited by the families of doctors, lawyers, and businessmen. Our street, Clubview Drive, abutted the golf course of the Columbus Country Club, and in the white-fenced green pasture across from our house pranced American saddlebreds and other magnificent show horses.

When I was five and my sister four, our parents divorced, an almost unheard-of event in 1946, and my charmed world turned cloudy. We stayed on Clubview Drive, but my mother went to work selling notions at Kirven's, a department store owned by members of my father's family. She hired a black maid named Ednell Allen Armstead, whom we called Edna. Sometime after Edna became my daytime mother, I began to notice and chafe against my mother's racism. Once in those early years, she spanked me at Kirven's for drinking from the "Negro" water fountain. The sign read COLORED, so I'd thought the water would be pink, perhaps blue. This is my first memory of my training in "racial etiquette."

From an early age, it rankled me that Edna had to use the back door and the garage bathroom, that she had to sit in the backseat of the car even when no one else was in the passenger seat. It wasn't that I was entirely tolerant; I could use the word *nigger* as easily as any of my friends. In early adolescence I went out with neighbor boys in the bed of a pickup and hurled eggs in the dark at hapless black people in their neighborhood, an action fraught with so much potential tragedy, it haunts me yet. And in my adolescent eagerness to integrate Edna into my world, I would thoughtlessly order her to sit up front when I drove her home. Wisely, I now realize, she refused.

"Red and yellow / Black and white / They are precious in His sight. / Jesus loves the little children of the world." On Sunday mornings, dressed in velvet and lace, the little white children of First Baptist sang "Jesus Loves the Little Children." Of all the church songs I loved this one most, and sang it nonstop and off-key in the backseat of my aunt Nana's green DeSoto, annoying my mother, aunt, my sister Barbara, and my double first cousins Bill and Steve on the endless, twenty-four-mile after-church drive up Georgia Highway 29 to my Hadley grandparents in Hamilton. It was later that I began to detect the contradictions between the song and our lives.

Through the 1940s and into the 1950s we made that drive, the four little cousins punching and poking one other as we drank in the sights from my aunt's crowded, wool-upholstered backseat. Acres of cotton fields, plowed and planted in fiery heat by Negro men behind plodding mules. Chained black convicts, pickaxes pounding rock along the narrow highway, chanting their mournful dirge. Miles of clay-coated green kudzu, dangling from power lines. A "Visit the Everglades" billboard with a picture of a glass-bottom boat posted on land owned by Big Mamma, my paternal grandmother. Mangled carcasses of roadkill all along the highway—possums, coons, dogs, and rattlesnakes grazed on by buzzards.

Halfway to Hamilton, in the middle of nowhere, our tires rattled across the wooden bridge over Mulberry Creek, just past the Big House—a large white two-story farmhouse with a deep wraparound veranda, where my father grew up. We'd turn left at Mamie's cabin, back in the woods on Williams land. There she'd be waiting, my grandmother Williams's old cook, likely the grand-daughter of a Williams slave, now skin and bones. With a wide, toothless grin, she'd reach out to touch us "babies" as she deposited her weekly sweet-smelling bundle of fresh laundry, tied up in a white sheet, onto the floor of the backseat. Tucked into its center was a jug of muscadine wine, which, as we cousins grew older, we found courage to sip secretly.

As Nana's poky car finally nosed into town, having stopped at least once for someone, usually my cousin Steve, to get a roadside whipping, we'd first pass the massive Beall-Williams-Mobley house, handed down in my father's family since the 1830s and still occupied by cousins. Then, to our left, on the square, we'd see the once-gleaming, twenty-one-foot marble Confederate soldier, now blackened by time and neglect, but still honored each Confederate Memorial Day when lines of elders and schoolchildren laid wild wisteria at his feet. "Fate denied them victory but crowned them with glorious immortality" read the words inscribed on its base.

Downtown Hamilton consisted of little more than four square blocks around Monument Square. Three elegant houses anchored and decorated three of its compass points, all of them large, boxy antebellums with stately columns, balconies, and spacious verandas that announced, "The best people live here." Two had belonged almost from the beginning to members of my father's extended family, to Williamses, Bealls, and Mobleys. Strewn among these landmarks were gabled Victorian farmhouses with gingerbread trim, white picket fences, and neat flower beds, as well as simple cottages, old stores, and warehouses smelling of seed corn and animal feed, smoked hams, and sturdy bolts of calico. A scattering of outbuildings peeked from behind and between the larger edifices—chicken coops and smokehouses, a tannery, a coffin maker's premises.

Among the public shops were a Williams uncle's drugstore, the post office, two gas stations, and Evelyn's Café. Evelyn was my mother's younger sister, a sexy, blue-eyed, tough-talking, chain-smoking woman. Around nine hundred people populated Hamilton proper in those days, six hundred of them black and three hundred white.

After bumping across the railroad track at the depot, we'd pass a bevy of Negro shacks raucous with orange hollyhocks in summer, and then we'd pull into our Hadley grandparents' gravel driveway. It was a plain, small house, six rooms—two front, two middle, two back—with screened porches back and front. Beside it blossomed G'mamma's riotous garden of snapdragons, sweet peas, roses, zinnias, and marigolds. Inside, her house was adorned with her creations: hooked rugs, French-embroidered baby dresses, knitted afghans, patchwork quilts, crocheted antimacassars, and needlepoint chair seats.

Though we'd eaten less than an hour earlier, the kids would make a beeline for G'mamma's red-and-white kitchen, where leftover fried chicken and biscuits, still warm in the oven, prepared by Hopie, her maid, awaited us. After that there were endless possibilities for pleasure. We could ride the cow in the back pasture or pretend the propane tank or cotton bales were horses. Or we could play fort in the smokehouse or Tarzan in the apple tree. Or we could swipe strawberries from our great-grandmother Deedie's garden (the "quarters," as it was once called), cut paper dolls from old Sears catalogs, read the *Saturday Evening Post,* shoot our cousin Buster's Red Ryder BB gun at birds and one another, duel with spears torn off G'mamma's massive Spanish dagger bush, or line the steel rails across the street with pennies so the afternoon Man O' War would flatten them as it chugged by.

But our favorite Sunday pastime was a visit to the courthouse with Dad Doug. By that time, Marion Douglas Hadley, my maternal grandfather, had been sheriff for more years than anyone cared to count. I was proud to be the granddaughter of a sheriff. Dad Doug was tall and lean, a Gary Cooper kind of guy with clear blue eyes, wavy brown hair, and a face deeply furrowed by the sun. He kept his badge in his wallet and his gun in his glove compartment, drove a regular unmarked Ford like everyone else, and wore the khaki shirt and pants and white socks of every other white farmer in Harris County, along with a straw hat in summer or a felt hat in winter. His only effort at a uniform was a thin black tie.

⁓

Every summer, my sister and I would spend a week or two in Hamilton. We ate breakfast at sunrise, awakened by G'mamma's call and the irresistible smell of bacon, eggs, toast, and coffee. Sometimes when we lay abed too long, Dad Doug would swoop one of us up by the feet and hold us upside down until we squealed. This playful side, however, was a rarity. Most often we'd be at the table in our pajamas, waiting, when Dad Doug would walk in, tousle our hair as he sat down, and say, "Hey, here, girls." Those are among the few words I can remember coming from his mouth, other than "Don't touch that gun," a remark he made specifically to our cousin Steve one day when he left us briefly in the car at his farm. Steve disobeyed him, and the gun lay in several pieces when he returned. We sat quietly as the two took a little walk into the woods. Nothing was ever said about it.

On our Sunday outings, he'd take us by Shorty Grant's Amoco station for moon pies, orange Nehis, or chocolate ice cream in paper cups with tiny wooden spoons. The station reeked of rubber and oil and gas fumes. Shorty was a little bowlegged man with a potbelly and a kindly way with kids. Snacks were always on the house for the sheriff's grandchildren.

In warm weather, Hamilton police chief Willie Buchanan, baggy trouser legs rolled to his knees to reveal pasty calves, a Jesus fan in one hand and a Coca-Cola in the other, would be sitting on the park bench in front of the courthouse. While the two men chatted on the bench or Dad Doug worked in his office, we children had free run of the stately mahogany courtroom. There we performed elaborate trials. Because we'd never actually watched a trial, except in westerns, ours were concocted in our wild imaginations or, more often, inspired by the gossip we overheard among the grown-ups on G'mamma's front porch. Since there were only four of us, sometimes five when Cousin Buster joined us, we took turns being judge, jury, sheriff, prosecutor, and criminal. Once or twice, when one of the two jail cells out back was empty, we'd extend our drama into that damp stone place with all its smells and whispers.

Summers in Hamilton were even better than our Sunday trips, for then my sister and I were allowed to splash in Mulberry Creek with the black Weaver children who lived on Dad Doug's farm. Best of all, we got to wait tables at Evelyn's. It was a simple place, long and narrow, with a linoleum floor, wide, flyspecked front window, and metal tables. Our aunt Evelyn was the star, flitting from kitchen to dining room, issuing orders to the cook, flirting, joking, scolding, and teasing her customers, most of whom were kinfolk either by blood or marriage. There were no menus, and the folks who came in for lunch simply ordered what they had a taste for—country-fried steak, ham, BLT, chicken salad. If the makings weren't in the kitchen, my sister and I dashed out the back screen door and into the grocery store to get them. No one seemed to mind the wait, caught up as everyone was in the gossip of the day or just doing their "bidness."

Despite a sluggish ceiling fan, the café was hot. Back in the kitchen, Hopie, the black woman who worked for Evelyn when she wasn't taking care of G'mamma or in jail for drunkenness, expertly shuffled half a dozen frying pans at once, sweat sliding like molasses down her ample shoulders. The dining room was filled with the hum of the men's serious murmurs, occasionally cut by the sharp exclamations of women, edged with mock outrage and the tantalizing whiff of scandal and secret, or sudden laughter that cut through the café like a burst of bright light.

Some days we'd stay in the house, reading, playing paper dolls, G'mamma's Singer ticking in the background as she made dresses our mother would force us to wear, that cigarette always dangling from her bright red lips, her canary chirping away in its cage. We perked up when the phone rang, signaling the soap opera about to begin. This was "Miss Berta" (as G'mamma was known to her many friends) at her best: the lifted eyebrow, the wry lip, the arch remark, the upward roll of the eyes, the flourish of a bejeweled hand.

Those woods, she once told me, referring to the unknown, are full of things you do not want to know about. But I did want to know. I squatted at keyholes or simply listened openly, my ear straining for some meaning in the rapid whispers and hushed drones of my grandmother and her daughters as they rocked on the porch or sat in the overheated parlor in winter, or when G'mamma took us to Little Sister Hudson's elegant antebellum house or the smelly little "old folks' home" where her aunt lived. Our fascination with the gossip at the latter was quickly exhausted by the suffocating heat of coal-burning fireplaces, even in summer, and the death grip of Aunt Betty's bony hands on our arms as she tried to show us her love and keep us from leaving. The best secrets came from G'mamma and her friends Flora Hardy, Miz Sprayberry, and Alex Copeland, who used to be the preacher at Hamilton Baptist Church but was now the organist. "Run out of town." "Born out of wedlock." "Buncha men showed up at her screen door." "Ran off with . . ." "Caught them down by. . ." The fine hairs on the back of my neck sprang up at these hints of scandal.

G'mamma was always busy with something, except when one of her migraines came on. When that happened she'd retire to her room, door closed, room darkened, a cool cloth over her forehead.

Evelyn and Hopie would tiptoe around and call the doctors, a married couple, until one or the other showed up with a black bag and a hypodermic needle.

G'mamma's mother, Deedie, lived in the back bedroom, next to the kitchen. She didn't gallivant with us and she didn't wait on G'mamma, her only child, when she was having her migraines. My great-grandfather Mr. Bob had been a terrible drunk, and I think she was just worn-out after all those years of riding herd on him. G'mamma called her father a "bridge builder." Later I learned that chained convicts built those bridges across the Mulberry and the Ossahatchee creeks and that "Mr. Bob," pistol and bullwhip at the ready, told them what to do and made damn sure they did it. Deedie's room was always darker and cooler than the rest of the house and when she wasn't out back in a calico sunbonnet, tending her strawberries, she was there, sunk deep inside herself, rocking and dipping snuff.

Deedie was plain as a paper sack, a simple country woman who knew more than she let on. I sensed that even as a child. She represented "history," and that, in my mother's family, felt a bit forbidden, a thing best locked in an old trunk; but it was a thing this curious child longed to unwrap, much like Deedie's old trunk, stuffed with yet-unwrapped gifts from years gone by. "Got everything I need," she told me when I asked why she hadn't opened them.

As I grew older, G'mamma's migraines got worse. She spent most of her days in bed, calling for Hopie, who'd left Evelyn's Café to become her maid, to notify the doctors. Everyone crept around her. "Don't tell Mamma," her daughters whispered about almost everything. One Christmas, just as lunch began, one of my cousins accidentally set the field across the street ablaze with firecrackers. It was a dry winter, and flames raced quickly through the brown grass. Platters of turkey, dressing, and candied yams were being placed on the crocheted tablecloth, and the outwardly calm daughters rounded up the kids to eat, hissing, "Don't tell G'mamma. Just eat like nothing's wrong." The smoke billowed so thickly we could smell it in the dining room, and while the men were out beating the fire with branches and blankets, the women and children said blessings, smiled, and ate as if nothing whatsoever was wrong. G'mamma didn't seem to notice.

I thought maybe something bad had happened to G'mamma long before. Once, when I was around ten, she said something mean about "nigrahs," and my mother shushed her, glancing my way and saying of me, "She likes them."

"Won't like 'em so much once one of 'em rapes her," G'mamma shot back, those haughty, smack-certain eyes boring into mine.

"Has one ever raped you?" I asked, both amazed and curious. "Well, no." She stammered a little, not expecting such a question from even this child. "But I was driving alone one night and, standing right out in the middle of the road, butt-nekked, was a nigrah man, right there in my headlights. Scared the living daylights out of me." That didn't sound to me even close to rape (which my mother had defined for me when I asked as "a man taking advantage of a woman," and the boys next door had later filled in the blanks), but I kept my mouth shut.

❧

I tiptoed back into Hamilton that summer of 1993, carrying articles about Norman Hadley's murder and the lynching just to remind myself, if need be, that I hadn't made the whole thing up. I didn't expect much cooperation, or even living memory of the event, nor did I expect to find documents. I figured few had been created and that those that had, had long ago been destroyed by flood or fire, the way it happens with certain pieces of paper in small-town courthouses. Those disappearances had become so common in recent years that an archivist at the Georgia Archives recited for me a law I should quote if I suspected something amiss in Hamilton.

Louise Teel was eighty-four years old that fall of 1995 when I returned with questions about the lynching burning inside me. A large, jovial white-haired woman, she was my mother's first cousin and the closest thing to a genealogist I'd known on the Hadley side of the family. I found all two hundred pounds of her planted in the recliner the army gave her cousin Helen when she retired as a nurse. Helen, once and always a missionary, had died sitting in that chair at Muscogee Manor less than a year earlier. Louise still cried when she talked about Helen, but Louise cried when she talked about most things, laughing and crying at once. Except for her mother, Sheriff Marion Madison, "Buddie" Hadley's eldest daughter, she was the only Hadley I ever knew who had any passion. She just loved life, loved to talk. A simple country woman, she'd lived most of her life with a husband from one of the meanest, most powerful moonshine families in Harris County.

I asked Louise if she'd ever heard of Norman Hadley. "Oh, yes," she said, as if I'd asked her what she had for lunch. "He was the one who was murdered." Just like that. "By whom?" I asked. "Oh, a bunch of nigras shot him. Then they hung 'em. I saw it. I was only two then, and everybody told me I couldn't remember anything, being so young, but I do. I remember that woman's tongue. I'll never forget that woman's tongue and the bullet hole."

"How'd it happen?" I asked.

"I wish I knew, Karen," she said. "I wish I knew. I asked that question all my life and all I ever got was silence." She stopped, shredded the tissue in her lap, and shook her head for a while. "Just silence. Or they'd say I had just made it all up. All I can say is they must have had something to hide."

CHAPTER TWO

Plantation Politics

The initial aim of Georgia's founder, James Edward Oglethorpe, and the colony's twenty trustees was to create an Eden in which England's "downtrodden" would find opportunity to become sturdy yeoman, growing grapes for wine and mulberry trees for silk. In 1732, sensing in advance these would bring Georgia to grief, Oglethorpe convinced Parliament to outlaw liquor, slaves, large plantations, lawyers, and Catholics.

His noble ideal quickly died. Oglethorpe screened applicants so carefully that few of the "unfortunates" made it through. Mulberry trees and grapevines proved resistant to conditions in the colony. From 1732 to 1750, the plantation forces pushed their case, and when trustees returned their charter to the Crown in 1750, and Georgia became a royal colony, the dream of a pure small-farm Eden evaporated. From the exhausted and shrinking lands of North Carolina and Virginia came planters and the families they'd enslaved. These included my Williams and Hadley ancestors, who sought the fertile black soil along the Chattahoochee River, and the pure, sweet whiskey-making waters of its tributaries. They waited impatiently in the northeastern counties, already cleared of troublesome "savages," until most of the Muscogee and Cherokee bands along the Alabama border were driven out or murdered and they could claim their 404 ½-acre plots, which they had already won in lotteries.

Georgia soon led the world in cotton production, thanks to the advent of the cotton gin and the depletion of soil to the north. A slave population of just under 30,000 in 1790 billowed to over 100,000 by 1810. On the eve of the Civil War, nearly half a million slaves accounted for 44 percent of the state's population; 75 percent of those lived in the fertile Black Belt, where Harris County was located.

From its beginnings in 1827, Hamilton, Harris County's seat, attracted residents devoted to law, religion, and education. Columbus, established one year later in 1828, just south of the county line, sat on the banks of the magnificent Chattahoochee, which flowed into the Gulf of Mexico. Developers envisioned a booming port city with Black Belt cotton plantations supplying a textile industry the equal of New England's. My paternal great-great-grandfather, General Elias Beall, was one of five commissioners named by the governor to lay out the city.

After a military career most notable for the number of Cherokee and Seminole he slaughtered or drove west, General Beall turned to starting Baptist churches around the state, becoming, in the words of one family genealogist, "a great Baptist exhorter." His son, Elias Harold, who in 1840 became a major general of the Georgia militia, settled in Hamilton, opened a mercantile, and carried on the tradition of starting and tending Baptist churches. In 1863, Elias Harold's daughter Mary Louise would marry Corporal Benjamin Henry Williams in a lavish wedding held in the midst of the Civil War. These were my paternal kinfolk.

Hamilton's establishment aspired to be a model of refinement, heaven to the hell of nearby Columbus, with its brawling bars and brothels, its teeming slums and smoky foundries and textile mills. In 1853, Hamilton Female College was created, boasting it would teach young ladies "to point an argument as well as to paint a picture," and offering courses in Ovid, Virgil, and Homer. The Female College brought the brightest daughters of the best families from throughout the region "to cultivate the heart" as well as the mind.

In addition, the county was blessed with an abundance of healing springs; spas and sanatoriums sprang up in her northern mountains. A recruitment brochure claimed Hamilton was one of the most healthful places in the state and boasted of her "moral, intelligent, and refined citizens."

The first wave of Williamses rolled into Hamilton aboard ox-drawn wagons somewhere around the time the county was incorporated in 1827. They were descendants of one John Williams, a Welshman who arrived in Virginia as an indentured servant but was given his freedom and a cow in 1655. The family who arrived in Hamilton consisted of "the bachelor uncle" Britain Williams, then in his forties, and Brit's two orphaned nephews. One was my great-great-grandfather, Thomas Arundel Williams. They brought with them twenty-seven slaves (including at least one large family of fifteen). Brit, his orphaned nephews, and slaves settled on some of the most fertile and beautiful land in the county, where they built a split-log homestead, slave cabins, stables, a barn, and assorted outbuildings. They called it the Blue Springs Road Plantation. Here they raised livestock, cotton, corn, potatoes, fruit, and other foodstuffs both for sale and for their own consumption. Among Brit's slaves were blacksmiths known far and wide for their expertise. Some set up a shop in the village, others on the plantation. They traveled freely around the county, servicing other farms and plantations.

This slave population doubled every ten years and by 1860

the Blue Springs Road Plantation claimed nearly ninety enslaved people, thirty-two of them under the age of thirteen. At Brit's death in 1863, at the age of eighty-three, he owned 2,200 acres and 94 slaves, making him, along with men named Lowe and Hood, one of the county's largest slave owners. The slaves alone were worth nearly $100,000, or some $4 million in today's dollars.

His twentieth-century descendants would revere Brit for taking in his orphaned nephews and great-nephews and giving each some college education. He was remembered as a kind and generous man; but what of the people who provided his wealth and who lived with him far longer than any of the great-nephews, men named Isaac, Mike, Austin, Jesse, Isaac, and Samuel, and women named Celia, Susan, Mariah, Sara?

The fact of enslavement is condemnation aplenty, yet some slave owners were more lenient than others. But little remains to document Brit Williams's relationships with those he essentially held captive for close to half a century.

His estate records reveal that some of the men were allowed to make and keep money: at the estate sale, Osborne, a slave, bought a blue dish for $5.50; Jordan, two counterpanes; Boy Frank, two valances and a counterpane for $15.00. Samuel, a blacksmith, and several others could read and write. Families appear to have been kept intact, with as many as four generations of several families still living together at emancipation.

Stories were told by Brit's descendants of devoted servants laughing and crying at weddings and funerals, happily joining their masters and mistresses at Hamilton Baptist, where they were listed as members though relegated to the balcony. Plantation records show regular doctor visits were made to slave quarters. In his will, Brit ordered "my blacksmiths" not be sold at all and that those enslaved people not specifically designated for the great-nephews who'd reached their majority be kept together on the plantation and their output used, if necessary, toward the education of the minor great-nephews. It appears that few, if any, of these slaves ran away to join "contrabands" during the Civil War as did many elsewhere and, at war's end, most if not all remained, three or four large, intact families on or near the plantation. The men kept the Williams name, as did the women until they married.

As a child, I'd been told by my Williams grandmother, some-what proudly, that my father's family once "owned slaves." My mother told me her family owned none. I'd learn through my research that was not true, though they owned far fewer than the Williamses had. Slavery was simply a concept to me, one to which I'd given little thought, until the day in the county clerk's office in the Hamilton courthouse, when I came across Brit Williams's estate listings, compiled by executor James Monroe Mobley after his death in October 1863. "1 negro man Dick, 63 yrs of age, $600; 1 negro named Cardy, 60, $300; Austin, 55, $1,000; Jesse, 40, $1500; Jordan, 30, $2,000." And on it went, noting the sex, name, age, and price of nearly one hundred human beings—men, women, and children. Even on these legal documents, they were not permitted their own space. Interspersed among their names were farm implements and animals: "13 hogs, 10 spotted sows and six pigs, 6 spotted sows and 4 pigs, $938.00" followed by Mariah, Sarah and Easter, then "1 lot raw hides 28 lbs@3.52, 1 log chain, 12.00, 1 barrell [sic] syrup, $320.50." Writing this down, I felt sick, as I do now. I feel sick whenever I think of those papers and that reality.

No record I've found attests specifically to the treatment these families received at the hands of the old bachelor or his several overseers over this long stretch of time. "The man must be a prod-igy whose manners and morals are not corrupted by this institu-tion," wrote slaveholder Thomas Jefferson of slavery. Whippings of slaves were routine on most southern plantations, including Jefferson's own; branding and other physical disfigurements were not unknown. When Brit and his slaves lived in Greene County, before migrating to Hamilton, an enslaved woman had her mouth sewn shut; another drowned her three children at the bottom of a well and hid herself there, and when discovered, she tried to pull her master in. The Williams slaves likely heard these stories and passed them down the line. In Hamilton, slaves, including, once, a lone seven-year-old girl, were sold at the courthouse door. Close by was the whipping post where owners paid the sheriff to lay thirty lashes across the backs of recalcitrant slaves.

In the 1930s, Rias Body, formerly enslaved in Harris County, told an interviewer with the federal Works Progress Administration of being tied "in the buck," a torturous position from which there was no escape, and beaten. But I find no signs of runaways from Brit's plantation, nor evidence of sales. No chains, manacles, or whips appeared on the estate list, which does not mean they were not standard pieces of equipment then.

Still, the plantation was an extremely lucrative business venture, with little to be gained by physically handicapping the workers. For forty years these families raised and handcrafted a bounty of profitable products. Enslaved women wove linens and kept beehives and raised chickens, goats, and rabbits. Boys and men hunted rabbit, squirrel, even bear and wildcat. Brit's blacksmiths, carpenters, and other skilled craftsmen traveled widely and unguarded as they served the county; it would not do for their owner to antagonize them. Most lucrative of all were the enslaved women whose childbearing doubled Brit's holdings every ten years. It is highly likely, given practices of the day, that the "free people of color" listed with him in the 1830 census were Brit's family and that it was a black or mulatto woman who was, in an unacknowledged manner, in charge of his house.

The several hundred people owned by my extended family embraced freedom eagerly while still remaining loyal to their former owners. On the April day on which Union troops, heedless of the fact that the war had ended, marched into Hamilton and burned down half the town eight days after General Robert E. Lee's surrender at Appomattox, the newly liberated Lewis Hudson took up a sharp rock and carved the date April 17, 1865, into a boulder. On their way in, they burned the Blue Springs Road Plantation house and barn to ashes and the newly freed black families stepped in to build it back. When Yankee soldiers set torch to the courthouse, black and white alike poured forth to douse the flames.

These are the kinds of "loyal darkey" stories my family and other white southern families loved to tell. I heard plenty of them as I made my rounds of Harris County—like Cheney, the Hadley slave, a mere girl whose family moved to another town at the first word of freedom, but who, allegedly loving her "white folks" so dearly, walked all the way back. They found her asleep in the buggy next morning.

Today I recall the story of the fires and know what hopes those freed people had for a bright future. Their savior, Abe Lincoln, was two days dead, but had that news, so slow back then, reached them yet? Did they have reason not to believe the hopeful stories they'd been told by the men in blue who'd set those fires, reason not to be alight with expectation that that forty acres and a mule would not, any day, be theirs? Perhaps some hoped the old masters would move to Brazil, where they could still own slaves. Or perhaps they had no reason at that moment to want anything but the best for everyone around, believing emancipation would soon bring equality. Some would be compassionate. They'd seen what the white women and children and old men had endured during the war, many starving alongside them, suffering the same deprivations. By helping put out those fires, they'd be helping themselves, building goodwill for the future. There were only a few weeks like this, optimistic weeks on which many of the emancipated would look back and weep.

I think of this period in history, in Hamilton, knowing what I now know, and feel nothing but regret that a more honest and brave-hearted people had an opportunity to turn history around and these not only failed to do so, but never even saw it. What a difference they could have made in the lives of future generations had they chosen love over fear and cooperation over conflict.

᳕

A few miles south of Hamilton, in Columbus, the Freedmen's Bureau set up shop, and freed people from that section of Georgia and Alabama flooded the city for their forty acres and a mule. Others, sometimes entire families, or "useless" women and children driven off farms, were looking for jobs or even just a crust of bread. Regional planters, including Hamilton's elite, urged the federal military commander to discourage blacks from foolish aspirations, which he did, in stump speeches around the state. They also managed to have the Freedmen's Bureau director appoint one of their own, Dr. E. C. Hood, to be county bureau agent. Within weeks, he'd lost face by hanging a freedman by his thumbs in the broiling sun for four hours and was fired, only to be replaced by another former slave owner.

Meanwhile, Columbus was on fire with political activity among blacks. Rev. Henry Turner, a free black since birth who had served Union troops as a Methodist A.M.E. chaplain and now served freed people as a newspaper editor and political leader, was barnstorming the state, rousing fellow blacks to rise up and demand their rights. Harris County blacks traveled elsewhere if they could to hear his speeches. Only once did a Radical Republican come to the village. George Ashburn was a former white overseer especially hated by planters for his demands that they all be stripped of land and rights. At the courthouse, Ashburn was warned to watch his words or have his friends bury him the next day. A close Williams friend, veteran Pomp Ramsey, sat a few feet from the podium at which Ashburn spoke, and kept his pistol aimed at Ashburn's head. That day Ashburn's speech lacked its usual sharp rhetoric, and newly freed slaves in the audience took in the lesson.

The next night, Ashburn was assassinated in bed at a Columbus boardinghouse and six Muscogee County Democrats were arrested by federal authorities. This became a national cause célèbre and one of many reasons why Congress in 1867 declared martial law in Georgia and ordered that blacks be allowed to vote for new state constitutions and officials. The South accused federal officials of torturing the prisoners, men they regarded as heroes, ratcheting up an already overheated hatred of the Yankee overlords.

Consistent with the Hamilton town fathers' desire to keep their former slaves away from bad political influences, none of the Yankee schoolmarms who'd flooded Columbus and surrounding towns had been allowed in Hamilton; instead the black children were taught for a time by the sheriff's wife, then by young J. Curtis Beall, a mulatto (or mixed-race person, in the vernacula of the day), freed from the plantation of General Elias Beall and his wife, Carrie.

But warding off bad influences on the blacks was the least of the power brokers' worries. Just after the war, wealthy white southerners embarked upon a new phase of warfare. Their immediate goal was to get Republicans out of the South and get the South back into the Union. In the long run, they'd regain the reins of power and prosperity, subject the freed people to a new form of servitude, and win redemption in the eyes of the nation.

In August 1868, white and black Williamses stood together in long lines under sweltering skies to cast the first biracial vote. On the ballot for two state representative slots were Brit Williams's formerly enslaved blacksmith, Samuel Williams; and William I. Hudson, a white man who'd held one of the county's two seats during the war and was therefore running illegally, forbidden from taking office by Congress, along with another white man. All over the South, white men boycotted these elections, but in Harris County nearly as many white men voted as black. Earlier the *Hamilton Journal* had given Williams a muted endorsement by informing readers, "all negroes running for office are not Radicals," and on the ballot he was listed as "Neg," rather than "Rad," which defined most black candidates. At the end of the day, Williams, who'd come to the county as a seven-year-old slave, and the white patriarch Hudson won their races.

Meanwhile in nearby Camilla, Georgia, and elsewhere in the South, white men massacred many blacks on this election day. Harris County remained calm, partially because whites believed they had nothing to fear. Most believed that their one Negro candidate, Sam Williams, was the puppet of the ruling clan and thus entirely trustworthy. Even better, many knew that Leland Stanford, who had a shrewd legal mind, had earlier been elected delegate to the state constitutional convention ordered by Congress and attended primarily by freedmen and radical whites. As head of the Bill of Rights Committee, he'd helped to mastermind a successful effort to remove a clause in the new constitution guaranteeing the right of freedmen to hold office. He had already tricked black delegates into trusting him by pretending to support Gen. Ulysses Grant for president. Twelve days after being sworn in, all but three black members of the Georgia General Assembly were ousted on grounds that the new constitution did not guarantee their right to hold office, and Sam Williams returned home to his little cottage near the square, took off his new suit, donned his old overalls, and went back to his forge and his hammer. He was the only one of the twenty-seven black legislators who did not sign a statement of protest against their ouster.

Partially to salve the wounds this treacherous defeat inflicted upon Hamilton's freed people, the white members of Hamilton Baptist helped black members in their desire to build their own church. A biracial committee met to make the decision. Sam Williams made the motion, directing black members to begin the process. A half mile west, down the Blue Springs Road, in a wooded valley that dipped away from Hamilton Baptist, they built an upright wooden structure with a baptismal pool nearby. A black preacher was hired. They named their church Friendship Baptist and it quickly became the heart of a large and bustling black Baptist community. Schools, burial societies, a women's association, lodges, and more churches would be spawned on and from this ground. Here freed people would sing and sermonize on the main floor and in the front rows, listen to hymns sung in their own voices from the choir loft, be married at the altar, and have themselves and their children baptized in a clear pool on the grounds, the way the white folks at Hamilton Baptist had been, rather than in the muddy Mulberry Creek, as had formerly been the custom. They consecrated their sacred font with the planting of an oak tree.

The U.S. Congress would not, however, be mollified with churches. The ouster of Georgia's black elected officials so enraged most members that they imposed martial law upon Georgia for the second time and ordered the state to readmit its elected freedmen to the state legislature. They also ordered them to send home those who were there illegally because of their participation in the Confederate government and their refusal to sign a loyalty oath, men like William I. Hudson. Sam Williams remained in office for what was left of his term, but like many of his colleagues—many of whom were beaten or threatened—he either chose or was convinced not to run for a second term. He did, however, become a vice president of the Negro Labor Convention, an organization dedicated to helping freed people negotiate for higher pay and better working conditions. Historians would later reveal this arrangement was backed by planters, who were able to pay, eager to lure the best workers away from poorer farmers, and determined to control any black organizing. If true, that would explain why Sam Williams, who lived short steps from James Monroe Mobley, could remain in Hamilton unmolested while doing this work.

Hamilton's high and mighty had far more to worry about than a lowly blacksmith. The election that brought Sam Williams to power also resulted in Harris County giving a majority to the Republican candidate for governor and a "yea" vote for the state constitution written by the freedmen, their erstwhile white Republican allies, and the few planters like Stanford who'd slipped in. All this signaled trouble ahead, and when General Ulysses Grant, running as a Republican for president of the United States in 1872, won Harris County with a combination of black and white votes, the local Democratic leaders knew their fight was far from over.

In truth, white Georgia Republicans had for the most part proved as treacherous to their black colleagues as Democrats; most had voted with Democrats to throw blacks out of the General Assembly in 1868, their chief interest being to expand their influence among whites. Nationally the party had always been the party of business, and the nature of struggle between Democrat and Republican was between planter and businessman. The only role either party ever really saw for the freed people in those days was that of political pawn.

The combination of supporting black churches and schools and allowing a few favored freedmen their political heads served

Hamilton's white leaders well for a time. They needed black votes and by hook or by crook, they got most of them. To ensure black men voted right, worked hard, remained loyal, and acted humble, the extended Williams family both gave and sold small plots of land to many of their former slaves, although—as was customary among white planters—much of this land was not registered in the deed books in order that it might be taken back at short notice.

One thing outside white control was an increase in black women not working for whites. Many registered as "farm laborer" in 1870 were "keeping house" in 1880. "Keeping house" was the phrase commonly used for white housewives. Black women serving in white homes were called "servant." This increase in black housewives, regarded with pride by blacks and their white allies, was viewed with hostility by whites, especially women, who increasingly had to scrub their own floors and peel their own potatoes and had long viewed the black woman's services as their birthright. That census, and many to follow, also showed a high number of young black and mulatto females living alone with single white men and giving their occupation as "housekeeper," or "cook."

Most freedmen continued to work white planters' land, but within two years after the end of the war, they'd mounted a region-wide struggle against the brutal "gang system" used under slavery. They settled on the sharecropper system, long employed by the planters with poor whites. In comparison to gang work, this seemed to offer more freedom but would quickly become a quagmire of endless, debilitating debt.

A century of pain and penury would follow, faced not only by poor blacks and whites, but by the entire South as the new slavery of sharecropping, undergirded by increasing racism and violence, a low-intensity continuation of the Civil War, took its toll on the region. While freed people struggled to build a new world for themselves within the harsh limits imposed, white planters and yeoman farmers proceeded immediately following war's end to reconstruct their former lives. My ancestors and their like, having lost the bulk of their wealth in slaves, clung to their land and grappled however they could for more, while instituting laws and practices that kept blacks as close to slavery as possible. As waves of economic depression washed over Georgia, Williamses and Mobleys—in their strategic positions as sheriff, judge, legislator, senator, lawyer, moneylender, clerk of court, and Democratic Party official—increased their property holdings exponentially.

The greatest source of wealth was, doubtless, the infamous convict labor system, in which hundreds of thousands of prisoners, mostly black, were sold to the highest corporate or individual bidder. Sheriffs, judges, justices of the peace, and other county officials throughout the South were in on this massive take, and my relatives, paternal and maternal, were almost certainly at this trough, though the higher their ranks, as with the Williams side, the greater their reward.

In 1872 Congress outlawed the KKK and the War Department shut down the Freedmen's Bureau. By 1877 a compromise won the White House for the Republicans and promised Democrats that President Rutherford B. Hayes would remove remaining troops from the South. This led to the exodus of many white Republicans, putting black rights back into the hands of white southerners. Reconstruction was dead and black citizens were left to the mercy of their former masters and the protection of the abolitionist network of the North, which continued its philanthropy.

The Compromise of 1877, fashioned in the U.S. Congress, assured southern whites political autonomy and nonintervention in matters of race and promised them a share in the new economic order. It also freed the white South to fashion a new form of slavery, using labor contracts, peonage, and discriminatory laws written into their state constitution. With large numbers of poor whites and blacks of every ilk flooding into Georgia's cities, the framers of Georgia's 1877 state constitution, including James Monroe Mobley, gave Georgia's rural counties power over the cities vastly unequal to their population.

In 1883 the U.S. Supreme Court determined that the Civil Rights Act of 1875, the only law forcing compliance with the Fourteenth and Fifteenth Amendments, could be used only on rare occasions; henceforth, civil rights became a local matter. As Frederick Douglass wrote, "We have been grievously wounded in the house of our friends." In 1895, Booker T. Washington, a man most southern blacks saw as a savior, rose in Atlanta to declare, in what became known as the Atlanta Compromise, that black people should settle for manual labor, the goodwill of the white man, and a gradualist approach to rights. A year later, in *Plessy v. Ferguson*, the U.S. Supreme Court declared racial segregation constitutional.

᪉

I lay all this out in detail because little about Georgia politics of the late nineteenth and early twentieth centuries—certainly not the lynching of a woman and three men in 1912 Hamilton—makes sense without understanding the shifting, yet reactionary class structure. In the beginning, the idea was that all white men could someday own a slave and that ownership would make them part of the aristocracy of white men. In the first three decades of the county's existence a lot of those dreams came true. In the 1850s, a Georgia farmer with two slaves and a small farm was five times richer than the average northerner. More and more white men acquired slaves. Cotton production became increasingly lucrative.

By the time the war ended, two-thirds of Harris County's roughly 15,000 population was poor and black; one-third were white, and of those, roughly 65 percent were poor. The fight over secession had inaugurated a new era of resentments of the poor against the rich. While many wealthy planters opposed secession, it was their class that misled the South into war with their fiery speeches and votes to secede, which is why the men who actually fought called it a "rich man's war and poor man's fight." The rich passed laws that made it possible for their sons to stay home. Many also refused their new government's orders to cease cotton production, honor blockades, send slaves to build fortifications, and grow food, measures that leaders believed were necessary to win the war. From the war's first year, southern editors predicted the South's failure would be due to planter greed and disloyalty. Later historians would also blame the loss on "states rights," which made it difficult for states to unite.

In Hamilton, daughters of the wealthy continued their studies at the Female College during the war, holding elegant Christmas balls and shopping for satins and sweets at well-stocked Beall Mercantile, while Henry's Confectionary, selling soaps, toiletries, and pharmaceuticals, refused credit and countless shopkeepers used the war as an excuse to gouge customers.

In these and other ways the rich all over the South inflamed the poor against them and contributed to the ultimate loss of the war. Because of this vast white resentment and the large numbers of white radicals in Columbus and counties surrounding Harris, planters saw fit to curry black votes in their own way, which included supporting their right to vote and paying for those votes. Due to their long history of slavery, freedmen were, for a time, far easier to manipulate than truculent whites and so the races were played against one another in dozens of ways over the next century as wealthy white men successfully maintained power.

The problem facing the former slave owners after the war: how could a small minority, at most 35 percent, or one-third—250 to 300 white men at most, after you eliminate all the war dead, women, and children—of the population maintain power? The answer: with the carrot—an acre or two of land, a dollar bill, an old dress, favors large and small—and the stick—no credit, no job, an unjust jail sentence, a small group of hooded, sheet-shrouded, gun-toting men circling a cabin on a dark night, a hapless "darkey" blowing in the breeze.

The political gatherings of the Harris County elite included large numbers of black voters, former slaves still laboring on large plantations who were hauled in on planters' wagons, seated at separate tables that groaned like the white folks' tables with barbecue, collards, corn bread, and yams, and lectured to on the largesse afforded them by their former masters. Shamelessly the whites played the Civil War card by having weeping mothers beg their Populist-leaning sons to remember the sacrifices of their veteran fathers and vote Democrat.

In Hamilton in 1893, Ben Williams, running for the Georgia Senate, arranged for a large chorus of the favorite "darkeys," as they called them, to serenade the dying William Hudson, whose seat Ben sought, outside his antebellum mansion on the square and thank him for his years of service in the Georgia House and Senate. These tactics, coupled with rampant vote-buying, worked to keep the old guard safe. But for myriad reasons, whites of every stripe would soon decide or had already decided the Negro should not vote at all: it encouraged them to be "bumptious on the street," as gubernatorial candidate Hoke Smith would proclaim; the Negro vote, many believed or claimed, was the cause of increasing charges against black men of the rape of white women, which led to increased lynchings; the black franchise made it harder for whites to completely control the labor-management relationship or, as they put it, "to get good help." Most importantly, they were too inclined to populist alliances, too fond of progressive legislation to increase spending on schools and taxes on the rich.

In 1877 a poll tax law had been passed, instantly eliminating large numbers of poor blacks from voting. In 1900 Georgia Democrats established a statewide primary system open only to whites. Since Democrats dominated the state, whoever won the primary won the general election. Blacks could still vote, but their votes were meaningless. Even that measure was not enough and soon cries rang out for total disenfranchisement. It would not be long before that most precious and essential of all rights would be entirely removed from the hands of southern black men.

CHAPTER THREE

The Unveiling

The old masters did something else to bind poor and rich whites together. Working with women, they created the Lost Cause movement, designed to glorify the antebellum South and the Confederate cause, honor the war dead, and provide poor and middling whites with a sense of aristocratic belonging. No longer were there privates and colonels; no more would be mentioned the deserters and the anti-Seceshers, the privileged rich and the put-upon poor; now they were all brave and simple soldiers—true patriots, not traitors—who'd fought the good fight to defend Constitution, hearth, and home (not slavery, which for public purposes was now deemed "wrong" and, even before the war, was said to be "in its last days"). Only because there were too few of them to fight on, they had so tragically lost. Beginning in the late 1880s, statues of this humble soldier were erected in cities and towns all over the South.

Each year Hamilton's largest public events—Confederate Memorial Day, General Robert E. Lee's birthday, and numerous gatherings of the United Confederate Veterans' Williams Camp Meeting, made up of every old veteran still living in the county—

drove home these messages, at the heart of which was the eternal crusade for white superiority. With whites unwilling to face up to the wrong their leaders had wrought by starting and continuing a hopeless war, or to bring their economy in line with reality, or to democratize their system after the war to welcome blacks and poor whites alike, the main thrust of southern life became the preservation of its traditions and the creation of myths. For fifty years they'd carried their propaganda north, laced with lurid tales of black inferiority, disease, and criminality. They'd been enormously successful in this. Since the early 1900s, mainstream, even liberal, magazines like *Harpers,* the *Atlantic Monthly*, and *Good Housekeeping* often played their tune. Chief propagandist at the outset was General John B. Gordon, who'd commanded Harris troops, led Georgia's Reconstruction-era Ku Klux Klan, become governor after the war, and was then the first southerner to return to Congress. Dead now for six years, General Gordon had been a distant cousin to a ragtag bunch of Gordons living out by the Chattahoochee River, men and women who would loom large in the tragedy soon to happen in Hamilton.

Lest the war and its just causes be forgotten, the old soldiers— all former slave owners—had ramped up their celebrations and their propaganda. At a turning point in black-white relations, a time when all black efforts at equality and unity were being systematically dismantled, Lost Cause activity was at an all-time high. And nowhere so energetically as in Hamilton, Georgia.

On Tuesday morning, November 29, 1910, several thousand people thronged Hamilton to witness the long-awaited unveiling of a Confederate soldier statue in the center of the square. For two years the village had thrown itself into a flurry of rebuilding and modernizing. Today the white townfolk strode about well dressed and proud, their heads held high amid so many city visitors because of a new Gothic Revival courthouse, the judge's new brick Investment Building, Mobley Bros. Farm Implements, and an array of freshly painted cottages ringing the square. In the evening, if the visitors tarried, they'd notice new acetylene lamps, which gave the town a welcoming appearance. This morning the air was frosty; the atmosphere festive. The brass band struck up at 9 a.m. and led the welcoming committee to the tiny train depot to meet guest speaker Governor (and soon-to-be U.S. senator) Hoke Smith, whose potential presidential candidacy added to the allure.

Only four years earlier, Smith, running for governor, had not been welcome here. Many blamed his heated racial rhetoric for the disastrous Atlanta race riots of 1906 and the town had supported his opponent. After his election, and except for making good on a campaign promise to the ultraracist Tom Watson crowd to disenfranchise black voters, he'd returned to his more moderate stances and once more won favor in the eyes of the Hamilton elite, most of whom deplored incendiary speech. They'd seen the damage it could do not only in the Atlanta riot (where the judge's son-in-law commandeered state militia troops) but in Wilmington, North Carolina, in 1898, where distant Williams cousin Colonel Alfred Waddell had riled crowds of white men to a frenzy, resulting in wide-scale death and destruction aimed at ridding the city of black leaders and officeholders. Even though the ends in that case were to their liking, they preferred more legalistic means.

Seated with Hoke Smith at the podium, in the shadow of the white-satin-shrouded twenty-one-foot marble soldier, was Master of Ceremonies Judge James Fenimore Cooper Williams, who'd led a sharpshooter battalion throughout the war. Next to him was his first cousin Miss Lula Mobley, corresponding secretary of the Ladies Memorial Association. At seventy years old, Cooper's tall, lanky frame was stooped. Mobley, almost child-size at fifty, was defiantly straight. She was dressed neck to toe in black watered silk. The shadow of the man who'd formed their political outlook, his uncle and her father, Colonel James Monroe Mobley, dead now for seven years, hovered about.

It was the ladies who'd raised the $1,360 to pay for the statue and the ladies and their servants who had put this occasion together, rising at dawn to barbecue pigs and possum and make potato salad. The purpose of the memorial was to show their devotion to those rebel vets both dead and still living and to teach their increasingly irreverent sons the true meaning of the Lost Cause. This gave them, many of whom were college graduates, a sense of purpose; they were the teachers and it was in the schoolroom and the Sunday school room that the most important work of indoctrination took place. In addition, the women's suffrage movement was making itself felt throughout the country and the men reckoned on Lost Cause activity keeping their women safe from that.

At 10 a.m. the brass band blared Dixie and a bevy of white-gloved ladies pulled the velvet cord that removed the white satin cloak from the gleaming statue. A gasp ran through the crowd. Hamilton had no public artwork, precious little private artwork, and no one could deny it was magnificent. The welcome address was given by Colonel Leland Stanford, the man who'd helped make it possible for Georgia's first black legislators to be unseated.

❧

And so it was on that brisk late autumn afternoon in 1910 that Hamilton's old masters remained masters and could say with straight faces that their war had been vindicated, despite the fact that, as the inevitable result of this great denial, their children— black, white, mixed—were at war with one another.

They had silenced the loudest and most threatening of the black leaders and once again docile Negroes labored in their fields, bringing forth bale after bale of the cotton they called "white gold." White-on-black violence had quieted down, except for that which arose out of the nocturnal cavorting of blacks and whites. In 1900 a conference had been held in Montgomery, Alabama, to discuss the problem of "white bullies" and "black brutes." White men had lost touch with their "plantation manners," likewise black men not raised in slavery. What was to be done?

While Harris County in 1910 was a hotbed of sex between black women and white men, it was the white-on-white "honor killings" that concerned the county the most. Here on the square, a decade earlier, City Marshal Will Robinson, a Williams in-law, had been shot dead by the clerk of court's son over a white woman. In 1908, just before the new courthouse opened, Henry Mobley, son of James Monroe Mobley, had shot and killed that same clerk of court's son in the drugstore on the square in another fight over a white woman. They'd all claimed self-defense and only Henry was tried, though quickly exonerated. The code of honor among these former slave owners or sons of slave owners, which painted self-defense in broad swaths and quietly glorified gore spilled in the defense of women, was alive and well in Harris County. It was a key piece of the Lost Cause ideology and one that the women, at least, were starting to see as unfortunate.

As the morning air grew chill, the crowd headed for the warmth of the courthouse. There, packed tightly as cotton bales, they clapped and cheered like children as Hoke Smith, having promised, "We are above politics," portrayed a halcyon future for a region sorely wronged and misunderstood by history. The South would rise back up to glory and the leadership of the nation, a virtual Camelot. In melodious tones and effusive language he praised Generals Lee, Beauregard, and Jackson, along with the humble foot soldiers of the local soil. He paid homage to the brave white women who kept home fires burning and the plantations producing during those four mean years but made no mention of the slaves or of black men like Alfred Williams, who'd accompanied the judge's brother Charles to battle. Now the courthouse janitor and living close by, Alfred would likely have observed the festivities from a doorway or against a balcony wall.

Sometime that evening, as he and his crew cleared the leavings from the box lunches off the lawn, soon after the judge and Miss Lula saw off on the 7:22 p.m. train to Atlanta the man they hoped would be the next president of the United States, the clock on the courthouse tower inexplicably stopped working.

CHAPTER FOUR

New Sheriff in Town

The unveiling of the statue was simply the beginning; the following year would mark the fiftieth anniversary of the war's beginning. Throughout 1911, a shiny new Hamilton came alive with Lost Cause festivities, coupled with more church revivals than anyone could remember in one year. At Hamilton Baptist, the young women swooned over Rev. Willie Upshaw, a golden-haired, silver-tongued, wheelchair-confined Atlanta evangelist, who urged them to repeat each day the biblical injunction in Romans 12:19, "Dearly beloved, avenge not yourselves, but rather give place unto wrath: for it is written, Vengeance is mine; I will repay, saith the Lord."

In March, Friendship Baptist consecrated its handsome new brick structure, finer than any church, black or white, in the neighborhood. During Rev. Forbes's long tenure there, 1,500 people would be baptized in its pool. The *Harris County Journal* announced that the colored Masons were building a new two-story building.

It was in the midst of all the hoopla—February 1911—that my maternal grandfather, Deputy Sheriff Buddie Hadley, moved his countrified family from a rented split-rail cabin in the honeysuckle tangle of Blue Springs to the stately old Mobley place, just off the newly named Monument Square. A month earlier he'd been sworn in for another term and the move into such palatial quarters tipped some off that he'd soon be running for sheriff.

"Convenient to church, near school, 2 wells, splendid water—all conveniences," the ad had read. The indoor toilet alone might have cinched it, but there was so much more. The idea of living in such a fine house would have both delighted and unnerved Emma Hadley, for it meant moving into the midst of Hamilton society. A plain-faced woman with piercing black eyes who wore her long black hair halfway down her back, Indian-style, and sewed her own dresses, would feel out of place among the college-educated, book-club-attending, operagoing women of her new neighborhood.

Still, she'd have appreciated the convenience of the shops, a good Baptist church for her children and herself (if not her husband, never a churchgoing man), and the safety of people nearby, all brightened by the new gaslights along the paths. Mostly she'd revel in the spaciousness of the house—four large rooms up and four down, high ceilings, fine draperies, carpets, a fireplace in every room (including a marble mantelpiece in the parlor), six elegant porch pillars, a deep veranda, and a front balcony. All this was a far cry from the linoleum floors, wood-shuttered windows, and outhouse of their former homestead.

Elegance, however, was second to safety for Emma and her children. Annie Laurie, her eldest, was newly married with a toddler, living up on Pine Mountain with a headstrong ne'er-do-well of a husband who'd just shot and wounded a Negro—in self-defense, he'd claimed. Worried for her daughter and grandchild, with smallpox on the spread as well, the practical Emma quickly brought them to live with her and Marion, as she called the sheriff.

Clifford, her eldest son, had just been hired at the Hamilton post office and planned to take lodgings at Susan Robinson's hotel, but that posed a problem since the somewhat peculiar young man found it difficult to eat in others' company. So now he'd also move in with the folks. And Bessie, a pretty teenager, would have a high school to attend and a boost to her marriage prospects.

The move signified a victory for Hadley, long considered down on his luck. In 1897 he'd moved the family to Pensacola, taking a job with his brother-in-law selling insurance to sailors heading off to war in Cuba and the Philippines. Emma's headaches, the futility of cotton farming in a depression, family feuds, and neighbors' vendettas had set his teeth and stomach on edge and so they'd left for the smell of the sea and the hope of prosperity. By 1899 they were back, tails between their legs, with nothing to show for the effort; most of the money they'd received from their share of the grist mill that Buddie and his brothers had inherited was gone.

In 1900, brother Joe had won the sheriff's post and hired Buddie as his deputy. He'd had to take up the plow as well, just to survive, but stayed in the job through two more sheriffs over the next decade, winning his share of plaudits in the *Harris County Journal* as he brought in more lawbreakers than others, tracked down fugitives in Alabama, even survived bullets through his hat and in his leg.

Sheriffing ran on both sides of my Harris County families. Between 1858 and 1956 the county saw two Williamses, one Moore, and three Hadleys in the office. For Williamses the job had been a launchpad to greater power, but for Hadleys it was the penultimate political position.

Hadleys were solid middle-class people. Buddie's late father, William Henry "Buck" Hadley, and his wife had raised their five children on a six-hundred-acre farm that abutted the Williamses' Blue Springs Road Plantation. Their farms lay seven miles southwest of Hamilton and seven miles east of the Chattahoochee River. Mulberry Creek snaked through Brit's place. While Williams boys were privately tutored and attended academies and college, Hadleys, if lucky, finished eighth grade in the one-room Hadley School. Their father, a master carpenter, respected miller, and justice of the peace, handled many of Brit Williams's business matters and was his friend. What Hadleys lacked in wealth and polish they made up for in character, common sense, and good disposition.

Unlike Williamses, who married laterally or upward, Hadleys tended to marry laterally or downward, making them perfect for bridging the crucial gap between the elites and the discontented whites of the county. Over the years Hadley family members had increasingly married into the more rough-edged clans living in the western districts near the Chattahoochee, in towns called Mountain Hill, Mulberry Grove, and Antioch. These included men called "wool hats," who ran afoul of federal revenue agents, drank heavily, and frolicked at night with Negroes, male and female. These were men who didn't care much for the law, unless they were the ones meting it out. Early on it became clear to Mobley-Hudson-Williamses that if they were to hold Harris County whites together politically, they'd have to use Hadleys. In addition to that, with Buddie Hadley they got a man black folks liked and respected. His father had been a small slaveholder but was known as a "good one." He'd lived most of his adult life in a section of Blue Springs highly populated with blacks. He employed dozens at his sawmill and was said to get on well with them.

As for Buddie Hadley's future, the move into town couldn't have been wiser. By the end of the year Sheriff Middlebrooks would retire and Buddie would throw his hat into the ring. In the meantime he'd be elected senior steward at the Masonic lodge and complete his initiation into the inner circle. Living in a Mobley house symbolized the kind of acceptance and financial backing that would be necessary to win future elections, but it would also create doubts in the minds of some family and friends along the river, men who did not always see eye to eye with the Hamilton elite.

Events had taken a troublesome turn in April, when an old Hadley friend, Edgar Stripling, rolled into town aboard the Central of Georgia. Stripling had left town as a fugitive felon and returned a conquering hero in handcuffs. His trial for the murder of another Hadley friend in 1896 had pitted brother against brother and torn the community to shreds; when friends helped him escape from jail most felt relief and good riddance, but fourteen years later he'd been captured in Virginia, where, incredibly, he'd served for years as Chief of Police R. E. Morris. Newspapers nationwide were turning him into a hero. Now the local brothers' battle over his fate would resume and Buddie Hadley would be drawn into it.

On January 10, 1912, a special election was held for numerous vacated posts. It had been a cantankerous political year and more than the usual positions were up for grabs. Buddie Hadley, the natural choice, was elected sheriff without opposition. Ordinarily this would predict sure victory in the May primary, but within four days, the celebratory smiles of his large extended family throughout the county would be wiped clean.

❧

When I began this quest, I believed I was looking for the woman my father killed. This was not a threatening prospect: my father was dead and, being a seeker himself, would likely have been intrigued at my dedication to finding out the truth. Instead, once I began to dig, I found myself poking about in my mother's family.

This posed more of a problem because my mother was very much alive and had, throughout my upbringing, brushed aside any questions I had about her family. I'd sensed that she was ashamed of many of them—their poverty, their lack of education and social standing. Just before I arrived home bearing the lynching articles, Mamma had been interviewed by her grandson for a school project. He'd asked her what she was most proud of in her life and she'd answered, "My children and my sheriff father and grandfather." Some time ago she'd written to congratulate me on an article of mine and added, very uncharacteristically, "I admire you for going after the bad guys." I didn't think she'd admire me for going after *our* bad guys, however. Still, at that point I held tight to the idea that, as the articles had suggested, my great-grandfather tried to prevent the lynching. Maybe we weren't the bad guys after all.

CHAPTER FIVE

Norman's Murder

The *Journal* had announced that December was as "pleasant as May for Hamilton's rose gardens," but by mid-January it was reporting that "winter is now upon us with icy grasp," and white petals lay brown and sodden on the ground. The village, so recently suffused with the sweet afterglow of church revivals, now hunched under dense clouds as a hard cold settled over the region. Mules stumbled along icy roads. Sleet pummeled the countryside and made any sort of outdoor work impossible. Men sat about idly. Some cut wood; others cleared land when rains slackened and bought mules in preparation for farming. Others nursed grudges. In order to drive up prices, Farmers Union leaders urged farmers through the *Journal* to order their tenants, mostly black, to hold back cotton and plant less next year. This was not popular among sharecroppers and renters already deep in debt. As an edict from an organization that forbade their participation, it was even less popular among blacks.

Schoolhouse meetings for January 15 were announced to prepare white farmers to go "with a member of the committee and get tenants to agree to this proposition."

"There is no excuse that is worthy of consideration," the announcement asserted. "A man who does not want to do a thing can find an excuse. A MAN WHO DOES WANT TO DO A THING CAN FIND A WAY."

The Hadley household was asleep when a fierce hammering and a God-awful holler came at the front door near midnight on Sunday the fourteenth. The news wasn't something the sheriff would be much surprised by; in fact, he'd half-expected it. His nephew Norman Hadley—more son or brother than nephew, a handsome bachelor playboy with a quick temper—had been shot twice in the head and left dead on the frigid front porch of a Negro woman's shack on Mulberry Creek.

Buddie and Norman were alike in many ways—handsome, fun-loving, irreverent outdoorsmen—but there was a big difference. Buddie had long had a stern wife, four children, and a trio of spinster sisters-in-law in his house, all of whom served to keep him in harness. He'd been raised by a solid miller father who built a school for his children and brought them up with middle class values. As a young man Buddie had taught Sunday school. Norman was a rakish, guitar-playing bachelor, raised by his mother's Gordon family in a moonshine culture out along the Chattahoochee River in a notorious section called Mountain Hill.

News of Norman's murder hit the new sheriff like an anvil. Norman was six months old when his parents married, a toddler when his father, Buddie's oldest brother, either died mysteriously or just disappeared. He grew up on the Gordon place, a plain pine-log folk house grandly named Twelve Oaks. His grandfather, George Washington Gordon, proudly claimed to have been the first white man born in the county. When Norman's mother remarried, he stayed on with the old folks and a houseful of aunts, uncles, and cousins. Gordons were God-fearing, whiskey-loving, quick-tempered folk. Hadleys were, through their mother's Moore

family, intermarried with Gordons six ways to Sunday and most
Gordon and Moore men distilled, drank, and peddled moonshine
down to Columbus and up to Atlanta. They often showed up in
the U.S. district courtroom in Columbus.

Georgia was for decades the largest moonshine-producing
(and, probably, consuming) state in the nation. The stringent
efforts of the temperance movement had turned most counties
"dry," thereby increasing illegal production. Brewing mash was
seen as a "right" and a "freedom," and the fact the North outlawed
it during the Civil War and began to send its agents after southern
moonshine men in the wake of the war made it more of a political
act than it might have been otherwise.

For the past two decades, even as he struggled himself, Buddie
Hadley had worked hard to rescue his nephew from this lifestyle,
doubling down his efforts since 1896, when Norman's uncles
Sambo and Mans Gordon, with Norman at their heels, had fired
at a federal revenue officer and barely escaped a long imprisonment. The following two years had seen a spate of arrests and trials
of Gordons and Moores, white and black.

Buddie related to his nephew like a father; he'd seen potential
in him and fought to be his better angel. He took him to Pensacola
with the family, hoping he'd join the insurance business. When
war broke out against Cuba, however, Norman had jumped the
train back home and signed up, serving a total of one day before
it ended. This past spring, Buddie included Norman on a fishing
trip back to Pensacola with the prosperous Williams men, hoping they'd see something besides sport in him and provide more
substantial prospects than the nightly Negro frolics, fraught with
booze, guitar blues, and mixed-race women, which so fascinated
his devil-may-care nephew.

Norman's murder was not something Buddie Hadley would
have wished for at any time. It was especially not something he

wanted on the honeymoon of a job he'd dreamed of for more than a decade.

It had been many years now since Norman was arrested for illicit distillery, which didn't mean he'd stopped, only that he'd grown smarter over the years and that Gordon and Hadley-connected sheriffs had managed to maintain a buffer between their whiskey-making kin and U.S. marshals. The current and former sheriffs in Norman's family—Buddie, his brother Joe, and his uncle by marriage Mitch Huling—had doled out the occasional deputy, jail guard, and bailiff assignment in hopes Norman, now thirty-four, might someday be sheriff material. But hopes for his future had begun to dwindle.

Then one hot night the previous September, Sambo Gordon, Norman's uncle and strongest influence, was found dead on a dirt road near the river, a dead black friend beside him, a hot pistol in each man's hand. The black man, Josh Caldwell, was Sambo's tenant, longtime gambling buddy, and partner in the moonshine business. Soon afterward fires began to break out in Mountain Hill and its environs.

First, the Negro society hall. Then a Negro church. Then a Negro lodge. Then a Negro school. Some white folks rushed in to help rebuild the school but these things take on a momentum. Gun toters' licenses were being issued to white men in record numbers. More men than usual were deputized as constables. A black ferryman turned up dead in the river; he was said to have been ratting to the revenuers. Somewhere in all this, a black man jumped on the back of Bose Moore's buckboard and was removed with a quick rifle blast from Bose's Winchester. Bose was Norman Hadley's uncle. Of the man, he said to his stunned children beside him, "He wasn't one of our nigrahs, and he had no business on this wagon." Even the blind could see that Mountain Hill was coming unraveled. Politicians began calling for policemen to patrol each of the rural districts of the county "for the preservation of order on Sunday especially and the routing of gamblers and rowdies." And the fact that Deputy Sheriff Buddie Hadley was making an arrest a day was small salve to heightened anxieties. "We never get tired of the war cry 'Quit your meanness,'" proclaimed the *Journal* in late August, concluding, "The Harris County jail is now too full."

Mountain Hill wasn't the only place that was roiled by gunfire; the entire South's 1911 Christmas had been riddled with violence. Newspapers, white and black, reported black leader Booker T. Washington's pleas to fellow blacks to suppress other black "gun-toters." Judge Price Gilbert of the U.S. Superior Court in Columbus lectured grand juries that things were so bad it was easier to convict a man for horse theft than for murder. Back in 1907 the *Harris County Journal* opined upon "too many homicides" and a lack of "fear of the hangman's rope." Primarily it was white men murdering white men and blacks murdering blacks, all claiming self-defense, and, especially in the case of whites, going free. Almost always the issue was a woman or money lost in a card game, or both. Juries, the editorial argued, were at fault, rarely convicting anyone of homicide. The "good people" wanted to put a stop to this, but every time someone came before a jury looking guilty he turned out to be someone's relative or neighbor; it was hard to be objective in such a small and interrelated community. Occasionally a politician would introduce a bill to expand jurisdictions in order to water down the blood ties, but such efforts never went anywhere.

January 14, 1912, had been the coldest day of the year. Late in the evening, Buddie Hadley was told that a Negro woman, Loduska "Dusky" Crutchfield, a tenant on the Gordon farm, had sent someone for "Mr. Norman." Sometime around 9:30 p.m., an unknown assailant or two pumped three bullets from two pistols into his body, propped him up against a tree beside the Mulberry

Creek or on the woman's porch (depending on the storyteller), and left him to die.

Sometime between the discovery of Norman's body and the wee hours of the morning when the *Columbus Daily Enquirer* was put to bed, someone had decided exactly who killed Norman, and a front-page headline announced not only the murder but the murderer. The evening *Ledger* followed suit, also naming unequivocally "a negro named John Moore." Moore, also a Gordon tenant, lived near Dusky and her husband, Jim, and their children, George, fifteen, and Lizzy May, twelve.

The two papers, however, disagreed on which night Norman had been killed: the morning paper said "Sunday," the evening "Saturday." While the first reports claimed Norman was killed "at High Bridge over the Mulberry Creek," later reports changed from "shot in the head by two pistols through his bedroom window" to shot outside "a negro woman's house," to "the shack of a man named Jim Crutchfield, who happened to be the negro woman's husband." Still, there were clues to the nature of the killing. The evening *Ledger*'s first report informed readers that the "killing is said to have grown out of an existing feud between certain negroes and white men in that particular neighborhood." Soon, however, the word *feud* would disappear, for in those days it connoted disputes among families and no one wanted anyone making that connection. A safer motive such as "a dispute over rents" was introduced and, for a time, stuck. Sharp minds would notice the switches and see right away that a cover-up was under way. If anyone troubled themselves to prod the newspapers to dig deeper or to offer conflicting information themselves, they got nowhere.

Sheriff Hadley's whereabouts on the Monday following the murder went undocumented. John Moore and his alleged accomplices were not brought in until late Tuesday evening, so presumably he was out questioning witnesses and potential witnesses while the trail was still hot. Because his and Norman's own closest family members were former and future sheriffs, deputies, and justices of the peace, most of them living near the scene of the crime, it can be assumed he had a lot of help in this matter and that the suspects, while not under arrest or confined, would not be going anywhere. Each lived on or next to the land of a Hadley, a Moore, or a Gordon.

So questions were asked and notes were taken and white men huddled in lodges and churches and barns while the women bathed Norman's handsome body, patted it with herbs, and dressed him in his only suit with the fancy little riverboat gambler's vest and cried and dipped snuff and cried some more and tended to Norman's mamma, Josie, who was close to death with grief. Meanwhile, others cooked up big steaming pots of pork and chicken and greens and large greasy pans of cracklin' bread.

While the women cleansed the body, the citizenry and the press cleansed Norman's reputation. Before it was over papers far and wide were calling Norman Hadley a well-loved, well-disposed, prominent citizen, from one of the best-loved, most-respected families in the county, a wealthy farmer. The "well-disposed" part was true, at least most of the time. The rest was pure fabrication and worked with many other factors to rile folks up more than they already were.

In truth, Norman Hadley was, at his death, little more than a near-penniless playboy-plowboy living hand to mouth on the largesse of his land-poor grandparents. At one time he'd been one-fifth owner of a 625-acre plot of land divvied up among his grandparents and their living children (with grandpa's name removed so he'd be eligible for his veteran's pension), but somewhere along the way he'd been eased out or bought out or had borrowed himself out. He grew up as the little orphan boy under their protection, always getting the biggest piece of chicken, the last slice of cake, never having to work for anything or pay for his misdeeds. When he was arrested on illicit distillery charges, his grandma Harriett put up for bail the farm she'd inherited from her biological father. The spoiled but charming grandson had never succeeded at anything he'd ever done—unless you count guitar playing, singing, poker, fighting, brewing and swilling moonshine, and loving all the wrong women. The 1900 census listed his occupation as "laborer," and in 1910 it was "odd jobs." He claimed ten dollars in total worth on his 1910 taxes and used his grandmother's land as collateral for the small loans he was always getting for seed and fertilizer. He'd never married and had no children, at least not any that anyone claimed.

But now dead, with newspapers large and small from Chillocothe, Ohio, to Paris, France, burnishing his image, Norman Hadley's failed careers as insurance salesman, soldier, and jailhouse guard would go unmentioned. His relative success as a distiller of illicit alcohol would likewise be left out. Before it was all over, Norman Hadley would be known worldwide as "a wealthy planter," or a "well-disposed, highly-popular young farmer." Norman was a man with a wicked sense of humor and would doubtless have relished his newfound reputation. Two days after his murder, on Tuesday the sixteenth, he would have the biggest funeral Mountain Hill had ever seen.

CHAPTER SIX

Though Silent He Speaks

By the time of the funeral, Norman had ascended into local saint-hood as the murdered-by-a-Negro nephew of the new sheriff, and so his burial had turned into a spectacle. Folks nobody knew were crossing the swollen river, traversing the mountain, and braving the slick roads from Columbus to stand in solidarity, ankle deep in mud, and pay their respects to a family under siege, though some simply came to gawk. Since word of his murder burst forth at break-fast table, in barbershop, lodge, church, parlor, and riverbank camp, vengeance lay like a rank perfume on the wet air of Mountain Hill.

The place, while chockablock with churches, had never been a model of decorum. In earlier days, proper folks were frightened to travel through. Columbus newspapers painted pictures of widespread drunkenness, gambling, and gunfights. White kin-folk who'd long ago left for holier regions wrote often, begging "the connections," as they called cousins, to join them in more "christianable" climes. In the late 1880s the *Columbus Ledger* hap-pily informed readers that Mountain Hill had transformed itself into a place of "orderly" and "upright" people. Somehow during the 1890s that transformation, if true, came unraveled, and the district once again resembled the Wild West. And it wasn't only the making and consuming of the demon rum that was causing the trouble and raising membership in the Woman's Christian Temperance Union (WCTU) and Anti-Saloon League; it was also the frolicking that went on between black and white after the sun went down, the ways in which, as one Gordon descendant would tell me in the 1990s, "the whites forgot they were whites and the niggers forgot they were niggers."

As sleet coated the cypresses surrounding the Gordon family cemetery, people gathered by the hundreds. Three Masonic lodges presided alongside the Woodmen of the World, whose fancy gravestone was an impressive marble tree stump entwined with ivy, adorned with a maul, an ax, a wedge, and a dove and inscribed *Dum Tacet Clamat*—though silent he speaks.

Rev. Brady Bartley presided at graveside. Bartley had already moved out of the district in disgust over its wild sinfulness, but he returned out of respect for the family. He'd lived next door to the Gordons almost his entire life.

Bartley was not the only good and temperate man who'd lately lost patience with Mountain Hill. Recently Rev. Cranford had preached on "a great wickedness" that stalked the district and of men who said "prove it on me" rather than beg God for forgiveness. Old-timers yearned openly for the days of the three-day camp meeting, where tear-stained men fell to their knees and confessed their crimes to large crowds and in great detail.

When Norman's uncle Sambo Gordon was murdered, the *Journal* obituary writer, routinely polite to the dead no matter who it was, broke tradition and admitted, "I do not say he had no faults. Far from it." Norman, on the contrary, was almost universally adored and good memories flowed freely this day.

Young women who'd long sought his hand recalled the sweetness of his tenor voice as he sang at Miss Ora's birthday party back in June. They had no need of embroidering, for Norman was a good son, a thoughtful grandson, a loving friend, and a most fetching man.

It's possible, however, that he was forbidden a church funeral. Many of his comrades had been removed by their churches, which served up their own sort of justice, "ousting" members for a wide range of immorality—cards, whiskey, women, cussin'—much of which had engaged Norman since adolescence.

Over time moonshine had become such a staple of the Mountain Hill area economy, alongside a lusty temperance movement, that a network of "wet" and "dry" churches had sprouted and ever-widening faults had formed beneath the surface harmony of families and friends. But family came first for these fierce Scotch-Irish folks, and, truth be told, almost all the white folks in those parts were kinfolk in one way or another.

Forbidden a church funeral or not, it's just as likely Norman would not have wanted one. His true church was the Masonic Lodge. The magic of organized manhood—its hoods, poetry, blood oaths, ancient rituals replete with quotes from Shakespeare in the deep forest—mesmerized him. He was an outdoorsman and it was only fitting that his service should be held in the weather, under the cypresses, encircled by giant holly trees.

Rev. Bartley said a few words but it was the Masonic brothers who ran the program. The evergreen sprig and the lambskin apron were laid upon the pine casket. The sprig stood for immortality, the lambskin for God's care. Norman's mother, Josie, was kept inside, nursed and comforted by her children and her tough old mother, too sick and grieved to stand. Within six weeks she'd be in a box beside her errant son.

Gordons were poor, homespun people yet were also deeply revered by their neighbors. The county newspaper's boilerplate on them, used frequently, stated they were "lineally descended from the Scotch Gordons so honorably mentioned in American as well as English history and of which illustrious stock our lamented Gen. John B. Gordon was a noble scion."

Scattered in and among the graves of the recently deceased Love, Brooksye, and Sambo were countless infant stones, fifteen in all, four belonging to Norman's tiny stepsiblings, most lost to disease during the tempestuous 1890s.

The fact that three Masonic lodges presided indicated strong feelings at work. Granted, Grandpa Gordon had been a member of Kivlin Lodge for fifty years and that fact had recently been celebrated in grand Scottish style, but if Norman had died of whooping cough or TB there'd have been no such outpouring.

Ordinarily the family's black folk—both "help" and friends—would have been there, gathered around the fringes of the crowd, to wish Norman farewell, and perhaps a few did bustle about the kitchen preparing coffee and cake for the visitors, but this funeral was different. A racial tension they could feel on their skin floated about the shorn fields and clay paths of the district, and blacks with any sense at all stayed indoors and kept quiet.

Had Norman been a young woman, raped and murdered, their anguish and the mourners' need for blood could not have been any greater. Being the nephew of three sheriffs and the grandson of another put him on a sacred plane. The Law, like the White Woman, symbolized the holy of holies of the South. In striking out at the beloved bachelor nephew of the beloved sheriff these "nigras" had struck deep into the heart of white supremacy. Never in the eighty-two-year history of Harris County had black folk cut so close to the quick of things.

Many of the mourners had fought beside one another at Gettysburg, Cold Harbor, and Monocacy, had fought under the very General John B. Gordon to whom this Gordon clan claimed kin, the John B. Gordon who'd proudly headed the state's Ku Klux

Klan during Reconstruction. Harris County's local militia was named for him. Some had doubtless listened well on Confederate Memorial Day as featured speaker Arthur Hardy implored them: "If ever again we are threatened with the scourge of the invader, if ever again a war of conquest is waged against us, we pledge you, in the language of the immortal [Irish poet Robert] Emmet, that 'we will contest every inch of ground, burn every blade of grass, and the last entrenchment of our liberties shall be our graves.'" They'd raised sons and grandsons to do just that, but lately they'd turned on one another.

It started back in the 1890s when men and women and children were forced to find work in the mills of Columbus and became infected with unionism and populism. Intrafamilial schisms appeared and widened around politics, and when the old planters ran for office they often had to put mothers on the podium to shame their errant sons back into the conservative fold. Beginning in the nineties, Hamilton candidates from the ruling elite received fewer votes in the Mountain Hill and surrounding districts than elsewhere in the county.

Tempers were even hotter than usual, with Edgar Stripling back in jail and folks taking sides over whether he should be freed or sent up for life. The fact that so many were kin made matters worse. Sick of scrapping, too many of the best people were packing up. Something was needed to hold folks together, keep them in place, something more than those Saturday afternoon scrimmages with the Gordon Militia, more lasting than the Lost Cause rituals. Something big and loud and final was needed to avenge the honor and good names of Gordon, Hadley, and Moore and put an end to all this crime.

Bound by white supremacist ideology, skin color, common rage, bolstered by the Holy Bible—not the *thou shalt not kill* but *eye for eye, tooth for tooth*—these Masons had long ago sworn blood oaths in their lodges to stand by one another, whether or not it was deserved.

The Woodmen also had strong bonds along these lines; their founder, Colonel William J. Simmons, an insurance salesman and former Methodist minister raised in southwest Georgia, was already trying out the ideas that would take form three short years from now atop Stone Mountain when he would resurrect the KKK.

Some had begun to see how divisions had risen among them, weakening them in the face of real enemies—how they'd wasted their powers in quarrels over cotton-holding and boll weevils and women and religious dogma and the drinking of spirits and the treatment of Negroes and land rights and inheritances and which moonshine man had turned in another moonshine man to the feds.

On a day like today these once-urgent matters shrank in light of the fact that so many loved ones, struck down in the prime of their lives, now lay dead at their feet. And so Norman Hadley was magically transformed from a handsome, cocky, guitar-picking playboy into a fallen warrior, his sacred name calling out for re-dress.

All the feuding factions of the neighborhood—most of them intermarried—bowed their heads together that day in the Gordon cemetery. It was a crowd—red-faced and rough, jut-jawed and fierce-eyed—containing both law enforcers and lawbreakers, cops and criminals. Lately black and white crime was on the rise but it was black crime that was noticed more; in the absence of a rural police force, every white man played the part. These men had been disciplining blacks and other whites outside the legal system all their lives. From white-on-white and white-on-black "whuppings" to white-on-white ousters from churches (and white-on-black church "ousters" during slavery) to lodge trials with various punishments, they did not see courts and jails as the only (or even the best) way to handle criminal behavior. Still, the county had not had a public lynching since a slave called Boy George was staked and roasted just before the war broke out. Harris County white folks prided themselves on a more cultivated form of "Negro control," and when time and again that failed, they took their bloodletting deep into the thick jungles out along the river, or into the river itself.

Sheriff Hadley wore several hats that day. As senior steward of the Hamilton Masonic Lodge he helped preside; as grieving uncle he wept and comforted and was comforted; and as sheriff he listened and watched. And he, a tall, quiet man with sky-blue eyes and a thatch of gray curls, was in turn observed, implored, queried, and counseled. The situation did not look good. Basic facts were still under dispute: where Norman was killed, when he was killed, why he was killed. What wasn't disputed, at least not openly, was by whom he was killed.

Some were puzzled as to why, with Norman dead in a pine box at their feet, his killer—already proclaimed guilty on front pages across the region—remained free. Not "at large," but not yet in custody. In other places, under similar circumstances, John Moore and his suspected accomplices would have already been strung up.

But this was the new sheriff's first month in office and some believed he, being their sheriff, deserved the opportunity to do things correctly. Others, however, wanted to put him to a test. It was a common urge in that era.

❧

Whatever the cues Hadley received that blustery afternoon, he went directly from Norman's grave to the rude tenant shanty of twenty-four-year-old Johnie Moore there on the Gordon farm and put him in his wagon. The fact that Moore stayed put within easy reach of angry white men was proof to some that perhaps the papers and whoever gave them the story were not entirely on the right track. Or it's just as likely that he had protection, perhaps called protective custody, during this brief span. Such were the tangled loyalties of the place where he'd lived all his life. For a black man, especially a mixed-race man like Moore in those days, the line between protection and prosecution was a fine one.

Shivering inside his wool pea jacket, Hadley laid both whip and epithets upon the back of his mule Jake as he wrestled the buggy through the sucking mud a short distance to the forlorn shack of thirty-eight-year-old Loduska ("Dusky") Crutchfield, who with her husband, Jim, was, like Moore, a renter on the Gordon's plantation. If any of the legal preliminaries had been followed, they'd have been authorized by the local justice of the peace, George Washington Gordon, Jr., Norman's uncle. Later the sheriff would tell reporters the suspects were taken in for questioning, and never throughout the entire ordeal would he use the word *arrest*. Possibly he consoled Dusky by telling her it was for her own protection; she was a witness, not a suspect. "The star witness" would quickly become her label, one that would stick into the twenty-first century. Later they would say she had agreed to name names.

Whatever Buddie Hadley said to Dusky Crutchfield, she got up on the seat of the buggy with him, a man she'd known since childhood and likely trusted, and together they went over and picked up another black farmer named Gene Harrington, a forty-year-old sharecropper and married father of one, on the farm of a first cousin of the sheriff. Harrington's fourteen-year-old daughter, Bertha Lee, was a stunning girl who'd attracted the attention of some of the neighborhood's white men, including Norman Hadley, and it was being whispered about that the father had a role in the murder.

Except for Gene Harrington, who'd long ago been arrested by

federal officers for moonshining but was quickly set free, none of the suspects, witnesses, or whatever Buddie was then calling them had ever before committed a crime, nor spent a night in jail, nor even been suspected of anything. Harrington was a church trustee; Moore and Crutchfield attended the same church he did. Jim Crutchfield, who brewed mash with the Gordons, had recently spent a year for that in the Atlanta jail. He, like Harrington, was a church trustee. His wife's record remained, until this day, entirely clean. They all had long enjoyed the protection of their white neighbors, moonshine partners, and employers. The time, however, that Jim Crutchfield spent in jail in Atlanta had signaled to some that this long-held arrangement was falling apart.

Hadley nudged the weary Jake slowly up Blue Springs Road toward town. He had to be wary. I do not know if he bound their hands with rope. I do not know what he told them, if anything. Perhaps he told them, as black men and women often were told in these situations, that they were being taken in for their own safety, that their names were out there. Someone had said something and someone else something else and soon it was believed that these three had something to do with it or knew who did.

All the sheriff had was hearsay. No weapon. No confession. At the moment, the woman seated beside him, his "star witness," was his best hope.

At the fork where the Blue Springs Road met the Lower Blue Springs Road, a short way from the jail, near Hamilton square, he encountered a masked posse on horseback. By the tilt of a hat, the crook of a nose, the rasp of a voice, he'd have known them all.

"Buddie, you better turn them niggers over to us now," one of the men said.

Blue eyes boring straight into those of the man in charge, Buddie stated that he loved his nephew as much or more than any among them, but that justice would be carried out in a courtroom.

He'd be down in Columbus in the morning, he assured them, asking Judge Gilbert for a special trial. The men would just have to trust him and should do so, for they had known him all his life and many shared his blood. For some reason, the mob moved aside. Perhaps they'd accomplished their purposes for the time: sent a message to the three Negroes that they had better cooperate (meaning "confess") or else, and thus made the sheriff's job a little easier. It would not be the first time a lynch mob had done only that, ensuring a conviction whether people were guilty or not. Or perhaps they did it to get a speedy trial. The only way one would be granted was if there was a compelling reason to believe a lynching was imminent. Or maybe they knew already a lynching was going to take place, but by letting Buddie Hadley look like a hero at this juncture, his reputation would be less harmed by a lynching. Hadley had only just made it through a special election. The real one was just around the corner.

Now Buddie Hadley sat in the freezing sleet, the new high sheriff, a country bumpkin who'd just moved his family into a mansion, rattling into town with a buggy full of his own family's dirty laundry, with a promise to face the fancy-pants judge the next day in his sumptuous Columbus chambers to convince the judge he had enough of a case to warrant the calling of a special trial.

No record exists of his wife Emma's reaction, or that of his grown sons and daughters, whether they knew of reasons for Norman's murder beyond the official "dispute over rents," though half a brain would tell them Gene Harrington was not a renter, so questions would have been asked. No one would be happy about the prospect of Norman's peccadilloes being paraded before town gossips and, possibly, northern reporters. Ida Wells-Barnett, W. E. B. DuBois, and the newly organized National Association for the Advancement of Colored People were known to send investigators or reporters who'd later make grisly hay of southern lynchings, even naming names. And that Ray Stannard Baker fellow of the *American Magazine*, who had so recently exposed the white South's hypocrisy in the matter of miscegeny, would be more than merely interested.

Buddie would have to be particularly protective of his fragile wife. When she was ten, her older brother fired a bullet into their father's head, killing him instantly. "The apple of discord," as newspapers would describe it, was a new stepmother's quarrels with Emma's older sisters, and the father's attempt to remove the sisters from the house. Though papers at the time opined that the young man should surely suffer severe penalties for so gruesome a crime, he was never even arrested, and had soon thereafter married Buddie Hadley's sister. The sisters he had defended, elderly and never married, now lived with Buddie and Emma, and none, including Emma, had ever gotten over that tragic event.

With only days on the job, the new sheriff had his back to the wall. All he could do was board that train in the morning and convince Judge Stirling Price Gilbert that there was good reason to call a special court and that he had enough evidence to convict either or both of the men he had in his buggy.

With the aid of jailer Zeke Robinson, a nervous young man with a new wife and baby, Buddie Hadley locked the three into the jail's only two cells—cages, really—cold and filthy and built entirely of steel and stone. Then he dragged his rail-thin, bone-tired body home for supper, acutely aware that from alleys and shop fronts, the sidewalk benches and the shadows of the Confederate soldier, eyes were on the jailhouse door. And those eyes would be there until his promise to them was fulfilled. Those eyes were multiplied by the eyes of countless villagers, both anxious and curious as to what the new sheriff was going to do with his strange predicament.

CHAPTER SEVEN

Negro Desperadoes

The day that I discovered the lynching at the Library of Congress, I learned that one of the victims was named Moore. I knew at the time that my mother's Hadley grandmother had been a Moore, but I didn't make the connection until much later.

More than two years into my research, in April 1995, I decided for no particular reason to return to the Moore family cemetery, but when driving there I couldn't find the turnoff. I'd passed it several times and was about to give up when a large buck leaped across the hood of my car and brought me to an abrupt stop, at the exact spot I was looking for. The last time I was there, with my elderly cousin Louise, she'd pointed out James B. Moore's stone because of its interesting inscription. This time I was dumbstruck to see the stone cracked open so wide I could peer into the murky depths of his grave.

Several hours later I found myself in the clerk of court's office. An ancient maroon leather ledger I'd pulled from a shelf inexplicably flopped open to a page that revealed not just any connection between black Moores and my mother's Moores, but a kinship connection. There, dated September 31, 1868, was an Indenture of Servitude between James B. Moore and his former slave Jane in which he agreed to care for her seven children, in exchange for their free labor until each was twenty-one. A check of federal censuses and other sources would later confirm that Johnie Moore was a member of my mulatto Moore family. I realized that all Moores, the "black" and the "white," had lived there where I'd "met" James B. I remembered the blood-red thistles that dotted that fenced-in plot, the well-kept grave of the former slave Cheney, unfaded plastic flowers placed atop the stone, and a strange unmarked grave next to James B.'s of large rough stones. Could that be Jane? I asked myself.

I sat in the Library of Congress weeks later and wrote in my journal: "How deeply imprinted upon our nerves is this ability to deny a child of our blood because some of that blood came from the 'wrong race?' I look at those black men and women all around me here and I wonder: 'Are you my cousin, half brother, or what?'"

&

Johnie Moore was, at twenty-one, the youngest of the three people the sheriff ushered into cold cells that January night. Although Moore had never been to jail, he'd heard plenty of grisly details from and about his notorious first cousins. "Negro desperadoes," the *Atlanta Constitution* called them. By now two of Jane Moore's four sons by James B. Moore had been murdered and Milford and Louis had been in serious prisons, not just this tin can of a lockup in Hamilton; site of so many escapes, it was a laughingstock throughout the state. Between them they'd served in Atlanta's infamous Fulton Tower, on chain gangs, at the state farm, and in the depths of the dreaded mines. Since boyhood, Johnie Moore had known the torments of hell that awaited him if he took the path of these relatives, so he'd stayed in school until he was fourteen, far longer than most white boys in the district, stuck to farming, avoided the moonshine trade and kept his nose clean, married young, lived next door to his mother, lost his wife, grieved, then found a new love, to whom he was now engaged. That's how he now happened to be sitting on cold stone that night of January 16, 1912. Word had spread fast the morning after Norman's murder, and since it was all in the family, so to speak, he'd been among the first to hear. If he'd wanted to run, he hadn't. That would have made him look guilty. He wouldn't have wanted that.

Johnie Moore was first cousin twice removed to a bevy of mixed-race Moore men who were blood kin to the sheriff. This connection to the white Hadley-Moore family came about during slavery. Buddie Hadley's great-uncle James B. Moore, a pig farmer and moonshine man, and his childless wife had one slave. Her name was Jane. By the time Jane was twenty-four and emancipation was at hand, she had six racially mixed children under the age of eight. They were Alfred, Milford, Louis, Susan, Genie, and Sogue. At war's end, she signed herself over to James B. as his indentured servant for life, and in 1868 she put her mark beside his on a paper granting him the children's care and services until each reached his or her majority. Moore, for his part, vowed to feed, clothe, educate, discipline, and govern them with humanity "as a father would."

Whether it was a familial attachment to Moore or sheer desperation wrought by those postwar years (sights of single mothers and their starving children thrown together in beggars' camps throughout the county) that drove Jane to sign away her children's labor for so many years, it turned out to be a wise decision: two years later the fifty-five-year-old Moore was felled by a heart attack, and Jane and her children inherited eighty acres of good farmland from his estate. Moore's wife quickly relocated to a mostly white section and hired as her servant a young white man.

Johnie Moore was the grandson of Jane's sister, who'd been enslaved by Buddie Hadley's grandfather, Thomas Moore. Through
the years, the mulatto Moores stuck together, remaining close to
their white cousins and working with them in the family moonshine business. Jane's eldest sons, Alf and his brother Sog, were
arrested several times in the late 1890s, as were Norman Hadley's
uncles Sambo and Mans Gordon, though never for shooting firearms at federal officers, as these last two were.

Johnie Moore was the only man in his beleaguered family not
stained by crime, whether as perpetrator or victim. He had every
reason to believe he was playing the game correctly and, indeed,
his upright life had won him the hand of a beautiful fourteen-
year-old by the name of Bertha Lee, the only child of the man who
now sat next to him shivering in the Hamilton jail, brought in for
questioning in the murder of Norman Hadley.

Gene Harrington was a tenant on the land of one of Norman
Hadley's uncles. Gene was an honest, hardworking man devoted
to his family. Like Harrington, the mulatto Moore men had, for a
time, led lives primarily free of courts and jails. Until the turn of
the twentieth century, they'd flourished, perhaps a little too much
for some tastes in the tightly entwined Mountain Hill community.
Slowly there had developed a love-hate relationship toward them,
among both blacks and whites. Over the past decade their criminal activity had become a problem for the several sheriffs of the
extended Hadley family. These included Buddie's older brother Joe
and Norman's uncle, Mitch Huling.

The love part of the relationship included some quiet socializ-
ing, financial and legal help, and sometimes lighter sentences; the
hate part involved an increasing discomfort with criminal behavior bolstered by a growing ostracism by whites of other whites who
consorted with blacks, even their own kin, causing many to push
these family members aside. Given all this, Johnie Moore would

have reason for both hope and fear at this crucial moment in his young life.

By 1900, the infant whom Jane Moore had cradled in her arms that day when she signed the apprenticeship papers had become a handsome, high-stepping man of thirty-one and was, of all her many sons, Jane's highest hope and dearest heart. Both literally and figuratively, Sog Moore was in high cotton. As the new millennium endured its first summer, the hottest in many years and verging on drought, Sog sat on what, for a Harris County black man, was a fortune.

On a hot day in August, Sog was shot dead in the doorway of Browns Chapel Church by an angry husband whose wife he'd just taken for a buggy ride.

Short months later Jane Moore watched one son kill another at a family Christmas celebration. Buddie Hadley's older brother, Joe, had just been elected sheriff. One of his first duties would be to arrest and help prosecute Jane's son Louis for the murder of her son Alf.

Court days in Hamilton always attracted a giddy crowd. With no theater, movie house, or even bars at this point, in a land in love with drama, court trials had long been a favorite form of entertainment. The better known the defendant or his victim, the larger the crowd.

Some of the townspeople liked "Negro trials" because of the glimpse they provided into an alien lifestyle that most white women, at least, could only fantasize about. In this case there was not only the black-white kinship issue, rarely discussed but widely known, but also titillating details, divulged under examination involving the "concubines" Juliet Baker and Emma Jane Bryant and their promiscuous living arrangements with the Moore brothers, good-looking, well-spoken men some white women could not help but notice.

Louis denied all guilt, but while he described events leading up to the shootings, observers could not but have noted, and perhaps been amused by the fact, that the racially mixed Louis spoke a finer English and displayed a keener wit than either white witness against him. That may or may not have figured into why the jury came to a guilty decision within thirty minutes; and it may or may not have figured into why, seven years later, the entire jury, the prosecutor, and the sheriff would sign petitions to the governor begging for his release and admitting they had been wrong.

Before Jane Moore had time to digest the murders of two sons and the imprisonment of another in one short year, her second-eldest and sweetest son, Milford, was brought before the bench in Columbus, where he lived. Milford had shot and killed his best friend, Coon Narramore, in a fight over Milford's longtime girlfriend, Pallie. Once again the fight that killed a Moore-related man was over a woman. This time, however, there was a fundamental difference: Coon was a white man. Making matters even more unusual, Milford was distraught over his death and many white men would take sides with the black Milford. Adding to the intrigue of the case was the fact that Coon Narramore was a cousin of the Hadley-Moore clan, making him a cousin as well of Milford Moore.

❧

In those first desperate hours in jail, it may have occurred to young Johnie that a certain powerful white family named Hargett might be his only hope, for it was Hargett lawyers who'd stepped in to handle Sog's estate, to defend Milford in court, and to get Louis out of prison.

Within three days after Sog's killing, Laney C. Hargett, one of the most prominent men in the county, petitioned Judge Cooper Williams to name him administrator of Sog's "considerable estate," worth around eight hundred dollars, a figure that would eventually swell to one thousand. Hargetts were the biggest frogs in that small pond called Mountain Hill and, as in my own family, their members ranged from lawbreakers to lawmakers, some of them both.

Laney's brother Flynn was the longtime secretary of the state senate, an influential and lucrative post if you played it right. He would remain there for many more years, pulling strings for friends, relatives, and himself in arranging pardons for prisoners both black and white.

Some Hargetts were feared and respected for their political power; others, especially the younger generation, for their tempers and trigger fingers. Some men in my family were said to carry Winchesters at all times in case they ran into a Hargett.

In his petition to handle Sog's estate, Laney C. Hargett had explained that "great loss and injury may happen" otherwise, referring to Sog's "estimable estate." Quickly, Sog's horses and mules and sows and barrows, his plows and mills and tools and dishes, and even his fiddle and silver watch were put up for sale; neighbors far and wide, black and white came to share in the spoils. His estranged wife received a share and his hundred acres was registered to his young daughter. The rest Hargett claimed for himself and others. The daughter's hundred acres was occupied by Flynn Hargett's son Fletcher and would eventually belong entirely to white Hargetts.

When Milford Moore killed Coon Narramore in 1901, Laney C. Hargett's son Hershall Vanderbilt, or H.V., as he was known, hired on as Milford's defense lawyer.

While preparing Milford's defense, Hargett learned that "the boys" from Harris were gathering around the Columbus courthouse, where Milford was to be tried, in preparation for a lynching if he was not found guilty and given either life in prison or a death sentence. His source, a bailiff by the name of Brewster Land, a Hargett cousin, had good reason to know what "the boys" would and would not do, since he had recently delivered a black prisoner accused of rape into the hands of these or other boys, who had immediately killed him out by the river on the Columbus side of the line.

Hargett believed he could get Milford off with a much lighter sentence, if not acquittal, because an entire cadre of powerful white men, including Coon's own kinfolk, were willing to testify to Coon's bad character and Milford's sterling one. This was something that had never before happened in these parts—and it was not going to happen now, because the lynch threats were real and Hargett and Moore both knew it, each being intimately acquainted with the people who made them.

And so Hargett deliberately lost the case, with Milford's resigned consent, and Milford was hustled off to a life sentence in prison, only mildly heartened by Hargett's promise to get him out as soon as possible.

Johnie Moore might have known what great efforts both Hargett lawyers made to free both Milford and Louis from prison. Laney Hargett, who represented Louis, had set up another brother, the true shooter, to confess. Crawford, also a mulatto, was born to Jane and presumably James B. shortly before his death. Laney sent depositions by Jane and the guilty brother, Crawford, along with piles of petitions, including names of the sheriff, the prosecutor, and the jury that had found Louis guilty, to the governor and the parole board. But before Crawford could be tried he became Jane's third son to be murdered. So Louis served out his sentence and had only recently stepped down from the train in the Hamilton depot, half a leg missing due to an accident at the convict-labor mines. As with many other things going on around Hamilton those days, his return had stirred up old animosities. Poor Milford, his heart almost gone was still being forced to labor in the mines, while H. V. Hargett continued to work hard on his clemency appeals.

If Johnie was innocent, he could rely on that shred of hope, the possibility of a Hargett coming to his rescue, but true innocence was a skimpy garment for a black man in Georgia in those days. Besides, big-city headlines had already declared him guilty. Regardless of any claims or alibis, he had to figure that that stain would stick.

Even if H.V. had had the time or the inclination to come to Johnie's aid, it's likely he would have been afraid of certain parties in Mountain Hill mad enough by now to kill anyone to sate their hunger to avenge Norman Hadley's death, including some of his own blood kin.

Within the Hargett clan itself were men well-known to be capable of putting away anyone coming to the aid of the men believed to be Norman Hadley's killers. In 1901, Flynn, Jr., and Laney C.'s brother Marshall had killed a man at a Valentine's party near Mountain Hill, allegedly for going after Marshall's wife. A younger Hargett by the name of Shaffer was fast gaining a reputation as a one-man lynch mob. Rumors said he was killing off black laborers who displeased him (or whom he didn't want to pay) and dumping their bodies in the Chattahoochee.

Something else might have kept the usually helpful Hargetts away from this case: they were blood kin to Norman Hadley's uncle Mitch Huling. It would not look good for them to stand up for someone accused of murdering the second of the family's men killed in six months.

CHAPTER EIGHT

Nobody's Negroes

The jail in which Dusky Crutchfield, Gene Harrington, and Johnie Moore were confined—a squalid little hellhole, reeking of despair and contempt—sat just behind the handsome new courthouse with the six massive Corinthian columns. Like much else in Harris County, it had a reputation. William Turner, the Atlanta transfer jailer who picked up prisoners around the state, described for the *Atlanta Constitution* the wretched conditions he'd witnessed—including prisoners sleeping with vermin and snakes. Turner said "the Harris County jail is the worst in the state" and accused the unnamed jailer, then Sheriff Ben Williams, of starving prisoners.

Soon afterward Williams was elected to the Georgia House, then the Senate. In both bodies he served a total of seven terms on the Penitentiary Committees, overseeing a massively corrupt convict labor system through which Lost Cause heroes like General John B. Gordon became millionaires. Sheriffs and other law officials all over the South were corrupted and enriched; freed slaves were reenslaved and their sons newly enslaved into a system that sentenced them, often for minor offenses, to draconian terms and almost certain death or dismemberment to provide free labor to Georgia's growing industries.

It had been a short three months since last October's grand jury took Sheriff Middlebrooks to task for the jail's broken plumbing and general filth. It called for repairs to "turn wind or rain," and a janitor for both jail and courthouse. Old Alfred Williams had been hired to keep them clean, but nothing else had been done. The grand jury had estimated that new plumbing alone would cost two hundred dollars, and white citizens of the county recoiled at any taxes, especially those spent on prisoners.

If there were ever any legal documents detailing how the three suspects were handled in custody, they have long since gone missing. It is unclear whether an actual arrest was ever made, whether charges were brought, and whether a preliminary trial, usually held by a justice of the peace in a store or his house, had occurred. The man in that post, Norman Hadley's uncle, was likely too aggrieved to perform his duties or too angry to be objective. His backup was Laney Hargett, with kinship ties to Gordons. Under law, until due diligence was performed and sufficient grounds for arrest were found, the detainees could be held for only seven days. This detail, if they understood it, may have given them a modicum of courage despite their desperate circumstances.

With no records available, only speculation is possible. One fact remains: no mention was ever made by the new sheriff, Buddie Hadley, or other law officials as to an actual murder charge against any of the three being held.

The prisoners' first night was a long one, with no heat and few blankets. They knew that in the morning the sheriff would board the early train for Columbus to ask the judge for a speedy trial. I can only speculate as to their state of mind in these early hours. They sat in the cold and the damp, possibly packed together with other prisoners. Since Dusky was being held as a witness, she was kept separate from the men, but there were only two cells and they were tight. The scattered thoughts of the three, when not focused on the mob members stationed outside and the fierce words they'd uttered at the fork of the road, would have been of their families: a husband, a wife, a fiancé, eight children among them. They'd seen enough to know that when mob thinking took hold, few distinctions were made as to guilt or innocence. They'd have known it was not uncommon for law officers to intimidate spouses and children to obtain needed evidence. Crutchfield was said to be a witness, while Harrington's role remained publicly undisclosed.

So far only young Moore was being named publicly as Norman's actual killer. His extended mulatto family had firsthand knowledge of both mobs and the court system, and knew how they often worked in tandem to produce guilty sentences. If he could think clearly in these tense hours, he'd know there were only a couple of ways things could go, none of them good.

Two years earlier, Eugene Harrington's name appeared on a subpoena as a witness to Johnie's mother Lula's attack on her landlord, J. G. Truett, though by grand jury time he had for some reason been removed. It's likely the prosecutor found him unreliable for some reason. Whatever the case, his refusal or inability to assist in shipping Lula Moore off to the state farm would possibly create enough white animosity to now deny him their support.

Dusky Crutchfield had seen enough of Harris County justice in her day to know she could go from witness to conspirator to murderer in a heartbeat; thus she likely entertained thoughts of possible white protectors, men like former sheriff Mitch Huling, whose grandfather had owned hers and who was married to Norman's mother's sister. It wasn't uncommon for sons of slave owners to stick up for sons and daughters of folks they'd enslaved. Perhaps she'd heard of letters that powerful white men wrote to the governor or the parole board when they wanted a black man or woman set loose, talking about how good the old black mammy was to their family and how they'd known this son or daughter since they were children together. But in those cases the Negro involved was usually the subservient sort, what white folks called "old-time darkies." Dusky was her own person. It would later come to light that she was a straight-talking woman, a deeply dangerous thing to be in those days. Rumors would soon circulate that she'd spoken too loosely of a matter involving a Mobley.

Federal census returns list her occupation as "none," a rarity among poor black women in that day. Her black women neighbors were listed as "farm laborer," "cook," "housekeeper," and "laundry." Dusky worked, but she worked at making moonshine, taking care of her kids (including a foster girl at one point), and running a juke on her own premises now and then, like many black folks in the district. These were all things which, in Harris County at least, were not enumerated on census forms. Many white men expected black folks to provide the fruits of these activities but were quick to call them "sorry niggers" when trouble arose.

Should it come to her needing white allies, Dusky Crutchfield's hopes wouldn't have been quite as thin as Johnie Moore's. She was, at this juncture, not a suspect. She'd lived on the Gordon place at least a decade, tended their stills, sometimes picked their crops, mostly entertained their men. She knew that Norman's mother, "Miss Josie," cared about her and knew Dusky wouldn't do a mean thing to her precious boy. She knew "Mr. Mitch," former sheriff Huling, Norman's uncle, could be devious and unpredictable but wouldn't be outright evil and kill or imprison someone he knew was innocent.

There was but a slim chance that Mitch Huling, with all that pressure on him to avenge the family honor, would stand up for her if the need came about. Besides, they were counting hard on her testifying against Johnie Moore, and she knew damn well that if she didn't, there'd be no white man on God's green earth to lean on.

There were lots of good white folks in Mountain Hill—some had helped pay for and even build St. James A.M.E., the church the four prisoners attended—but most of them were women without any power at times like this, mad about all the race-mixing and moonshine to boot. Also, almost every white man, woman, and child in the neighborhood and beyond was in some way related to the Gordons.

If she could calm down enough to draw back and take the long view of her neighborhood, she'd recognize it was almost entirely peopled by the big moonshine chieftains: Mr. Sam Teel and Mr. Lum Teel and the Kennons and the Cannons, the Hargetts, the Huckabys, the Brawners, and Norman's Gordon uncles, all kinfolk. Then there was Mr. O. K. "Kenny" Land, kinfolk, who hated moonshine but could be dangerous to them for just that reason. She'd know these men were mixed within themselves, kind as Lord Jesus one day and mean as cottonmouth rattlesnakes the next. But once they all got together on one thing, there'd be no stopping them.

Dusky Crutchfield had never seen a lynching, but she'd heard plenty about how inflamed men's minds became, how bonfires got set in their bellies and they were possessed like "haints." Nothing could stop them then.

CHAPTER NINE

Vendettas

Beginning on that January night of Norman's murder, whites' memories would be reshaped by this fresh outrage. Previously unconnected incidents slowly, steadily rearranged themselves into an obvious and long-running "Negro conspiracy."

Added to Milford Moore's 1900 murder of the white Coon Narramore was the 1907 killing of Narramore's half brother Dozier Huckaby, also a Hadley-Moore cousin, by another black man, Gene Bryant. The murder occurred at Bryant's parents' place, where Huckaby and a white friend, Jule Howard, had gone looking for liquor and frolic. Before the sun came up Huckaby lay dead: shot, stabbed, and brutally beaten with a gnarled cudgel, his loyal dog beside him.

Bryant went missing and was captured by Norman Hadley's uncle Sambo Gordon, who pocketed a handsome hundred-dollar bounty for his trouble. Soon afterward, Jule Howard was also arrested, much to the dismay of many whites who cringed at the rare fact of a white man and a Negro being tried for the same crime, as well as the thought of a white man joining a black man to so viciously bludgeon a fellow white. Separate trials resulted in a life sentence for the black man and twelve years for the white. The following year, however, after much harassment of his parents, the imprisoned Bryant signed a deposition testifying to Howard's innocence. It took another three years, however, for lawyers to obtain a pardon, and in early 1911 Howard was released.

Feelings about this case were reignited by Howard's homecoming, and the ongoing eye-for-eye calculations currently under way noted that not only was the black Bryant's dead victim white and a kinsman of the Hadley-Moore family, but worse (despite some skepticism that the confession had been voluntary), Bryant's silence had kept a white man in prison for four unnecessary years. In all these many ways, dots were being connected.

None of this was news, but somehow, with Norman having been murdered, it all began to look different—more purposeful, more conspiratorial, more *racial*. It had taken them this long to see it, so closely intertwined they were to the black folks, often failing even to see them as black, so many of them being only barely so. Until now they'd categorized the killings as part of the "moonshine wars" that erupted periodically throughout the tangled undergrowth along the riverbank. All these men had been partners in crime. In 1903 Sambo Gordon, Jule Howard, Gene Bryant, Josh Caldwell, and Dozier Huckaby, along with other kinfolk, were arrested en masse, hauled into U.S. District Court, forced to pay fines, and released back to their businesses.

In addition to this mountain of "evidence" of a Negro conspiracy, ancient resentments still simmered in those with especially sharp memories, memories of blacks who'd slipped the net so many years ago. There was the slave named Spence in Whitesville who'd beheaded his own child to keep the white owner from punishing him, then beheaded the owner, then disappeared. There was Alex Moss, who'd mortally wounded a young white man at a Negro party in 1889. Newspapers predicted a lynching each time, but nothing happened, likely because powerful white allies of both men prevailed, a common occurrence in what many called "the gray system" that reigned in this and many parts of the South. It was also in the year 1889 that the black cook Mary David was tried for the poisoning death of her white employer and two of his friends. David got only jail time because some white folks wrote to the newspapers that she could have done it mistakenly. Those were the days when mitigating circumstances made a difference in black folks' cases. In light of the current situation, they wouldn't count for much.

When these vendettas first began out by the river in 1900, nothing racial was made of them. Everyone knew they were in-house, as we'd say today. But one major and mostly unmentioned factor fueling racism and increasing segregation was the reality of black-white intimacy and the political need for whites to deny and distance themselves from it. In adjacent counties, when blacks got out of line, they were lynched. But here, some began to notice, they were either killed or got off scot-free like white men. Those with their mouths set on vengeance against black men had often been let down. The greatest letdown of all had come in 1903, when Miss Berta's cousin, John Cash—a bachelor living with his mother—had "stampeded" a Negro church at Blue Springs. Drunk, he demanded the congregants shut up and get out. Their singing, clapping, and praising was said to have irritated him. The pastor pleaded for mercy, but many of the worshippers whipped out their guns and mowed him down on the altar. Newspapers reported five hundred shots were fired. Though Cash died, no charges were brought. No revenge was sought. Until, perhaps, now.

Many of these men never had had any respect for the court system, preferring their own ways, but now even previously law-abiding men were feeling put out by the difficulty, if not impossibility, of putting criminals to death or even keeping them in jail for long. In 1908 Tom Spence, a black man, was tried for rape of a black woman; no black man had been charged with raping a white woman in Harris County since Boy George at the start of the Civil War. Spence was sentenced to hang, but the Georgia Supreme Court gave him a new trial and found him innocent. The week before, clumps of white men had sat around the jailhouse waiting for him to swing and had now been let down by the decision. The fact was that only one person had ever gone to the gallows legally in Harris County. That person was Hilliard Brooks, a black man executed in 1899 for the murder of a black businessman. On the other hand, when Henry Mobley, James Monroe's son, was tried and quickly acquitted that same year for killing Cooper Truett in a "sensational shooting affray" inside the City Drug Store, nobody but the dead man's family blinked.

Perhaps it was the pass that most white men got for committing crimes and the uneasiness it had to cause, within themselves and the larger community, that led government officials to focus so intensely on black crime. Also, I believe a widespread fear of blacks by whites, produced by their unpunished crimes against them, also served to increase whites' focus on "black criminality." We understand better today how unconscious or unaddressed perceptions of individuals and groups can be projected onto others in harmful ways. I found only one man, a fearless Columbus newspaper editor named Julian Harris, who once, in the 1920s, used this idea to explain KKK behavior.

While we may have a stronger grasp on this phenomenon, we still haven't remedied it, as evidenced by our mass incarceration of African Americans entirely out of proportion to their population.

The Mountain Hill district had long been a breeding ground for white outlaws, some of whom had attained the stature of heroes. Back in 1889, Frank Huckaby, Dozier's father, a white man, was murdered by a cocky young gunslinger named Will Wallace. It was in that year that Wallace and his gang also took to terrorizing blacks in Mountain Hill, assassinating one Ransom Gordon while he worked in the fields. Gordon had been a follower of a black teacher who'd already been run out of town; his school was burned down. The day after Gordon's funeral, Wallace stopped a black preacher on the road and forced him at gunpoint to reenact Gordon's funeral, then shot off his mustache. Enraged at all this (since it scared their farmhands and threatened white livelihoods), some of Mountain Hill's better white people called upon the governor to put a reward on Wallace's head. He disappeared but was caught and jailed in Hamilton, where, however, his friends engineered a Christmas escape. Soon afterward he taunted lawmen by riding through Hamilton firing his rifle into the air.

After he was captured he spent two years in rooms off the warden's office at the notorious Columbus stockade, where he'd be rewarded for stopping a breakout. Upon release he found redemption as a detective and a bailiff. In 1893, a long interview with Wallace appeared in the *Columbus Sun-Enquirer* embellishing his Wild West image and enhancing his fame with tales of daring and machismo while living in Texas. Soon thereafter he was murdered in Alabama by Negroes he'd been hired to catch for conspiring against several white planters. This elevated him to near sainthood among his young male admirers in Mountain Hill.

It was shortly after Wallace's death, in 1896, that another Harris County man with close ties to the Mountain Hill section, the recently returned Edgar Stripling, had taken up the outlaw-hero banner. In the bright heat of a summer morn, Stripling—then a substitute Columbus policeman—and his lieutenants battered down the doors to a Columbus courtroom. Jessie Slayton, a black man, was on trial for raping a white woman. Stripling dropped a noose around Slayton's neck and dragged him down the stairs and onto Broad Street, where he and his mob hanged the already-dead man to a tree.

Governor W. Y. Atkinson, an ardent foe of lynch mobs, arrived in town the next day for a wedding and angrily announced an enormous reward of five thousand dollars for information leading to the arrests of mob members.

These were depression days and no one needed that cash more than the farm families of Harris County's western section. Many knew Edgar Stripling had led the mob, yet none reported him.

One year later, Stripling made front pages by murdering a white man he claimed had insulted his wife and sister-in-law. Billy Cornett was shot at close range through his bedroom window as he was unlacing a shoe. Stripling was tried in Harris County, where the crime occurred, found guilty, and slapped with a life term. So stringent a sentence for a white man in a matter involving defense of self and wife or "the unwritten law," as it was called, was almost unheard-of in Harris County. Within days friends engineered his escape from the Hamilton jail. Again a reward was offered and it, too, went unclaimed. Stripling remained in the county for several weeks, undetected and unreported, while arrangements were made for him and his large family to leave the state. If anyone knew his whereabouts, they did not say.

Now, fifteen years later, he was back in the Columbus jail while a massive campaign, headed by none other than Laney C. and Flynn Hargett, Jr., stirred public outrage to produce a gubernatorial pardon for the unrepentant ("I'd do it again!") Stripling. The themes of the current campaign—the righteousness of honor killings, protection of white womanhood, rights of the community over the courts to determine guilt or innocence—served to inflame the attitudes swirling around the Norman Hadley murder.

Beyond the murders already identified as part of the black "conspiracy" against white neighbors, another one was added: Sambo Gordon's September 1911 killing by his black friend and moonshine partner Josh Caldwell, a quick and angry duel that left the two men dead in the road near the Goat Rock Dam. Sambo and Josh had grown up together. They'd been buddies and business partners. Several years earlier, Josh Caldwell had run away to Chattanooga to avoid testifying in a moonshine case. These were hotheaded people who were not inclined to sit down and work out their differences.

Sambo Gordon was one of those men, like his cousin Norman, who lived in two worlds at once. In the daytime he was "Mr. Sambo," the boss man, the landlord, arguing over rents, over cotton production, over broken farm plows and poorly treated mules, sometimes using the strap on the backs of his "boys." At night he was one of those boys, drinking their liquor, winning their money, or losing his to them in games of poker and faro, wooing and bedding their women at will. He'd been married not so long ago to an unhappy-looking woman named Pansy and they had a little girl, but none of that had straightened his ways.

It was six o'clock on that August evening of 1911. The sun had not yet gone down, but the drinking was well under way. Still, he was "Mr. Sambo" to Josh, or perhaps that is just the way the eyewitnesses, almost certainly black, reported it in order to avoid further hard feelings. Just as it was passed down in Sambo's family that he had gone to the barbecue to meet Josh on some business errand; just as it had been explained in court that Sambo was at Alfred Moore's shack the day Alf was killed to console "Aunt Jane" over the earlier death of Sog; and just as, more recently, an attempt would be made to have Norman shot in his bedroom rather than at a Negro shack. So it was handed down through the generations that Josh said to Sambo: "I got you. I got you, Mr. Sambo." And Sambo said back, "I got you, too, Josh."

In different ways, old resentments and rage were also reignited by the 1909 prison release of Louis Moore, then the 1911 release of Jule Howard. Incorrectly or not, Howard symbolized a white man wronged by a black. Moore was another matter altogether, for Sambo Gordon's testimony had helped send Moore to prison wrongfully. But the fact that he'd returned home only shortly before Sambo's killing stoked rumors that Moore was behind it—just one more on a mounting load of logs being laid for a sacrificial fire.

And so it began to build. Black-white killings took on a distinctly racial odor, a combustible quality, that had been more or less absent when they occurred. Men gathered in feverish knots outside Pratt's Store by the river, behind the churches, in the lodge hall to insist that something must be done.

In the chill air of January 1912, the recently memorialized war came to mean a lot more to them than it normally did. Suddenly everybody was remembering who served with whom, and now it was not those sorry Narramore boys but Private Oliver Narramore's two sons who had died at the hand of Negroes. People started counting white men dead by black men's hands and mourning in particular how they'd all gone more or less unavenged. Coon Narramore, then his half brother Dozier Huckaby. Sambo Gordon. Normally the Narramore/Huckaby branches were overlooked on the Hadley-Moore family tree, but now it would be mentioned that they were kin.

Law enforcement in those tangled swamps was often boiled down to a popularity contest—folks simply liked Bryant's victim better than Bryant. Now, the Sambo situation was a problem because he could be a snake in the grass, but standards were standards and he was a white man. Moreover, with the recent celebration of George Washington Gordon's fiftieth anniversary at Kivlin Lodge having everybody so fired up with Gordon love and loyalty, followed quickly by the cold-blooded killing of the presumably innocent Norman, something had to be done. Though poor Buddie Hadley had only just been elected sheriff, did anybody really want to mess up his honeymoon by undermining his authority? Besides, they'd agreed to give him a chance with the judge and a speedy trial. Nothing would happen just yet.

CHAPTER TEN

Brazen Iniquity

As I interviewed elderly black women and men throughout the county, one subject kept coming up, usually unbidden: interracial sex and procreation. The people I approached simply knew from experience that the lynching I was asking about had a sexual component to it. Seated on her front porch in a pair of her grandson's oversize Nikes and a pink cotton wraparound, Verna Hudson gave me what she called "the real nitty-gritty on white folks." She told me all the ways that her black family was related by blood to the white Hudsons and how common it was back then for "old white bachelors who lived with their mothers or sisters to come sit in colored women's houses." She was eighty-six years old when I met her. On the day General James H. Wilson's troops burned Hamilton, it was her great-grandfather Lewis Hudson who grabbed a sharp rock and wrote the date—April 17, 1865—on a large boulder a short walk from where Verna still lived. He was one of the first men to line up at the courthouse that long-ago day in August 1868 when the freedmen got to vote.

As Verna told her stories, I thought about Big Mamma, my Williams grandmother, an olive-skinned woman who once confided to me as a child that her most horrible memory was of the time she got off a plane that also carried prizefighter Joe Louis and was asked by a reporter if she was his mother. The fear of discovering oneself to have "Negro blood" was widespread among southern whites, who were aware that many mixed-race people had "passed" and that any one of them might have been an ancestor.

Learning as a child that being mistaken for a black woman was Big Mamma's worst memory said to me that being black, or even being seen as black, was the worst thing that could happen. And there was plenty around me to reinforce that idea. Black people had the hardest jobs (if any at all), received the harshest treatment at white hands, made up most of the chain gangs I saw regularly along the roadsides, and were routinely the object of my white family's scorn or ridicule. Early in life I was aware of the contradiction between what I was taught about black people and what I knew about the few who were in my life, such as Edna, other friends' maids, and our yard man, Roosevelt, all of whom I liked and trusted. Edna, I loved. But it would take years before I learned all the ways white people had constructed and then taught one another a caricature of blackness in order to stay in charge.

❦

Of all the potentially combustible issues simmering in Harris County in the winter of 1911–12, the most volatile was the issue of sex—forced, semi-consensual, and consensual—among black women and white men. Miscegenation had been a key ingredient in the war of words between North and South since the 1850s. Abolitionists had sought to shame slave owners, noting that while they regarded slaves as subhuman they frequently and callously spawned children with them, often working them like animals or selling them down the river. Slave owners' wives had sometimes confided in their diaries on these matters. Just over the Muscogee

County line from Harris, Laura Beecher Comer, a relative of the abolitionist Henry Ward Beecher and his sister Harriet Beecher Stowe, author of *Uncle Tom's Cabin*, complained to her diary during the Civil War, after learning of her husband's bachelor habit of eating and sleeping with slaves. Sex between white men and black women was commonplace in Harris County, long before and long after the Civil War. The "old bachelor" Brit Williams told the census enumerator in 1830 that a free "woman of color" and three free "children of color" shared his residence. His slaves, eventually numbering nearly one hundred, were all listed as black, though numerous slaves of his extended Beall, Hudson, and Mobley family and other elite families were categorized "Mu" in federal censuses.

Before his death, "Uncle Render" Hutchison, who lived out by the river near Mountain Hill, had ordered an eighteen-foot, four ton, granite obelisk erected at his gravesite and bragged to friends and neighbors that he wanted it known he'd personally bred more slaves than any other white man in the county. In nearby Talbot County, during slavery, Joseph Edgar Biggs had gathered his black and white children and told them they were brothers and sisters. Cautioning that they could never reveal this publicly, he urged them to stay close through the generations.

Miscegenation became a matter of heated public debate between blacks and whites in the early days of Reconstruction, when, in response to white lawmakers' efforts to force black men to support their wives and children, black Republicans started calling for white men to support their black children and mistresses.

In New Orleans, black concubines went on strike to force financial support for their services. Beneath such movements lurked the specter of interracial marriage. Such talk so terrified whites that most southern legislatures passed laws against it at war's end before blacks could be elected to office.

In 1867, Rev. Henry M. Turner, premier leader of Georgia's freed people, told a large outdoor assemblage at Macon that "all we ask of the white man is to let our ladies alone, and they need not fear us." As if that were not enough, he'd further enraged whites by telling his audience of between six and eight thousand people, "I am half white and half black, so I can speak to both races."

In Savannah, blacks mobbed a white lodge, demanding the protection of female virtue. Newly freed black men across the South were taking umbrage at the fact that, while they were falsely accused of raping white women, white men granted themselves total immunity in the matter of black women. Few whites agreed, at least publicly; many argued that black women were natural seductresses who lured weak white men into liaisons for economic gain. Most refused to use the word *rape* in that connection, but at least one prominent Georgia lawyer spoke up during Reconstruction to say, "It is all on the other foot. The colored women have a great deal more to fear from white men." He was a rarity; most white men claimed the practice stopped at war's end and that what vestiges remained were the work of white trash.

During Reconstruction, lurid articles describing southern-based radicals, black and white, marrying or cohabiting with the opposite race began to crop up in white newspapers, occasionally revealing—always with great disgust—a marriage between a white southern woman and a black man. From then into the twentieth century, the Macon paper often reported on police busts in neighborhoods where black and white cohabited, and was always careful to note the lowly station of the whites.

In 1886, the *Columbus Daily Enquirer* reported a grassroots Louisiana antimiscegenation movement, which was "approved in high places." The article read like a how-to, but nothing similar would take hold in Georgia for another twenty years; nor did it amount to much in Louisiana then. It was about the same time, however, that a bill was passed in the Georgia General Assembly to forbid blacks and whites to attend the same school; this was aimed at white children, primarily in Atlanta, who were enrolled in black schools by their Yankee schoolteacher parents. Editorials in support of the law equated integrated schooling with eventual interracial sex, just as any interracial activity was equated with sex by influential whites. No law specifically segregating white and black, except in marriage, had heretofore been deemed necessary. This would be the start—accelerated by the U.S. Supreme Court *Plessy v. Ferguson* decision in 1895—of local and state laws segregating public facilities such as trains, parks, pools, and benches.

It was during the late nineteenth century that white church women began to speak out and seek legal remedies on behalf of black women and girls—including repeated, failed attempts to raise the age of consent from ten to fourteen, a move opposed by white men who feared blacks would use such a law against them. In tandem with that grew white men's proclamations of the sacred nature of the white woman. While there were certainly white women raped by black men, the numbers never reached the mammoth proportions frequently claimed. This rationale worked so well that for decades it would remain the chief propaganda item to justify lynching and discourage social relationships between blacks and whites. It would also, for a time, muffle any white advocacy for the protection of black women and girls.

CHAPTER ELEVEN

Heroines

The tide began to turn in the 1880s when a black Memphis teacher named Ida B. Wells began to write antilynching articles in a church newsletter. Her columns drew the notice of white Memphis papers, which reprinted some of them. She came to the attention of Thomas Fortune and his National Afro-American League, the first black national organization to address the terror already beginning to sweep the South. Wells's incisive research and clear voice would be the first to disprove the myth of the black rapist and to show the countless other reasons blacks were lynched. From that decade well into the twentieth century, her voice would remain the most powerful and persistent.

Wells's interest in the topic caught fire in 1891, when businessmen friends of hers were lynched. In response she bought her own paper and assumed the role of investigative reporter. Through her research into the actual reasons behind lynchings, she found that alleged rape accounted for only 23 percent and that many of those were false charges. Once a believer in the "black rapist" myth, she now viewed it as a pretext for eradicating successful blacks, giving the lie to white claims that black hopes lay in self-discipline and hard work.

The fearless Wells, who in 1884 bit the hand of a conductor who ejected her from a "whites-only car" and sued the railroad (successfully, until her case was overturned by a higher court), kept on fighting: She wrote a pamphlet called *Southern Horrors,* won the support of Frederick Douglass, the most famous black American of his day, made several tours of Europe, and gained an international audience for her views. She regularly referred to the fact that many southern white women had consensual sex with black men, which infuriated white leaders, who routinely denied it even though white southern newspapers often reported these liaisons.

When she published an article on this subject, her newspaper office was incinerated and Wells and her co-owners were run out of town, warned that there'd be a rope waiting if they returned. From her new home in Chicago, she continued to publish well-researched reports, many for the *Chicago Tribune,* which exposed the truth behind lynchings. Wells took to the road throughout the United States and England to form antilynching leagues and, while in Britain, called for boycotts of southern textiles.

Columbus, a major textile manufacturing center, kept a close eye on Wells and its two dailies occasionally printed her speeches on their front pages. She was no less hated by the white northern press: a *New York Times* editorial once called her a "nasty-minded mulatress" for suggesting white women might consciously consort with black men, who, the *Times* assured readers, were "naturally prone to rape."

The antagonism of white Georgians toward the now-married Ida B. Wells-Barnett spiked in 1897 when she sent a white Pinkerton detective to Newnan, a short way from Harris County, to investigate the famous Hose-Strickland lynching. His report revealed that while Sam Hose had killed a white farmer, either in self-defense or in a moment of rage at being denied permission to visit his dying mother, the farmer's wife had not, as widely

reported, been raped on a floor covered in her husband's blood—
had not, in fact, been raped at all. That rumor, given credence
by the mainstream press, had created enough rage to bring two
thousand people (many of them on specially scheduled trains) to
participate in a savagery in which Sam Hose was barbecued and
his body parts widely distributed.

When Wells-Barnett's heroic efforts to stop lynching bore little
fruit, she counseled blacks to equip their homes with Winchester
rifles until they could save enough to abandon the South, provok-
ing additional antagonism by white southerners.

While Wells-Barnett's activities were grabbing headlines, another outspoken black woman, Anna Julia Cooper—a cousin to
my Williams family—wrote *A Voice from the South,* which excoriated white slave owners, explaining all the ways they had debil-
itated black people, continued to play them against one another,
and contributed to their downfall.

I discovered my connection to Cooper in a most unexpected
way, while looking for black women of this period who'd spoken
out against the sexual predations of white men. I found her 1886
plea for the protection of "the colored girls of the South" who live
"in the midst of pitfalls and snares, waylaid by the lower classes
of white men with no shelter, no protection nearer than the great
blue vault above." Something told me to look into her background
and I quickly learned from her own writings that she was the
daughter of an enslaved woman and her owner, George Washington Haywood. From my research into old Williams letters at the
University of North Carolina, I knew he was a cousin.

Anna Julia Cooper was the granddaughter of Eliza Eagles
Haywood, who had published erudite tracts with the Raleigh
Tract Society, and in the late 1700s mused in a journal whether,
if given the chance, women and Negroes might not be as capable
as white men. At age nine the precocious Anna Julia had been

sent to St. Augustine's, a school started by white Episcopalians for freed children on grounds formerly part of a Haywood plantation. She'd learned to read at an early age and within a few years was teaching other children; upon graduation, she enrolled at Oberlin College, where she'd become the second woman to insist on taking the male course. Married and widowed early, now named Cooper, she returned to Raleigh to teach at St. Augustine's and to make a name for herself as a popular speaker. In *A Voice from the South,* which was published in 1892 and won praise across the color line, Cooper mounted a line of attack on white southerners, which surely caught the eyes of her prideful Lost Cause cousins:

> Without wealth, without education, without inventions, arts, sciences, or industries, without well-nigh every one of the progressive ideas and impulses which have made this country great, prosperous and happy, personally indolent and practically stupid, poor in everything but bluster and self-esteem, the Southerner has nevertheless with Italian finesse and exquisite skill, uniformly and invariably so manipulated Northern sentiment as to succeed sooner or later in carrying his point and shaping the policy of this government to suit his purposes.

Continuing this previously unheard-of line of public attack on white supremacists by a black woman, she added wryly, "If your own father was a pirate, a robber, a murderer, his hands are dyed in red blood and you don't say very much about it. But if your great-great-great-grandfather's grandfather stole and pillaged and slew and you can prove it, your blood has become blue and you are at great pains to establish the relationship."

This would have enraged the Beall-Williams clan in Hamilton, whose greatest pride was their ancestors' military legacy, just beneath the surface of which lay slaughter, plunder, and pillage of countless numbers of Native American and African peoples.

In 1892 Anna Julia stood before a teeming crowd at the World's Convention of Women in Chicago and spoke against white men's predatory behavior toward black women.

The painful, patient, and silent toil of mothers to gain a fee simple title to the bodies of their daughters, the despairing fight, as of an entrapped tigress, to keep hallowed their own persons, would furnish material for epics. That more went down under the flood than stemmed the current is not extraordinary. The majority of our women are not heroines—but I do not know that a majority of any race of women are heroines. It is enough for me to know that while in the eyes of the highest tribunal in America she was deemed no more than a chattel, an irresponsible thing, a dull block, to be drawn hither or thither at the volition of an owner, the Afro-American woman maintained ideals of womanhood unshamed by any ever conceived. Resting or fermenting in untutored minds, such ideals could not claim a hearing at the bar of the nation. The white woman could at least plead for her own emancipation; the black woman, doubly enslaved, could but suffer and struggle and be silent. I speak for the colored women of the South, because it is there that the millions of blacks in this country have watered the soil with blood and tears, and it is there too that the colored woman of America has made her characteristic history, and there her destiny is evolving.

Her well-received book and the Chicago speech catapulted Cooper into the international spotlight. Of her presentation and others at the World's Congress of Representative Women in Chicago in 1893, Frederick Douglass remarked from the audience, "When I hear such speeches . . . from our women—our women—I feel a sense of gratitude to Almighty God that I have lived to see what I now see."

At the Exposition and in her book, Anna Julia Cooper established herself as the nation's first black feminist by asserting that black women, because they had endured more, suffered more, survived more, had more to teach black and white men and white women than the reverse. She was talking to black people about the schemes of white folks to divide and demoralize blacks; she used her "inside knowledge," her excellent education, and her fine mind to unmask and humiliate them.

In the last decade of the nineteenth century and the first of the twentieth, as the name Anna Julia Cooper continued to pop up in the *Washington Post* and the *Atlanta Constitution* as a founding member of the National Association of Colored Women's Clubs, the larger Williams-Haywood family undoubtedly squirmed at any possibility this brilliant, accomplished, though, alas, "black" scholar, orator, and leader might in some way attach herself to them. This sort of potential reckoning haunted a wide sector of white men and women in the South. Some of the Haywood family sought to exorcise the threat by burning copies of her book, which had been sent to them anonymously. As for the ever-polite and ladylike Cooper, not once did she express public disdain for her white family, though in private papers she wrote "My mother was a slave and the finest woman I have ever known . . . presumably my father was her master, if so I owe him not a sou, And she was always too modest and shamefaced to ever mention him."

❧

By the 1890s the Williams family was well entrenched in Columbus society. Ben was a state senator and his brother Charles, a prominent physician, headed the Georgia Medical Society. One of

Ben's wife's Beall cousins was married to a man of great influence in the city, William Young, president of Eagle & Phenix Mills. Another cousin was married to the brother of Gunby Jordan, the city's most influential industrialist and banker. An elegant section of Columbus had been named Beallwood. Ben's son and brother had fine homes in another upscale section, south of downtown, along the river near where General Beall had first laid out the city. Because of the populist diatribes against the rich, wealthy people at the time avoided the limelight. Certainly they did not want it known their ancestors had spawned black children now educated beyond their own and speaking to an international audience about the crimes of the white fathers.

Anna Julia Cooper was not the only offspring of slave and slave master who'd set white relatives' teeth on edge. In Wilmington, North Carolina, Alex Manly, believed to be a descendant of former North Carolina governor Charles Manly, a Haywood cousin, published the *Daily Record*, the only daily black newspaper in the world. In 1898 Manly took up a prominent Ida Wells theme: "Every negro lynched is called a Big Burly Black Brute," he, or possibly a staffer, wrote in the *Record*, "when in fact many of those who have been dealt with had white men for their fathers and were not only not black and burly, but were sufficiently attractive for white girls of culture and refinement to fall in love with them, as is very well known to all."

In 1897, in a burst of anger at Georgia newspaper columnist Rebecca Felton, who'd gained national attention with her diatribes against black rapists, calling for "a lynching a day if that's what it takes," Manly wrote of the white men of North Carolina: "You set yourselves down as a lot of carping hypocrites; in fact you cry aloud for the virtue of your women, while you seek to destroy the morality of ours. Don't think ever that your women will remain pure while you are debauching ours. You sow the seed—the harvest will come in good time." The intemperate remark became the perfect pretext for the armed takeover of government already planned by former congressman Alfred Waddell, yet another Haywood cousin, and a committee of Wilmington's most powerful whites, including Uncle Alfred Williams's granddaughter's husband, Preston Bridgers, who acted as its chief fund-raiser.

At a planning meeting in the Municipal Auditorium, Waddell and his men decried the large numbers of blacks and Radical whites in city offices, reeled off lists of petty humiliations whites endured each day at the hands of black officials, determined they would have all blacks in the state disfranchised, plotted to drive out the city council, and made lists of blacks and whites targeted for removal. Using Manly's editorials to bring white ruffians in the streets to fight blacks, the men fomented their "riot."

On November 10, 1898, Waddell led a mob of four hundred "Red Shirts" into a black Wilmington neighborhood, entered Manly's newspaper building, smashed its presses, and burned it to the ground. Manly's light skin had allowed him to escape the city earlier, but large numbers of successful, educated blacks, already carefully chosen for exile, were rounded up and marched to the depot. Twenty-five others were killed, including the white Republican deputy sheriff. This was followed by days and nights of all-out warfare. In the end, the hard-wrought gains of freed blacks were almost entirely destroyed and thousands of lives had been wrecked. Far and wide in the white world, the defenders of white womanhood were lionized and the black editor Alex Manly was blamed. Undaunted, Manly served briefly in the office of Congressman George White, a black North Carolinian, writing civil rights legislation; but the remainder of his life was plagued with failure.

In the meantime, Anna Julia Cooper had begun to make public pronouncements decrying mobs and speaking specifically about the Hose lynching, calling the mob "hyenas." She also had choice words about the Wilmington riots and murders—with no mention, however, of her white relatives' involvement. At a 1902 Quaker conference, Cooper blasted President Theodore Roosevelt and his attorney general for bringing "no federal aspects" to the lynching mania. By now she was living in Washington, D.C., where as principal of the M Street School, she was attracting attention for her success at sending black students to Ivy League colleges. She was the only woman invited to join the American Negro Academy, a circle of prominent black intellectuals, including Du Bois.

In 1904, Mary Church Terrell, a black woman who'd achieved an even larger public presence than Cooper, her neighbor and colleague in Washington, D.C., and who was now honorary president of the National Association of Colored Women, published an antilynching article in the *North American Review*. In it she blasted white ministers for their silence on and sometimes support for lynching, saying that the practice was converting white southern women and children to savages. She blamed whites' hatred of blacks and a general state of lawlessness of the South. She took up one of Cooper's major themes, the invasion of Negro homes by white "gentlemen" who consider "young colored girls" their "rightful prey."

If white Hamilton was listening, and by now they were hyperalert to the subversive outcries of "the enemy," their ears were burning.

CHAPTER TWELVE

Race Wars

Sex between white men and black women in the South was taboo before 1906, but the Atlanta riot of that year—a watershed event for race relations—thrust the subject into national prominence. During a four-day carnival of mayhem, thousands of white Atlantans ran wild through downtown streets. Their anger had been stoked by hysterical and mostly erroneous newspaper accounts of white women raped by black men. Ten blacks were killed; hundreds, black and white, were injured; windows were smashed and trolleys wrecked. The city's carefully cultivated reputation as the pinnacle of a New South lay in ruins.

In the wake of the Atlanta riots, the vitriolic rhetoric of certain press and politicians would be held chiefly responsible, but that wasn't the only thing causing the increasing racial antagonism in rapidly industrializing Atlanta. The economic gap between the races was growing ever larger. Race was being used to pit white against black in mills, factories, and on construction sites. More than one hundred thousand blacks had left the state in the past several years and the Georgia Industrial Association was actively seeking European settlers.

White working-class resentment, stoked by the anti-union tactics of white business owners and government officials, was sky-rocketing. The recent segregation of the streetcars and other public facilities in Atlanta and the threatened segregation of housing were sources of ongoing agitation by black leaders. Atlanta newspapers regularly ran accounts of black crime, prominently positioned and luridly headlined. Also, in Atlanta and elsewhere, police abuse of blacks was out of hand.

The white police force routinely swept blacks off the street for no particular reason, hauling them into court, often trying them in groups with no lawyers. While many were virtually sold to the private coal mines, rock quarries, and brickyards, others were sent to the dreaded Atlanta Tower, an overcrowded and notorious city prison, or put in chain gangs for short periods. Almost all received small fines, resulting in a handsome purse for the city. Fifteen thousand such arrests were made in 1905.

It was in this edgy atmosphere that a controversial play, *The Clansman,* opened at the Atlanta Opera House in February. The play had already been banned in some cities, and Atlanta's black leadership was vehemently protesting the Atlanta performance. Its producers could not have picked a worse time.

Written by preacher-turned-playwright Thomas Dixon, a man Hamiltonians knew well, since he'd married a Columbus woman, the play featured black rapists of white women and extolled the KKK. Dixon was a popular speaker on the Chautauqua circuit, where he called for race war and gloated that the North was joining the South in matters of race. Three years earlier, Dixon's *The Leopard's Spots* had been the reigning hit on Broadway. In a letter to a friend about the book version of the play, Dixon had written: "It is the best apology for lynching, it is the finest protest against the mistakes of Reconstruction." *The Leopard's Spots* sold well over a million copies, as would *The Clansman* within a few months of publication.

On that February night in Atlanta, the audience watched blacks depicted as savages lusting after white maidens, corrupting the political process and dominating the white citizenry who desperately tried to rescue civilization. In the final moments, as robed Klansmen galloped onstage astride white horses to save southern womanhood before a blazing cross, the crowd went wild.

When playwright Dixon stood in the footlights at the play's end and memorialized his father as a member of the Klan, he received a standing ovation. Judge Cooper Williams, who went to Atlanta each month to pick up the vets' pension checks, was in the audience; with him was his protégé Arthur Hardy, *Harris County Journal* editor and a man enamored of Dixon, who was already plotting his own novel on the subject of race.

By September, Atlanta's racial temperatures were soaring. Six white women had been accosted or raped or had claimed to have been raped by black men. Two suspects had been lynched. Newspaper banners became battle cries and circulation soared. "Mob of 2,000 gathered at Lawrence home anxious to burn Negro . . . Let the women arm themselves . . . A reign of terror for southern women . . ." *Atlanta Journal* editor Charles Daniels called for a new Klan to monitor black behavior and lynch assailants. Amid the frenzy, his power and popularity grew and he was sworn in as deputy sheriff as the county police force was tripled. Over a four-day period, a mob of white Atlantans, estimated in the thousands, ran wild.

White newspapers reported black women attacking white men with parasols. State troops under the command of the judge's son-in-law, Ed Pomeroy, were called out. Newspapers compared proud, reborn Atlanta to St. Petersburg in the throes of revolution.

Before, during, and after the riots, white newspapers, theaters, and political podiums resounded with vicious calls for lynching, deportation, castration, and sterilization of blacks. Even the normally temperate *Harris County Journal* went off the tracks as editor Hardy published on his front page an inflammatory letter to the *Atlanta Georgian* titled "Scripture Justifies Lynching," which proposed that back rapists be castrated.

The *Columbus Sun-Enquirer* took to the idea and championed it on its editorial page. The Columbus City Council followed up by taking under consideration a bill to do just that. Hamilton's leaders, perhaps stunned by how quickly they were being roused to violence, declared a moratorium on rabid racism in the pages of the *Journal.*

Later, men of stature would blame the riot on the heated rhetoric of Smith's campaign, Dixon's play (which was still enjoying wide audiences throughout Georgia), and the *Atlanta Georgian* and its editor, John Temple Graves.

They might also have blamed the riot for fueling the growth of the Niagara Movement, begun less than a year earlier by W. E. B. Du Bois and other black intellectuals. Three years later it would become the NAACP, the first widespread national formation of blacks and their white allies to take on lynching. Until this point most black leaders had been hesitant to make a big show of strength, fearing it would only rouse whites to more violence and hurt their cause.

Watching politicians like Hoke Smith and other formerly trusted whites fomenting antiblack violence, Du Bois, the country's first black Harvard graduate, now a professor at Atlanta University, concluded that blacks could no longer trust the South's good white leaders to protect them. His first glimmer of that reality had come after Sam Hose's lynching seven years earlier, when Atlanta newspapers had also acted as cheerleaders for a lynching and he'd been stunned to see Hose's knuckle bones displayed in an Atlanta butcher's window.

During and after the Atlanta riots he and his colleagues expressed these sentiments more loudly and frequently. Kelly Miller, a colleague of Du Bois, Terrell, and Cooper and a Howard University professor, rejected Booker T. Washington's insistence that good white southerners could handle these problems, and called for federal troops to step in. He argued that if they didn't, blacks should arm themselves and fight back. Du Bois himself had sat on his front steps with a shotgun across his knees to protect his wife and daughters during the Atlanta riots. He and other black leaders began to counsel self-defense. Whether it was because of this counsel or sheer desperation, increasing numbers of rural blacks were taking up guns for self-protection.

Du Bois had recently completed a massive U.S. Bureau of Labor study of "the distribution of labor, the relation of landlord and tenant, the political organization and the family life and the distribution of the population" in Lowndes County, Alabama, a hundred miles from Harris. He'd worked on this for a year, seen several of his black agents driven out with shotguns, interviewed thousands of farmers of both races, studied every land record and every justice court case since 1850, and done what no one had dared to do before: he'd taken the machine apart. His study would show how it worked, right down to the last nut and bolt.

Two white agents had conducted intensive confidential interviews that would show the sex relations among black and white, as well as the political dynamics that drove labor relations, land ownership, and the economy and wrapped black people's lives in barbed wire.

This unprecedented report would never see daylight. Just before Baker came to town, Du Bois learned that his report had "disappeared" within the Labor Bureau. He'd gone to Washington to fight for its release and been told it "touched on political matters." It was a piece of dynamite, of course, which when lobbed into

Congress would certainly drive deep fissures into the North-South alliance, so carefully constructed since the war.

Eight years earlier, a similar, though less scientific report Du Bois wrote on commission for *McClure's* magazine had met the same fate. Soon New York philanthropist George Foster Peabody, the Columbus native with vast influence over the General Education Board, one of Atlanta University's largest funders, would warn Du Bois to stop inflaming blacks against whites. He would inveigh upon Booker T. Washington to speak against Du Bois and finally, in 1909, arranged for Du Bois to lose his job. In 1911 the determined and creative Du Bois rewrote the censored report as *The Quest of the Silver Fleece,* a novel.

In the wake of the Atlanta riot, in a madcap rush to avoid race war or, as former Georgia governor William J. Northen began predicting, "the utter collapse of western civilization," temperance groups such as the WCTU and the Anti-Saloon League blamed liquor. Mayor pro tem Ed Pomeroy and others shut down Atlanta's saloons. Quickly, however, white saloons were reopened so as not to turn away convention business. Bars allowing whites and blacks were closed for good and black bars were closed for long periods. The Georgia prohibition bill, covering both races, pushed relentlessly and unsuccessfully for decades, was signed into law in the immediate wake of the riots to take effect on August 1, 1907. In this season of heightened Negrophobia, its passage was heralded as whites making a personal sacrifice in order to save the dissolute Negro, whose welfare they must oversee.

Black voting was viewed by many as contributing to "Negro uppityness" as much as interracial carousing and alcohol selling. Consequently, upon his election, Governor Smith spearheaded a voting law requiring literacy and property ownership, which cut almost all blacks from the rolls. By 1910 only eleven black men would be qualified to vote in Harris County. In addition, the new white agenda for blacks—put into operation with the defeat of populism—deemed any education beyond industrial training useless and even dangerous. Tuskegee Institute president Booker T. Washington, the darling of the white business community, made countless speeches essentially urging blacks to gratefully accept their naturally inferior position in America.

With all of this in play, astute black leaders of the time had to wonder if the Atlanta "riots" were not prearranged by white leaders determined to stamp out any remaining vestiges of "Negro domination." One of these leaders, an editor named Max Barber, was driven from the city much like Alex Manly, not by a crazed mob brandishing torches but by a soft-spoken banker, James W. English, who called him into his office and told him that he could leave with his family or kiss his wife and children good-bye forever. Two years later, English would be exposed in state senate hearing rooms as a major beneficiary of the state's barbaric convict labor system.

❧

In 1907, around the time that Dozier Huckaby was murdered near Mountain Hill in a fight with a black man and a white man over a little "ginger-colored baby," former governor William J. Northen began organizing grassroots clubs. His goal was to bring together the best of the whites and the blacks to protect white women from black rapists, blacks from other blacks, and blacks both male and female from brutish white men who might lynch or rape them.

In the same year, far away in St. Francisville, Louisiana, after a white man murdered another in a fight over a black woman, a mass meeting was held in the courthouse to formulate plans to suppress "the keeping of Negro concubines by white men."

Northen's credentials were impeccable and he enjoyed wide-spread support within both races. He'd presided over the Georgia

Baptist Convention since 1895, served several terms as head of the Southern Baptist Convention, and was a trustee at Mercer, a Baptist college, for forty years. He was governor of Georgia from 1890 to 1894 and served many years before that in the state legislature.

In the midst of the riots, he'd called together the most prominent black and white ministers in Atlanta at the colored YMCA. In February, he attended the Georgia Equal Rights Convention, the inner circle of black leaders in the state, a group allied with Du Bois and his Niagara Movement. These men were not, however, willing to accept Northen's—and all white southern leaders'— insistence that blacks accept white supremacy as the sine qua non of any pact.

For most of that year Northen traveled the state, urging the formation of organizations called variously "civic leagues," "law and order leagues," and "legions of honor." Newspapers closely followed his progress and he was exultant over his success. At seventy-one, with a flowing white beard, he seemed anointed by the Almighty to the task. In a Jeremiah warning of the imminent fall of white civilization, he spoke strongly against lynching and proudly of his efforts as governor to stop it, but like many of the old patriarchs who'd never come to terms with their own racism, he confused people with his double messages. One day he'd be blasting the mob; the next day he'd be talking so venomously about black lawbreakers that he seemed to be rallying the mob to action. But 1907 marked the first time that he'd led forthright public discussions of the white South's biggest taboo: miscegenation, particularly between white men and black women.

In his pilgrimage, Northen enlisted select groups of "sun-kissed white men," by which he meant high-minded Christians and "law-abiding Negro ministers and Negro laymen" who are "fully and heartily ready and anxious to help solve the awful conditions which confront us." He called on whites to follow his example;

they should not hesitate, he said, to salute a law-abiding African American and "tell him I am his friend and will be his staunch friend as long as he behaves himself as a member of the community." This recognition, Northen suggested, "helps the Negro to make himself a man." Working together—with whites fully in charge—the white and black "first classes" would codify the population of each county so that they would know "definitely and fully, the character of all the people among whom we live." Only "law-abiding" blacks had access, he contended, to the information necessary to make a complete and accurate list of the "vicious and villainous Negroes," who "lounge around dives and dens and clubs during the day and commit burglaries and assaults at night."

"Law-abiding" black men, Northen told his audiences, had the special task of helping to unearth "a large body of low down, filthy, morally corrupt, and physically rotten white men who have Negro concubines." Once exposed, every "last one of such white men" was to be sent to the state penitentiary for twenty-five years. Punishing these men was absolutely vital, Northen emphasized, because "we can never settle the problem of the races as long as we allow corrupt white men to ruin the homes of Negroes and make for them a lot of instant strumpets and wenches of pure, clean women."

Such talk surely shocked the people of Harris County, even those who hated the practice of interracial sex. The notion that black men, even "law-abiding black men," should have any say in this sensitive matter would have curdled the blood of most white men in Harris County. Already Georgia's black leaders were demanding the integration of police forces, and in nearby Macon these demands were being answered. In 1889 Hamilton's own respectable black men had organized a posse to hunt down a white child molester. "Mobs of negroes armed with shotguns, pistols, etc., have nightly visited the premises" of the suspect's father-in-law for the past two weeks, reported the *Atlanta Constitution*. That Sunday night, "100 armed negroes went to his residence and demanded entrance and searched the house." No attempt was made to stop them and the culprit was quickly turned in by another white man. No record was found of the outcome; he was most likely put on a train, the solution for many complicated situations in those days.

Still, this black toe dipped into white men's waters caused concern. A year earlier, in Charleston, South Carolina, two black men had lynched a white man who "outraged" a black woman, and Rev. Henry Turner's Equal Rights Convention passed a resolution of support and voted to raise funds for the men. More recently, the news of armed blacks protecting their neighborhoods during the Atlanta riot dredged up memories of an earlier scare, when one of the Hamilton elite had announced that Negroes had stolen the local militia's arms cache. Though he'd quickly reversed himself, those old fears of black insurrection born during slavery and passed down to newer generations sullied the air more than usual these days. Behind all this was the knowledge of the cruelties whites had heaped upon black heads—not least of which was what white men had done to black women—and the long-standing, deeply suppressed fear that their turn would come. Slowly they were waking to the fact that perhaps this turning of the table might already have started, catching them unaware.

By the fall of 1907, Northen had visited more than ninety counties and organized civic leagues in many of them, according to his weekly reports in the *Atlanta Georgian*. Northen was not, however, invited to bring his campaign to Harris County. He'd been swept into the governor's office in 1890 on a tidal wave of populism and, despite his disavowal of the movement years ago, he'd not been forgiven. Some years earlier, when the *Atlanta Constitution* announced he'd be addressing the Harris County

Farmer's Alliance—an organization largely Populist but taken over by crafty conservative Democrats—its president, Judge Cooper Williams, wrote politely but firmly to say the governor had never been invited to Harris County. Williams men knew how to hold a grudge and this had all the earmarks of one. Or maybe they were just smart enough to surmise that since Northen was loudly advocating incarcerating white men for having sex with black women, half of them would end up in the penitentiary if his ideas took hold. Another strike against Northen was that some years earlier when he was governor and advocating stronger antilynching laws, he'd had the temerity to announce to the world that there were "100,000 white murderers in Georgia," referring to lynch mob members who'd gone unpunished.

Whether to invite Northen would not have been a matter of any debate in Hamilton. White women especially shared his concerns, but not his determination to expose white offenders, and besides, Hamilton had always done things its own way. In their minds, they had good relations with their black folks and their black ministers; they regularly sent white ministers like Rev. Willie Upshaw and their own Rev. Alex Copeland into black churches to reassure the restive ones. As for this business between white men and black women, sooner or later they'd deal with that in their own way as well. But they certainly weren't giving black men a say in the matter. The sheriff at this time was Mitch Huling; he and his deputy, Buddie Hadley, had family up to their necks in these matters.

Harris wasn't the only county to turn its back on him; still, Northen found no shortage of supporters. One day he was in Jasper County, the next in Putnam, often in two or three counties in the same day. He met with bankers and ministers and merchants. He published their names and gloried in their willingness to sign on to his ever-increasing army of Christian conquistadors. Many were his old populist allies and many conservatives were driven to support him by the recent embarrassment and fright they were given by the Atlanta riots, and the resulting embarrassing national revelations of white southern men's biracial sex lives. Chief among these was a magazine series called "Following the Color Line."

Before the embers died on Atlanta streets, a "muckraker" named Ray Stannard Baker stepped off the train in Atlanta. Already famous, Baker had worked at *McClure's* with the legendary Lincoln Steffens and Ida Tarbell. Baker had recently started the *American Magazine*, intending to push it to the forefront of American journalism with a series on the Atlanta riot and its causes. Muckraking, or "yellow journalism," was feared by the plutocrats while the masses saw in it hope of great societal change.

Du Bois was one of the first men Baker interviewed. Du Bois found Baker naïve but shared the findings of his study in hopes this white man with a large bullhorn would be willing to bring them to light. His bottom line, as he told Baker, was that inequality—not sex, alcohol, black crime, or miscegenation—was at the heart of "the Negro problem."

Baker, who followed Northen's campaign and accorded him much space in the series, was largely cut from Northen's cloth, and believed that what was needed to solve the race problem was simply an equal application of criminal laws and an abundance of kindness and decency on everyone's part. He did nothing to dispute the white supremacist beliefs undergirding the system he criticized. Disregarding Du Bois's position, he nonetheless revealed more truth about the relations between white men and black women than arguably any white journalist before him. His goal was not to detail the humiliation this posed to blacks nor the role it played in weakening black communities socially and economically, but to demonstrate the hypocrisy of the white South's claim of "white supremacy" as their excuse for discrimination and injustice. He described a growing antagonism towards miscegeny and talked about how the old practice of white men—including prominent judges, governors, and wealthy planters—keeping their black families on the side was still alive and well.

He described a visit with a prominent white man who expressed great bitterness against Negroes and argued that they must be kept down. The next day another man showed him the "neat cottage where the other man's Negro family lived." "I saw this man's colored children in the yard," he said.

In 1906 Baker's incendiary articles began to appear. Bits and pieces would be reprinted in pamphlet form by committees to advance Negro interests in the North and passed from hand to hand to the delight of many, for here at last was proof the Negro wasn't the only problem. The white man, mostly the "cracker," but in part the planter, was getting his due; Baker, desiring this class's patronage, hastened to brush off what little damage he'd done.

He advised readers: "The hatred and fear of such relations have grown most rapidly, of course, among the better class of white people. The class of white men who consort with Negro women at the present time is of a much lower sort than it was five or ten years ago and than it was in slavery times. Negroes are awakening to this, too. I found several Negro communities, where women's clubs and other organizations were trying, feebly enough, but significantly, trying to stem the evil from their side. It's a terrible slough to get out of. These women (concubines) are honored rather than ostracized, have advantages, thus status among Negroes."

However, the "hatred and fear of such relations" Baker referred to among the better classes, was not, Northen found, enough to galvanize them to action against it. He often expressed his frustration at these "sun-kissed men" who showed up to lend their moral support to law and order but remained silent when asked to make efforts.

Others wrote to him claiming that their counties had no rapes, no lynchings, no problems. They did not see this as their task and did not wish to draw attention to the widespread miscegenation they all knew existed in the county. The inner circle preferred a code of silence where race was concerned. So much of what the crusading preacher-politician Northen said came too close for comfort: things like the undemocratic nature of the legal system, that white men had taught black men their wastrel ways, and the need for good whites and blacks to put bad whites and blacks under a special watch to prevent crime before it could occur.

It wasn't the antilynching aspect of Northen's campaign that kept him out of Harris County so much as the anti-miscegenation piece. Black leaders like Turner, Du Bois, Wells-Barnett, and Cooper, along with a few white Yankees, had long preached that message, but for white southern leaders the subject had been mostly, until now, taboo. Taken with Northen's message and pulling strings from his gilded peaks in Manhattan, George Foster Peabody counseled his Columbus friend, Gunby Jordan, to form regional commissions to attack the problem. These attempts were quickly thwarted by southern governors who wanted the matter, however crucial, to remain local. And, indeed, it would not be long before this inflammatory issue would find public utterance in Harris County.

CHAPTER THIRTEEN

Clutch of Circumstance

It is October 1996 and, while conducting my research, I am staying with my mother in the house on Clubview Drive where I grew up. Mamma's attitude on race has not changed. Edna still works for her and still enters the house through the back door, though now, when I take her home, she sits up front beside me. She tells me stories of police roundups at black nightclubs in earlier days, where men were locked up long enough for "police to have their way with the women." Sometimes Edna would be locked up along with them. I can remember our phone ringing late at night and it would be Edna calling Mamma begging her to come get her. My mother never went. I like to think that she called her sheriff father and had him put in a call to a friend at the station to let Edna go, but I can't be sure. Edna also tells me that she picked Mamma to work for because there was no man in our house. That had been her big sister's advice when she first left home to find a job. "It's safer that way," her sister said.

While my mother was determined not to aid my quest for the truth, she sometimes forgot herself and handed me a treasure. The best of these was her revelation of the "two-family families" of

Harris County where "a white man would have a black family and a white family and the children all looked alike." I remembered that as a teenager, I had remarked on how I often saw black people who looked like white people I knew and suggested to her that "maybe God made two of each of us." She told me I was crazy. Now here she was telling me about these families, even naming names—Hudson, Jones, Land. She said to me: "If you find that in our family, I don't want to know."

❧

In the midst of Northen's crusade and Baker's articles, Hamilton lawyer-author-orator Arthur Hardy sat down in his cottage across from Hamilton square to pen a novel.

A voracious reader, Hardy was aware of the growing acceptance of open talk about miscegeny. He knew full well he'd moved to a county filled with all manner of sex among white men and black women, past and present. He'd been excited to see how Thomas Dixon's books and plays pillorying white southern men's interracial peccadilloes were winning him international fame and great fortune. So in 1908—the year the new courthouse was completed—he hastened to finish *Clutch of Circumstance,* which, while set in the Reconstruction era, would hold modern miscegenators' feet to the fire.

Dixon's *The Leopard's Spots,* which Hardy bought and read in 1902, portrayed white southerners' "sin" of miscegenation as a curse that led inevitably to black men raping white women and the utter downfall of Western civilization. At the same time, a new generation of blacks, creative, educated, and outspoken, men like Charles W. Chesnutt and W. E. B. Du Bois, were writing on the subject from their own perspective, enticing white writers to bring their white supremacist fire to the battle.

Spots struck a strong chord with the ambitious Hardy, who

began to slip short articles on the theme into the *Journal*. But when his sensitive new wife, Irene, became apoplectic over a racially mixed infant who looked entirely Caucasian and lived next door, Hardy could no longer resist his creative urges and wrote a novel based on an old Harris County family.

This "plump, rosy, fluffy little baby" next door was, it turned out, one-sixteenth Negro; her father, grandfather, and great-grandfather were white and "of good family"; her maternal lineage, increasingly white as well, was nevertheless "negro." Irene was distraught at the notion that this fair child was doomed to life as a black person.

Hardy dedicated the novel "to my wife, whose pity for a helpless babe, and whose indignation toward an unnatural parent suggested and inspired the story." Now his book would go out into the world and inspire white men to stop their evil, philandering ways. Through the white northerner of the novel, who points out to his blind southern cousins the curse of miscegeny on themselves and their illicit offspring, Hardy would open the blind eyes of his own townspeople and those beyond. If he harbored fears that certain white leaders in the town would take umbrage, this did not stay his hand.

Surely there would be gossip about who old "Col. Gurley," who fathered the "comely" Angelus by an enslaved woman, represented. He'd have known the possibilities were manifold among Mobleys, Williamses, Copelands, Whiteheads, Hutchinsons, Lowes, Hudsons, and Bealls, all of whom had seen café au lait babies born to their enslaved women. No one of the county elite needed to feel singled out, however; "Col. Gurley" could easily represent any one of dozens, many long buried beneath this soil. Besides, Hardy's book was written for the common enlightenment and surely they would honor his motive.

If there'd been any doubts in the young author's mind as to

his book's local reception they were immediately dispelled. "[T]he book of the decade, yes, of this generation," the *Harris County Journal* proclaimed. Invitations poured in to speak at school commencements, Sunday school classes, Lost Cause events, and ladies' book and poetry clubs. But with the book's subject being too taboo for public discourse, he was asked to speak on subjects such as the Bible, the nation's history, and the Civil War.

In the midst of all the fanfare, Irene Hardy was taken to Johns Hopkins Hospital in Baltimore for "nerves."

I asked my mother if she knew about Arthur Hardy's novel. *Clutch of Circumstance,* she replied without a second thought. My cousin Buster, now called Doug, on the other hand, had never heard of it, though Hardy, who mentored my scholarly cousin, had bequeathed to him much of his library. To me this illustrates the change that came about with my generation. I believe a conscious decision was made at some point to protect us from this seamy history so we could live free of its weight. Still, it lay close enough to the surface to tease and even haunt some of us, especially me.

CHAPTER FOURTEEN

Special Court

Early on the morning after Sheriff Buddie Hadley locked up Dusky Crutchfield, Johnie Moore, and Eugene Harrington, he climbed aboard the Central of Georgia for the short trip to Columbus. Hamilton had not faced so serious a crisis since the burning of Boy George and, soon afterward, the Yankee invasion. The stumble-tongued sheriff would need assistance when he confronted the venerable Judge Stirling Price Gilbert, so he was accompanied by Arthur Hardy and Ben Williams, Jr., a wealthy planter.

Only a week had passed since Hadley had placed his work-hardened hand upon Judge Williams's Bible in the Hamilton courthouse and sworn to God to uphold both the Georgia and U.S. constitutions. Now he sat in the plush seats of the train with that judge's nephew and Hardy, whom some considered partially responsible for the local upsurge in antimiscegenation fervor—smoking cigars and nervously mulling the upcoming meeting. No public mention had been made of legal representation for the suspected murderers, but Hardy regularly represented poor blacks in court and was possibly there in that capacity.

The outcome was anything but predictable. None knew just yet how the judge would take to this new sheriff. Already Hadley had failed to take into custody men seeking to prevent him from carrying out his duty, a clear violation of law. Likewise, he'd ignored another law requiring him to call out a posse to protect prisoners threatened by a mob. Likely he figured he'd used horse sense and knew that to make arrests would only incite others to further efforts against the prisoners. These things had to be weighed and balanced. Besides, Hadley had been dealing with a dozen or more masked men—what chance would any charges stand in court? Support for the mob's cause was growing all over the county, and though some of the mob members were now walking around unmasked in broad daylight watching the jail, they'd still be, now and forever after, "parties unknown," nameless, faceless instruments of the public will. Never in the history of Georgia had a man even been charged with a lynching, much less with the attempt to lynch.

The lynch threat was used more often than not simply to control the legal process and likely that's all it was here, especially since most of this mob was the sheriff's own kin. Hadley had to reckon he was approaching the judge not as lawbreaker but as a hero of sorts, just as the papers had portrayed him, for he'd stood his ground and, for now at least, spared the lives of one woman and two men. He'd kept the matter, more or less, in the hands of the law.

Harris County had another hero, Judge Marcus Beck, who now sat on the state Supreme Court. Beck, a Hamilton native, had personally used his status as superior court judge in Zebulon, Georgia, many years ago to rescue a black man from a lynch mob. Perhaps the men on the train spoke of it, imagining that this was what their new sheriff had done.

Still, this situation had its own twist. These three petitioners were savvy men and knew they'd be asking Judge Gilbert to back them up on a promise made to a mob, even though they knew that Gilbert despised mob rule with every fiber of his being. Two years earlier, before a Columbus grand jury, he'd called mobs "scalawags . . . and the scum of the earth."

Riding down that day to confront the judge, they knew they held a two-edged sword. None of them wanted a lynching, and for a variety of reasons. Mob violence was bad for business. It made sheriffs look weak. It made white southerners look barbaric in the eyes of the North, especially the investors and new residents the business community sought to attract. More pressing, it scared off black servants and field hands needed for the conduct of normal life. The town's main industry, Hamilton Female College, now called West Georgia A&M, would suffer if masked men with torches and pistols terrified the young ladies boarding nearby or, worse, roused blacks to riot and caused anguished white parents to remove their sons and daughters. Such turmoil would send family members and other "better people" scurrying to Columbus for safety and civilization. Already too many, including younger Williamses, had set up housekeeping in the city's richer neighborhoods, seeking better schools and the finer culture of the rapidly growing city.

Nevertheless, there was no firm consensus on lynching among whites. Proper folks spoke against it, but many privately condoned some. Many of the more refined whites even thought in terms of "good" and "bad" lynchings. "Bad" ones snared innocent people or people accused of minor infractions. "Bad" ones barbecued bodies, sliced off parts, drew large raucous crowds—including women and children—and produced photographs often printed in Yankee newspapers. "Good lynchings" were for blacks accused of raping white women or killing law officers, in which case a message needed to be sent. Mixed messages about lynching were sent all the time. The *Harris County Journal* remained mostly silent on the question but had, on occasion under Hardy's aegis, reported lynchings almost in a how-to style, only occasionally furrowing its brow. Under the New South order—with black leaders led by Booker T. Washington urging followers to submit to "good whites" in exchange for those white leaders' protection of blacks— more whites felt compelled to speak out against the practice.

The "special court" involved the calling of a grand jury to seek indictments for a specific crime and the holding of the trial at that time. In the past they'd been held within days, even hours, but now a new law required a minimum thirty-day wait. The "special court" was one of those measures good men supported as a way to curtail lynching, but others protested, with cause, that it prostituted the legal system, turning judges and juries into legal mobs. When officials begged lynch mobs to "let the law take its course," as my great-grandfather had done at the fork of the roads one day earlier, they were understood to be promising death under a legal guise. That view changed a bit after a wait was required by law in the hopes mob tempers would cool and adequate evidence would be gathered for a fair trial.

As their train slowly chugged into downtown Columbus, the Hamilton men could not help but notice the city's renaissance. Everywhere they looked they saw brick streets, handsome new homes, refurbished mills, new banks, and shops. In 1903, *Harper's Magazine* had sung the Queen City's praises. Columbus titans, observing and fearing the great union movements and worker uprisings under way across America, had worked hard to satisfy its mill and foundry workers with factory schools and libraries.

Since the 1890s, when textile barons had reaped riches on the backs of women and children paid as little as fifty-six cents per week, they'd successfully fought off, both with payoffs and goons, the National Union of Textile Workers. Fearing race riots on the heels of the Atlanta riots, they hired Rev. Ashby Jones at First Baptist. Jones was one of Atlanta's most prominent spokesmen for racial peace. His first Columbus sermon, "Atlanta's Lessons for Columbus," expressed white leaders' thinking: There will never be racial equality. Whites will always be superior and must be the guardians of black people. Blacks are not capable of the vote. And lynching is not a solution to "the unspeakable crime." He urged his listeners, and they were many, to form biracial groups for working on problems. With Rev. Jones as their spiritual guide, the city fathers—funded by their favorite philanthropists, George Foster Peabody and Levi Strauss, New York millionaires raised in Columbus—built the nation's most elegant YMCA for black people. They poured money into the large black A.M.E. and Baptist churches and brought Booker T. Washington and prominent black ministers to town to speak to both races.

Since Reconstruction, wealthy whites had supported those black churches that agreed to keep politics out of the pulpit. Nothing had changed. Sermons continued to focus on honesty, thrift, and industry, and parishioners were often told that to win respect they must be respectable. Women's clubs formed in Columbus churches, sometimes bringing in as many as eight hundred women to hear lectures on how to raise their sons or keep clean houses, and other messages of "upliftment."

Columbus newspapers, controlled by the families who spearheaded economic development, also sent messages to white housewives on racial control. Recently the influential Gunby Jordan had called on white housewives to stop sending food home with their maids. Such access to free food made black men lazy and unwilling to work, he argued. He was especially concerned that the brickyards, crucial to his development plans, were having trouble finding workers. Until 1909, when the infamous convict labor system was shut down, only prisoners worked these hellacious jobs. Now new ways were being sought to coerce non-prisoners to take them.

Meanwhile, black leaders were expected to soothe whites' anxieties. When a black minister used the *Daily Enquirer* in 1907 to ask whites to release black employees to attend Emancipation Day ceremonies, he assured them: "[W]e do not anticipate anything that may cause an unfriendly feeling between the white and colored races," adding that event speakers would "denounce a class of young men who do not work but loaf and do everything possible to degrade the race."

The Hamilton delegation recognized that Hamilton was no longer its own little fiefdom. In recent years the county had been increasingly affected by Columbus development, which reached physically into that section of their county along the river both ruled and sullied by the moonshine cabals now causing the current troubles. The very forces the Populists had opposed—syndicates, bankers, giant corporations—had slipped into Columbus and, unlike anything General Sherman or Abe Lincoln envisioned as their troops stormed the city, were now laying claim to streetcars, utility companies, railroads, and anything else promising hefty, long-term profits. Men who lived on Beacon Hill, had studied at Yale and Harvard, Oxford and the Sorbonne, vacationed in the Alps and on the Mediterranean, were quietly taking part or full ownership of sectors long owned and controlled locally, both private and public. And their reach didn't stop at the county line.

As they invested millions upon millions to build dam after dam up the Chattahoochee, they were also acquiring thousands of acres of some of the richest cotton and moonshine land in Harris County. The possibility of harnessing the river's vast potential had been envisioned before Columbus was even laid out. It had taken a half century to make that dream come true. But since 1908 profits had increased astronomically, and now the pressure on Columbus residents to give the Yankee investors what they wanted—and be happy about it in the bargain—was tremendous.

One day before Norman Hadley's murder, officials from Stone & Webster, as well as General Electric, Westinghouse, and other behemoths of the newly emerging electrical industry, gathered at a spot called Goat Rock in Harris County to survey construction of the latest hydroelectric dam. Ordinary residents of Columbus had opposed the increased electric rates this modernization was causing and Gunby Jordan, the project's chief promoter, along with other city fathers, was eager to impress both corporate investors and leaders from the area with the progress that this new technology would bring to all levels of society.

Given all these considerations, the beleaguered sheriff might have longed for the old days, when a sheriff could throw prisoners to the mob and be considered a hero. That still happened in some places but was more risky in these changing times. Governors were deploring these actions, embarrassed by an increase in publicity up north that made it harder to bring in Yankee dollars. Just recently some Georgia politicians had called for sheriffs to be made financially culpable for lynchings, and several blacks in other states were suing white officials.

In 1893, Gov. Northen had approved a law making "mobbing or lynching" a felony, subject to imprisonment for one to twenty years. Should death occur from "mob violence," the person or persons causing such death were to be tried and subject to penalties under state law for murder. The law also charged peace officers with responsibility for stopping mob violence, and if necessary summoning citizens of the community to help by using every means in their power to prevent such mob violence. Failure to act by either sheriff or summoned citizen was declared a misdemeanor offense. Northen had pushed the bill through the General Assembly, though its passage had done nothing to stop the lynching of black people.

But recent events had spurred louder demands for stricter

enforcement and efforts were under way for stricter laws. At that moment, in fact, certain Georgia editors were howling for Sheriff W. B. Stark's impeachment in Walton County, and two Alabama sheriffs had recently been impeached and removed from office by that state's Supreme Court for negligence in protecting prisoners against mobs. The most glaring example of a change was the 1906 federal government action against Sheriff Joseph Shipp of Tennessee, recently sent to prison after a unique U.S. Supreme Court trial that drew the attention of every sheriff in the South. Shipp, a Georgia native, had stood by as a mob took a man from his jail. The man's case had been accepted on appeal to the federal court and that had given President Teddy Roosevelt the chance he sought to act against lynching. This did not bode well for states' rights. White men of even middling intelligence knew that if they did not put a stop to lynching, the federal government would find a way to move in.

Since the turn of the century, congressional liberals had sought federal antilynching laws and lost. Increasing white southern control over that body had made any legislation that interfered with white men's control over black lives in the South nearly impossible. But the barbarism of lynch mobs throughout the 1890s and into the new century, coupled with the birth of the NAACP and its sophisticated use of publicity to win public sympathy, had the South's more practical white leaders worried. Only one week earlier, the *Chicago Tribune* had named Georgia the number-one lynching state in 1911, with twenty-one of them, and this wasn't the first year it had received this unwanted attention. By the time it was all over, Georgia would sit at the top of this list.

Judge Price Gilbert, for his part, had waged his own campaign against the practice. Son of a slave owner from Stewart County, he subscribed to the New South credo, believing that a segregated industrial economy, heavily financed by northern banks, would solve the economic, social, and racial woes of the region. A staunch but not outspoken white supremacist, he would later describe in an unpublished manuscript his belief that blacks were incapable of the full rights of citizenship, such as voting and jury duty. He did not, however, believe, as many respectable whites still did, that mob violence sent messages to blacks and kept them under control. Rather, he preached incessantly against it on the grounds it weakened the law, its servants, and civilization.

Gilbert served as solicitor general from 1895 to 1906. In that period there had been dozens of lynching threats, and five men he had either been prosecuting or was set to prosecute had been lynched. All but one were black. Since his appointment to the bench, there had been three mob attempts on the jail in Columbus alone, all of them repelled or outwitted. The sartorial, Yale-educated, deeply Methodist Gilbert found all of this harrowing and intolerable. But until two years ago he'd done little more than lecture grand juries, civic clubs, and churches in his six-county jurisdiction about the importance of the legal process and the criminality of lynch mobs.

Then, in 1910, he had ratcheted up his message. On hearing a mob was gathering outside the Columbus jail, he quickly called a grand jury and ordered the sheriff and jailer to "meet it with cold lead." To avoid this, the sheriff smuggled the prisoner to Atlanta. The enraged mob refused to believe its prey—a black man accused of raping a white girl—was gone and, two hundred strong, they stormed the jail with sledgehammers and firearms.

Jailer A. A. Phelts did as the judge ordered and was mortally wounded in the process. The judge, grieving over the death of his friend of fifteen years, called a special grand jury to declare that should another mob form when the prisoner returned for trial, he would not plead with its members but would himself join the ranks of the sheriff's men and personally fire into the mob. As it turned out, the sixteen-year-old rape victim went to Atlanta to make a second identification of the man and declared he was not her attacker. Another man was subsequently arrested and convicted. Newspapers and preachers sang Gilbert's praises. Not only had he stopped a lynching and saved the life of an innocent man, but he had also prevented dozens of Columbus men from making murderers of themselves. Most important, the papers crowed, he'd protected the sanctity of the law.

At First Methodist the next Sunday, Gilbert's pastor raised his face to heaven, stretched forth his arms, and proclaimed in stentorian tones, "Thank God, we had a man upon the bench. A real man and no sham. And yet I dare say some of you censured him. Ain't you ashamed of yourself? Let no man among you do else than stand by such a man and in upholding him uphold all that's best. Thank God, we have a man and not a pea-hen politician for a judge." A town meeting was held to oppose mobs. Ministers praised Jailer Phelts as a hero and martyr who "gave his life for justice."

But for Gilbert, the price came high. A longtime friend was dead. Phelts was a husband, a father, a longtime loyal servant of the justice system. Grief-stricken and outraged, the judge called upon the county to raise a thousand dollars for the family and to build a monument in the jailer's name. Gilbert's wife fell ill under the pressure. When newspapers, including Harris County's, had recently encouraged Gilbert to run for governor, he declined, giving his wife's poor health as the reason. By the time the Hamilton men rolled into Columbus, Judge Gilbert had become an icon, hailed by many, hated by many. As the contingent filed into the Columbus courthouse—magnificent with its five imposing Corinthian columns, occupying an entire city block, well over three times the size of Harris County's proud edifice—Buddie Hadley's insides had to be churning. The men all knew Judge Gilbert would welcome their quest about as much as he'd welcome a bucket of horse manure raked across his Persian carpet.

A highbrow gentleman of the "Chesterfieldian" type, Gilbert had constantly sought through wise and gentle admonition to appeal to the better instincts of people, and here they were asking him to take a mob's word that it would wait for a trial. To call in a special guard or to move the prisoners would say to the mob: "I don't trust you. It would say to the sheriff and his backers, all friends of the judge: 'I don't trust you.'" The sheriff had made a promise to the mob—many of whom were his own kinfolk—and now he and his backers, certainly with some chagrin, came as the mob's mouthpiece.

The conversation that transpired within the judge's chamber that morning can only be imagined, but numerous factors would have already played a part in the participants' thinking. At the moment a major controversy roiling the state concerned a double lynching in Walton County the previous June. This one had caught the attention of the Hamilton men for many reasons, including the fact that the Fifth Militia, commanded by Judge Cooper Williams's son-in-law Ed Pomeroy, was called from nearby Atlanta to protect an accused black rapist.

A black man, Tom Adams, accused of raping a white farm woman and threatened by a mob was removed from the Walton County jail to nearby Atlanta to await trial. By trial time the large mob had grown so belligerent that, under Georgia law, the sheriff and the judge requested that the governor order a large contingent of militia to accompany the prisoner by train to Monroe.

The sight of these troops guarding an accused black rapist in full view of their Confederate statue enraged large numbers of Georgia citizens. Amplifying their anger was the fact the prisoner slept in the courthouse, protected by soldiers handpicked from four militia companies at an announced cost to the taxpayers of one thousand dollars. Three large photos of these scenes splayed across the front page of the *Atlanta Constitution* stoked matters more. Judge Brand of that circuit complicated the situation further by apologizing to white citizens for having to do this. When the trial had to be postponed for lack of a witness and the prisoner was returned to Atlanta, the mob, now numbering more than one thousand, made it clear they would strike when he returned, with or without the militia. This time the sheriff assured the judge he had matters in hand and the judge chose to believe him. The governor twice notified the sheriff and judge of his concern, given news reports of an impending lynching. No, they assured, him, there's nothing to worry about.

Chained to two deputies, the prisoner was returned to Monroe for trial. The mob stopped the train just outside Monroe. They dragged all three to the site of the alleged rape, released the deputies, and lynched the prisoner. Just to make sure the legal system knew who was in charge, they then marched to the jail to lynch another black man, this one accused of a minor crime. The sheriff's wife tried to talk them down and a farmer tried to stop them, but to no avail.

After this, all hell broke loose among friends in Monroe, a town forty-five miles from Atlanta, with the sheriff's people pitted against the judge's friends and everyone forced to take sides as to who bore responsibility. City newspapers, preachers, and politicians raised a howl, calling for stronger laws as well as the judge's and the sheriff's heads. Legislators tried to push through an investigation that would judge and prosecute the guilty parties, be they judge, sheriff, or governor.

Newspaper editorials blazed away at the irresponsibility of both judge and sheriff, and a prominent Atlanta minister invited legislators to a Sunday night sermon to announce that the soul of Georgia had been wronged, men had become beasts, and civilization was at the brink. Many of the legislators showed up and enough were sufficiently outraged to pass a law forcing the removal of a prisoner to a safe venue should mobs threaten.

In Walton County, Judge Brand had spoken publicly about his refusal to call up the militia: "I don't propose to be the engine of sacrificing any white man's life for all the negro rapists in the country by assuming a responsibility that the law does not impose upon me." This was not the sort of remark to ever issue from Judge Gilbert's mouth, but the men from Hamilton had reason to hope he'd take a lesson of caution from the Walton County situation and make no move to order troops. The latest law was not yet in effect, and under current law it was up to the sheriff to request that the judge appeal to the governor to do so. A more recent law allowed prisoners to request extra protection, but that one would not take effect for several more weeks. The current law mandated that the sheriff request of the judge either a change of venue or a call-up of state troops if there was clear and present danger of a lynching. Upon such request, the judge was ordered to request troops from the governor or change the venue himself.

In Hamilton's case, the mob had promised the sheriff there'd be no lynching if a special trial was called. He had, in return, promised not to request troops, a special guard, or a change of venue. This is what he'd tell the judge, and the other two would back him up. This, they hoped, would be enough for Gilbert to just let things be.

In addition to the Walton County lynching, the Hamilton trio knew of another incident, which, like Walton County's, gave them reason for both hope and dread. It was the one that Edgar Stripling, a Columbus substitute policeman at the time, commandeered right there in Columbus on a sunny June morning in 1896. It was one Judge Gilbert had not likely forgotten, as one of the victims had been snatched from under his very nose.

Hadley, Hardy, and Williams knew well the details of this drama and many of its players. Certainly the novelist Hardy would see the similarities between it and their own situation. It had involved a powerful Columbus family. A young white woman, a member of the Bickerstaff-Flournoy-Howard family, whose hands steered much of Columbus government, press, and industry, was allegedly raped by a black man.

This happened near the river in the very section under development by some in this family, a section still occupied by poor whites and blacks but increasingly being carved out as a residential haven for the rich. Gunby Jordan had just bought five hundred acres from the Hadley-related Narramores and built a handsome lodge. Nearby, a posse hunted down a suspect, the woman made a positive identification, and the man was jailed. A crowd of five hundred or more thronged the jail grounds screaming for blood. Judge Burlington Butt stood before them and offered a special trial. In 1896 there was, as now, no law mandating a thirty-day wait and the trial was to be held in four days. When the crowd jeered the judge, business leader Richard Howard took center stage and reminded them of just which powerful family was in charge.

The *Daily Enquirer* editor was a Howard kinsman named Flournoy Crook, who also held prominent business and political positions. On the pages of his paper the next morning, Crook reassured citizens that this distinguished family had matters in hand. It included a letter from the alleged victim's husband, laying out his impeccable family connections. No reference was made to the 1890 murder trial of Richard Howard, his brother Robert, and a Bickerstaff cousin for killing a brother-in-law at the racetrack in full view of several thousand people, including the city marshal and the mayor, who had tried to stop them. Following a heavily attended and widely reported trial in which the men claimed "self-defense" and were portrayed as gallant guardians of their sister's honor, they were acquitted and returned to their prominent positions in the community. Now, with their imprimatur, the militia was sent home.

The use of local militia troops to guard black prisoners was highly controversial, given that most came from the "finest families" and had signed on for social, political, and career reasons, expecting their most arduous duties to come during summer camp training and performances at annual Confederate Memorial services.

The captain of one of Columbus's two militia units was the Howard brothers' close friend and next-door neighbor. As the troops had fended off the mob, the young guards were called "nigger lovers" and "traitors" by mob members, and rumors had abounded of imminent defections should this duty be extended. On the morning of Jessie Slayton's trial, four days later, only eight unarmed sheriff's deputies accompanied a visibly trembling Slayton down Tenth Street to the Webster Building. The unpaved street was lined with several hundred armed, angry, and cursing men, many of them drunk. Thirty minutes into the proceedings, the judge announced that the alleged victim would be called to testify, a taboo among people in that day due to Victorian attitudes toward sex and the intimate nature of such testimony. Word of this quickly reached the street and an outraged mob rampaged the virtually unguarded courtroom. Prosecuter Price Gilbert stood by helplessly as the shrieking defendant was dragged away. After hanging Slayton from a tree, they stormed the jail to snatch another accused rapist, one who'd been tried three times and was awaiting another trial. William Miles's last sight would be of a dead Jessie Slayton, hanging from a branch, his face shot entirely away. So far the similarities between that situation and Hamilton's were obvious: powerful families were seeking a special trial, no militia, no special guard, no change of venue.

In case this wasn't enough of a precedent to give the delegation hope they'd get their way, there was also the family connection. Ben Williams, Jr.'s uncle lived nearly next door to the judge; his uncle Dr. Charles Williams lived short blocks away, as did his brother Tom; all traveled in the judge's social circle. In addition, the Gilberts were close friends of the Mobley family. The judge's wife and daughter summered each year at Miss Lula Mobley's charming antebellum home on Monument Square in Hamilton. It was a welcome respite from the heat and the clamor of the growing city. They loved the square, where the children could now play around the base of the statue; the hand-churned peach ice cream Miss Lula made for her Juvenile Missionary Society classes; the small-town happiness of First Methodist; the drives up Pine Mountain to pick violets. For them, as for me in childhood, Hamilton was a storybook village, devoid of the ugly underbelly that Judge Gilbert often observed from his bench in the courthouse.

Gilbert knew well the cutthroat methods of the Mountain Hill men, the moonshiners who'd been ducking and dodging the law most of their lives. He'd prosecuted Milford and Louis Moore, sentenced Gene Bryant and Jule Howard, and knew how easily those trials or sentences had been subverted. How quickly jurors changed their minds and petitioned for the release of men they'd sent to prison. How easily men and women were coerced to lie under oath. How lynch mobs in the shadows caused defense lawyers to blunt their case. How much witness tampering took place before trials began and throughout. How little sunlight there was, in fact, between a lynching and a court trial. He'd never admit it out loud, but every judge in Georgia had to know in those days that the main reason to oppose lynching was that it made the court system look weak and invited anarchy in other realms, such as manufacturing.

In addition, a change of governors was slated in a week. Acting

Governor Jack Slaton would be replaced by former governor Joe Brown, a man who'd used militias frequently during his last two terms, delivered numerous speeches, and wrote several articles denouncing both labor unrest and lynch mobs. Best to get this thing settled down one way or the other before he came to power.

Gilbert also knew that the hotheads of Harris County were not confined to Mountain Hill; he knew there were a dozen or more Mobley and Williams men in their twenties and thirties living in Hamilton, many with a history of being quick on the trigger. He also knew that jailer Zeke Robinson was Ben Williams, Jr.'s brother-in-law, a young man recently married with a new baby. Williams now sat before a judge who'd recently lost his friend the jailer to a lynch mob. Would words from Williams be required? In addition, it was Gilbert himself who'd demanded that they build a new courthouse and now surely he would not insist that accused black killers of the sheriff's nephew be protected there under armed guard by militiamen likely to be their own kinfolk. The men had not been able to imagine that someone so intimately connected to their village might create a situation that could very well result in another jailer's death and a brothers' war smack in the middle of the Hamilton square. They also knew that Gilbert, despite his tough talk and many opportunities, had actually never called militia out to protect prisoners.

Though he'd never fought a battle, Price Gilbert was a military man to the core. For years he served as captain of the Columbus Guard and he currently sat on the State Board of Military Advisors. In 1896 he'd seen the damage this kind of duty could do to a militia company. He knew as well as any that these men joined for history, for society, for careers, for glory, to please old veteran parents and grandparents, to meet well-situated young women, to play baseball at the park for cheering crowds, not to protect Negro criminals.

Another argument against using the militia to curtail lynch mobs was that it rarely worked and sometimes caused more trouble than it solved. When troops were rushed to Statesboro (a city outside Gilbert's jurisdiction) in 1904, the sheriff had thrown his prisoners to the mob and the militia captain had stood by as one was lynched in full view of him and his troops. After that, still in the presence of militia, a mob of fifty drunken men had rioted for days, killing and whipping innocent blacks. The Methodist minister had expelled two of the mobsters from his congregation and twenty-five others withdrew in protest over that. He'd testified in court against the militia captain, who was court-martialed. The whole business had torn the town apart. Just recently the captain had been pardoned by then-governor Hoke Smith. No one sitting in these chambers this morning wanted any of that for Hamilton. Gilbert had no reason to believe that Sheriff Hadley, in that circumstance, would not do exactly as the Statesboro sheriff had and hand off the defendants to the mob. He had no desire to put either the still-grieving sheriff and his family nor Columbus troops, men whose families he knew well, in such a position. So the fiercest of all the antilynching judges in Georgia decided to believe the three when they vowed that no trouble was expected.

In case any of them had harbored doubts as to what the judge's position would be, they needed only read that morning's *Daily Enquirer.* Though the Superior Court judgeship was much coveted by many able members of the bar, given Gilbert's popularity none had yet dared contest for it. As of this morning, that had changed. Eugene Wynn, a popular lawyer and former Recorder Court judge had thrown his hat into the ring, announcing he'd run for Gilbert's Superior Court seat in the May election. Wynn had a strong following among Harris County residents. Though Georgia Methodists had praised Gilbert in 1910 for imposing heavy sentences on violators of the prohibition law, his sentences were not draconian enough for the Anti-Saloon League, which might now throw its considerable weight behind Wynn.

Before becoming solicitor general, Price Gilbert had served as a state legislator. He left because he hated politics, but Georgia's system of electing judges kept him mired in that world. His life's ambition was to sit on the Georgia Supreme Court. This required a gubernatorial appointment. To place a governor in the position of calling out the militia, in this case, would not be a popular call. A longtime militia man himself, Gilbert knew the havoc such decisions caused, both at high levels and within the ranks.

Gilbert would have known well where this Norman Hadley trouble began and he knew well the whiskey men who ruled the county's western district. Though Democrats like himself, they were wool-hat men who'd flirted with populism, had close ties with "negro desperadoes," moonshiners like themselves, and smelled too much of whiskey and anarchy for this silk-hat Democrat's refined tastes. Inside that lethal mix were also former law enforcement men—bailiffs, jail guards, constables, deputies, a sheriff. None of them had liked him calling on the Columbus sheriff and jailer to meet a mob with gunfire. Across the state, law officials had protested that order; some viewed it as kowtowing to federal agents who'd earlier warned of a lawsuit if federal prisoners housed in the Columbus jail were harmed.

Compounding his woes, the Anti-Saloon League was on his back. He often spoke out voraciously from the bench against saloons and brothels—including the fact that powerful Columbus men owned many of these places—but that wasn't enough. Rev. Solomon's ("if you're not for us, you're against us") zealots wanted blood; they wanted Gilbert to sign oaths promising draconian sentences to wrongdoers. Gilbert said no to their demands and they'd declared they'd unseat him. It's likely he'd heard rumors that Norman Hadley's uncle Mitch Huling, now living in Columbus, was considering a run for the Muscogee County sheriff's office. Already it was known that Brewster Land, with blood ties to most of Mountain Hill, would seek the spot; it was Land who'd handed over a prisoner to a lynch mob back in 1901.

These and other potential costs of standing on principle surely weighed upon Gilbert's mind in the hours leading up to this meeting. Those principles would be at war with the realities of his life. He'd often told grand juries that the sensibilities of family and friends should play no part in the execution of the law. He gave speeches in which he spoke of the necessity for judges and legislators to eschew politics when it came to making and executing the law.

There was also the possibility of an unmentioned factor: dynamite. In the wake of the 1896 Columbus lynching, the *Atlanta Constitution* had proffered a reason the mob had been practically given a welcome mat to the courtroom and the jail. Some men in the mob worked in the granite quarry near the site of the alleged rape; they had access to dynamite and a threat to use it had been made. Perhaps fearing copycat events, Columbus papers did not mention dynamite. If it had been a factor, the high-toned judge would still hold that memory and see it as a real possibility. Perhaps the trio even made some mention of it.

Given what they knew, the men who came hat in hand to Gilbert's chambers that morning of January 17, 1912, had good reason to believe Price Gilbert would not exercise his prerogatives to call out the militia or attempt to remove the prisoners from the jail to a safer location. Details of the discussion would not have been part of the public record. All we have is what the sheriff told the press in its aftermath, what the *Ledger* reported that evening, and the written record of the judge's decision to call a grand jury forty days hence to empanel a petit jury to try unnamed persons in the murder of Norman Hadley.

Outside the courthouse, Sheriff Hadley explained to the press in his earnest manner that the prisoners would not be moved, for fear they would be mobbed by people watching the jail, but neither would they be lynched, because the mob had given their promise. They would be tried in special court, where he would show evidence that all three were either culprits or accomplices in the murder of his nephew. By now, it seemed, Dusky Crutchfield had joined the two men as a suspect.

CHAPTER FIFTEEN

The Die Is Cast

On the following morning, Marion Madison "Buddie" Hadley and his son Douglas stood in Judge Cooper Williams's office in Hamilton. Douglas, a handsome twenty-one-year-old newlywed who'd until now been driving a taxi in Columbus and had just become his father's only deputy, placed his hand on the Bible and swore the oath his father had earlier sworn, to "in all things well and truly without malice or partiality perform the duties of the office of deputy sheriff of Harris County, Georgia." State laws gave sheriffs primary responsibility for the safety of prisoners. On that day the man who would become my grandfather swore to God that he would protect the three held in jail. After that, father and son took the sheriff's horse and buggy back out to Mountain Hill to pick up a fourth prisoner. That morning's *Daily Enquirer* had informed its readers that Sheriff Hadley "does not doubt in the least that he has the guilty parties," but it had failed to mention he did not have them all in hand.

The fourth man, Burrell Hardaway, was a preacher, but not the sort the black folks at Friendship Baptist enjoyed, not a man like Reverend Forbes, whose only job was to shepherd his flock. Hardaway was a self-proclaimed preacher, struck holy in a Mountain Hill cornfield where he still worked as a tenant farmer except on Sundays and Wednesday nights, when he preached at the almost brand-new St. James A.M.E. church, which white folks of the neighborhood had helped to build. Some fancy black ministers called men like him "shirt-tail" or "jack-leg" preachers, and distanced themselves for various reasons. In the case of Burrell Hardaway, the distancing began the second some heard he'd been preaching from the pulpit against Norman Hadley and other white womanizers of black women and girls. It was an unwritten rule among the white-approved black Methodist and Baptist churches of Columbus and Harris County that ministers did not say things to agitate race relations. After his arrest, the whites would call Hardaway a "so-called preacher," if they mentioned his vocation at all.

It's not known when Burrell Hardaway's misdeeds leaked out, possibly through the questioning that went on in those jail cells, possibly through widespread intimidation of other Mountain Hill black people by dozens of self-appointed white law enforcers eager to bring someone to justice. Back then it was common for whites to plant black spies in places they could not go, always needing to know what blacks were up to, so perhaps a paid informant rushed the news to authorities at the first mention of Norman's death.

Hardaway's subversive preaching would certainly have brought to mind another fiery black man, one named Jackson, who'd come to Mountain Hill in the 1880s and opened a school. Word spread that Jackson bragged of having a white wife and urged blacks to insist on social equality with whites. He'd been run out of town and his school was torched. Most likely it was Jackson who inspired the preacher in Arthur Hardy's *Clutch of Circumstance*. The fictional preacher rants endlessly about the white planters who impregnate black women and suggests to his black parishioners they pay them back in kind. Hardy's fictional preacher had also told his congregation to stand by their guns.

By now the phrase "Negro conspiracy" was being used. The sheriff himself had referred to it when speaking to reporters. Rumors raced through the county that "Before Day Clubs" were back. This figment of white imaginations, the idea that blacks organized to slaughter whites "before day," surfaced throughout Georgia whenever white men sought a pretext for large-scale mayhem against blacks. In 1904 the specter had been falsely raised when the *Atlanta Constitution* reported that Harris County blacks in the western district held secret meetings to plan widespread depredations targeting two white farmers for death. Something similar happened in 1895 when the sheriff wrote the governor about plans for a Negro uprising. That news traveled swiftly to newspapers across the country, some as far away as Pennsylvania, announcing "race war" in Harris County. The embarrassed sheriff quickly admitted a mistake and retracted his story.

It's possible that Burrell Hardaway took several pages from Hardy's book, in particular those about the black preacher railing against miscegeny and the white ones denouncing numerous other evils. One can only imagine the horrors he had witnessed and heard about that drove him to such taboo boldness against white men's predations.

Shortly after Hardy's book came out, an outspoken preacher was lynched in nearby Talbotton. It had been a little over a year since former governor Northen had visited that town, long a Populist stronghold, to form one of his Law and Order Committees. One day an elderly, blind, black preacher, whose name was never revealed, stepped off the train wearing a black silk coat, red vest with a gold watch chain, red top hat, diamond ring, and gold-tipped cane. Needless to say, he made an impression.

The preacher took a room with William Carreker, a well-off

black farmer, and soon the white planters noticed a "bad attitude" on the part of their "hands." They'd never really relaxed from the scare of the racially volatile 1890s and so put their black spies to work on the problem. Rumors spread that the preacher was telling blacks they were still enslaved and must declare their independence. That way they could wear a gold watch and a diamond ring like his.

Corrective measures were called for. A "Committee of the People" formed on the grounds of the Methodist Church just after services on a Sunday afternoon. Fifty men on horseback galloped over to the farmer's house and demanded the preacher be produced for a flogging. He would then be run out of the county, they explained.

When the mob leader, a wealthy planter named Will Leonard, persisted and beckoned the mob to move in, a shotgun blast from inside the door sent him to the ground. His head was blown entirely off. The committee made a quick retreat and law officers later found Leonard's body at Carreker's front door, hogs feeding on his brains. Carreker turned himself in to the sheriff immediately and was taken from jail by a mob that night. The next morning townspeople gathered to gaze at his dead body as it swung from the cross arm of a telephone pole in the town square. The old preacher was found four days later in Big Lazer Creek, his bound body weighted with rocks and mangled by bullets, his gold watch and diamond ring nowhere to be found.

These incidents and others had embedded themselves in both blacks and whites in next-door Harris County. They had not, however, hindered the crusade of Preacher Hardaway. They had indeed perhaps galvanized it.

❧

It was on the third day of the imprisonment of Crutchfield, Moore, and Harrington that their preacher arrived in handcuffs, the door locked behind him. And now the Hamilton jail contained four black people, one a fearless preacher, and another, as it would turn out, a fearless woman.

By now rumors were flying around the county that, during the time her husband was in prison, Dusky Crutchfield had gone about calling herself "Miz Mobley." It may or may not have become common knowledge that Henry Mobley, the son of James Monroe Mobley, had paid bail for a moonshiner arrested in 1910 with Dusky's husband, Jim. The man went free, likely due to testifying against Jim. With Jim in prison, Dusky moved near Henry Mobley's place and had all Jim's letters from prison sent to the nearby Cataula post office, where Norman Hadley's mother was postmistress.

Whether any of that would have disqualified her to testify against the other men or whether Preacher Hardaway got to her with his Bible and his ire, we'll probably never know. It could be she just got sick of white folks' lies and empty promises. If they came at her with that conspiracy line, acting like they knew she'd been part of it, that would have done it. This wasn't a woman to be accused of a crime, especially if she knew a white man had done it. If she did, she'd no doubt have said so and that would have been a death sentence in itself. Especially if that white man was yet another kinsman of the sheriff, a high probability given the widespread kinship connections of the crowd Norman traveled with.

The combination of those four—Johnie, the sheriff's cousin; Dusky, the concubine of a leading citizen; Burrell, the preacher who would not be hushed; and Gene Harrington—father of Bertha, the object of Norman Hadley's hot pursuit at the time that he was murdered—was not ideal for a trial certain to be publicized as a drama akin to Thomas Dixon's *Sins of the Fathers*, which had recently drawn record crowds at the Springer Opera House in Columbus. Already the story of Norman Hadley's "murder by Negroes" was receiving national, even international, attention. With its potential for testimony about predatory white men, their young Negro prey, a Hamilton Mobley and his sassy black mistress, and a black preacher telling it like it was, this would be a trial made in heaven for the likes of Du Bois, Wells-Barnett, and Baker, and one made in hell for Hadleys and Mobleys and their extended families.

Even the *Atlanta Constitution,* eager to profit from the growing public taste for real-life scandal, had recently published a lurid book about Edgar Stripling, called *Georgia Jekyll and Hyde,* which was selling like hotcakes, bringing far more attention to reticent Hamilton than it preferred. So far, no article had hinted at Norman's black womanizing ways; no mention had been made of the fact that all three men were suspected because of their ties to the fourteen-year-old Bertha, whom the thirty-four-year-old Norman Hadley was chasing. The whites in the family and the whites in the county would want to keep it that way.

It may be difficult for modern readers to understand just how fundamentally white supremacy was undermined by interracial sex between white men and black woman or to fathom the depth and strength of the denial. Opening this thing up to the world about Bertha Lee Harrington and Norman Hadley would mean, in their minds, the unraveling of the entire foundation that undergirded their sad and disillusioned lives. Like churlish children who, being forced awake from a starry dream, lash out violently at the one who awakens them, they had to do something, they had to punish someone. When questioned, Dusky Crutchfield refused to name any of the three men as Hadley's killers. The preacher and Johnie Moore continued to accuse each other, or so it was said. Regardless, Solicitor General George Palmer, whose duty it was to prosecute one or more of them, would have realized early on that he had no case. Once he learned that the name of Mobley was being bandied about by this woman and just what her connection was, that folks had begun to call her "the concubine," the prosecutor would have no question that this woman, willing or not, wasn't the sort of witness this case required.

Even if there was evidence of guilt, they'd never be able to bring it to court, not with the defendants claiming they were protecting a black woman from a white man's sexual advances.

As the *Atlanta Constitution* would soon reveal, no actual charges were ever brought against any of the four. All were being held "under suspicion." According to the law, they could only be held without charges for seven days. Time was quickly running out.

It is possible that Prosecutor Palmer learned from Crutchfield, at whose house the murder had allegedly occurred, that another white man had been there and then ascertained his identity. It is also possible, even probable, that Palmer had come to the realization that none of these four people had anything at all to do with the murder. It is not likely, however, that Palmer, facing a contested election in May, would have wanted to announce that all four blacks were innocent and that he was bringing a white man, possibly another relative of the sheriff, to trial. If the sheriff was in on the possibility of a white suspect, it's not likely that in the glare of that spotlight and with those guns at his head, he'd have confessed to it. From the time he walked out of Judge Gilbert's chamber, he stuck to his story that he could prove them all guilty, either of the killing itself or of conspiracy to kill.

The days following the preacher's arrest were busy ones in the county. Farmers did light winter work in readiness for what they hoped would be early spring planting. The Robert E. Lee Lodge near Mountain Hill celebrated their hero's January 19 birthday. Miss Lula's WCTU women met to talk about the upcoming trip to Washington to lobby for Prohibition. Preparations to rebuild a black school recently burned in Mountain Hill got under way, with both blacks and whites joining in. White farmers met at local

Seattle Public Library
Capitol Hill Branch
(206) 684-4715

09/24/18 03:12PM

Borrower # 1207844

Snapshot /
0010081504689   Date Due: 10/09/18
acbk

Reykjavik nights /
0010086242731   Date Due: 10/09/18
acbk

A double life /
0010093015385   Date Due: 10/15/18
acbk

The night ferry /
0010093802394   Date Due: 10/15/18
acbk

The family tree : a lynching in Georgia,
0010086684270   Date Due: 10/15/18
acbk

Birds of prey : hawks, eagles, falcons,
0010090940445   Date Due: 10/15/18
acbk

TOTAL ITEMS: 6

Visit us on the Web at www.spl.org

schoolhouses to plan ways to convince their tenants to withhold cotton from the market in order to drive up prices. In Atlanta, a change of governors was afoot, with Joseph M. Brown to replace acting governor Jack Slaton on the twenty-fifth.

Throughout Georgia, ordinary white folk were voicing their dislike of miscegeny. One south Georgian wrote to a newspaper: "Deeper than physical fear must the blow be struck. Look at the hordes of mulatto children swarming in the cities, the towns, and even the country, and say how far is the white man responsible for conditions. If he stoops to the black man's woman, what then when the black man dares to lift lustful eyes to the white man's woman. Can the Anglo-Saxon exterminate the children of his own blood, half-breed though they be? Let him who is without blemish cast the first stone."

The white women of Mountain Hill were harshly stirred by the recent talk about interracial sex. One even wrote, in a newsletter, a snippy little piece about men getting away with some unnamed deviltry that would never be tolerated in women. What got to them the most was the part in Hardy's book about these disowned children of mixed race rising up to punish their white fathers. The novel had warned them of the turmoil to be visited upon them for the sin of miscegenation. For decades many of the whites and the mulattoes had been close, helping each other, as much like family as it was possible to be in those days.

But now whites were beginning to see that they'd been too lenient, too kind, had even brought about their own destruction. Some had begun to turn on the mulatto Moores back in 1910, when Johnie's mother, Lula, had been arrested for trying to kill another black woman. When she'd been released without a trial it got a lot of folks' goats, baffled as they were by the whys and wherefores of the system. Now that her son had supposedly killed Norman Hadley—and no family had done more for those mulatto

Moores than Norman's family—most folks were just fed up with the entire bunch.

There was something else nobody discussed. Many of the sheriff's white Moores were swarthy people. Some looked like gypsies. The sheriff's grandmother, Fada Moore, had come down with dozens of other Mountain Hill residents from Edgefield, South Carolina, a place famous for mixed-race folks who "passed." Who's white and who's black? These were questions being asked, quietly yet increasingly, in the newly segregating South. But for most of Harris County's whites—on a conscious level, at least—it was the murder of a sheriff's nephew that sealed the deal.

Law enforcement was under siege. They knew that the previous year there had been two lynchings not so far away, one in Eufaula and the other in Union Springs, both in Alabama. Both involved law officers allegedly killed by blacks. In both places white men had quietly slipped into town around midnight and quietly taken the law into their own hands. No one got named. No one was punished. During the Atlanta riots, *Atlanta Georgian* editor John Temple Graves proposed a municipal unit to monitor blacks' movements and lynch them when necessary. If a big-city editor like that could think it was right, then wasn't it? And if their sheriff had said he knew for a fact that these folks were guilty, had told it to the judge, had told it to the papers, then surely these folks were guilty. Who would deny family members the right to avenge their loved one's murder?

The motives for a lynching abounded, enough to fill four barns. One or more for every man who'd make up the mob.

For those in the know, there was Norman's real killer to protect. In 1897, right after the Columbus lynching, Governor Atkinson had addressed the General Assembly on the subject and detailed how black men were lynched to protect guilty white men. This wouldn't be the first time.

There was a need for miscegenators to declare their whiteness, a need for antimiscegenation forces to send the word to black and white folks alike about "the brazen iniquity."

There was the increasingly attractive idea—popularized by brilliant ministers, writers, politicians—that the Negro was a subspecies not able to handle the niceties of a democratic society. Now that he could not vote, why, many wondered, should he have a court trial?

There were the temperance forces who found the prospect of stringing up blacks associated with moonshine to be titillating. For some it was a campaign ploy, to show prospective supporters where they stood on these matters. For others it was simply a way to jab a thumb in the arrogant Judge Gilbert's eye. Others just wanted to make a big, bloody billboard to say to blacks, "keep your mouths shut and bow to the racial hierarchy."

Then, certainly, there was the need to protect families' reputations, a county's reputation, the South's reputation, to rid themselves of the guilty consciences these four symbolized. There was also their holy calling to avenge murder. They'd grown up on eye-for-an-eye theology and no one gave a damn if they got the wrong eye. There was, above all, the need to draw a thick bright line between black and white. The races had come too close and their separation called for something loud and violent.

For most of their lives these men and this woman had enjoyed the protection of white people, mostly Moores and Gordons. Events had placed them outside that protection. Norman's mother, Josie, was dying; anyone else who might speak for them would, in this explosive atmosphere, hold their tongue.

One powerful man with multiple motives was former sheriff Mitch Huling, Norman's uncle. Huling, having lost the last sheriff's race to Buddie Hadley, was now residing in Columbus, planning a run for sheriff of Muscogee County. A fierce foe of moonshiners, he had a violent temper, was quick with fists and guns, and had unusual ways of getting his man. In 1908, while he was sheriff, the county paper gave him the entire credit for a county in "the best moral condition it's been in in 40 years." He'd have hated seeing that now in tatters.

As for Sheriff Marion Madison "Buddie" Hadley, the man sworn to protect the prisoners, he'd take this as a loyalty test—perhaps a whiteness test, perhaps a class test, though by this time Hamilton's upper crust was as ready to be done with this impudent black woman who called herself "Miz Mobley" as anyone. He'd also seen the dollars and cents involved. Mobleys provided his ten-thousand-dollar security bond, as well as campaign cash and some loans. He had a large family and an overwrought wife to think about. He didn't want any of them to suffer the infamy that would come with such a trial.

Whiteness was at issue, but manliness even more so, and the two were so intertwined in the white man's bible by now that it was impossible to separate them. The elders would remember what happened to the men who fought to save the life of Boy George, burned on a tree in January 1861. Several days after the heinous deed a crowd of Hamiltonians met and passed resolutions deploring the act and the men who did it.

In the tiny brick courthouse on the south end of the square, the mob leaders and defenders then held their own meeting, where they too passed elegantly worded resolutions, calling themselves "a law-abiding people" justified (even ordained by God) in their action. Hailing their manhood, the mob questioned that of their detractors and reminded them of what every true white male southerner must do in such a circumstance, especially where kinship was concerned.

Detail after detail of the entire matter was published in the Columbus papers. Now, fifty years later, in these tense hours, some men and women around the square would recall James Monroe Mobley's oft-repeated lesson—learned at the wrong end of a mob—from those long-ago days: that when the community wants a lynching, the community will get a lynching.

It's unlikely, however, that Miss Lula Mobley wanted to see Dusky Crutchfield lynched, regardless of her embarrassing revelations about the family. As a longtime member and officer of the WCTU, Miss Lula had been engaged since the 1880s in efforts to stop white men's widespread, chronic rape of and cohabitation with "colored" women and girls. Perhaps she'd read Anna Julia Cooper's book. Regardless, Georgia's own Rebecca Felton, also a WCTU leader, had throughout the late 1880s and 1890s lobbied the members and the state legislature for laws to protect, first black women and children in prison from assaults by white guards, and then all women and children.

Long under the tutelage and the thumb of her powerful father, Miss Lula was in her seventh year without him and was only now beginning to find her own voice.

CHAPTER SIXTEEN

The Lynching

Whatever went on behind those bars, those closed doors, those hushed parlors, those rude cabin walls, those official offices, by Monday afternoon, January 22, men had knocked on doors and issued invitations and the new sheriff had been alerted that he'd "best catch the afternoon train to Columbus." In other words: get out of Dodge to avoid being associated with this act of vigilantism. Three days after Robert E. Lee's birthday celebration and one day after attending church services, the farmers began gathering in front of the courthouse. The weeks' long rain had stopped and temperatures rose to 50 degrees Fahrenheit. It would be a balmy evening with a bright moon.

Most had ridden in on horses and mules, many following the Blue Springs Road and the Lower Blue Springs Road, paths followed by General James H. Wilson's Yankee marauders fifty-one years before when they came with their torches to burn down the town. These men, sons and grandsons of those who fought those troops, now had their own torches, their own just cause. Their generals for the evening had plotted matters every bit as carefully as had Wilson's a half century before. Late in the afternoon, from a respectable distance they'd seen the sheriff off on the train to Columbus.

All day they'd trickled into town, forming small groups in front of the courthouse and in the square, smoking, swigging 'shine from brown-bagged jars, scanning the horizon, and playing a knife-throwing game called mumbledy-peg. Norman's stepfather's gun shop was a popular gathering spot. Everything was in order. Invitations had been issued and most accepted. Woe be unto the man who refused. When the time came, they would not speak among themselves or holler in anger or joy. It had all been arranged.

By midnight, townfolks—children, at least—would be deep in slumber. The leaders would use hand signals, learned in the lodges. Most would just follow along, do as told. Men not in lodges were not invited; the brotherhoods ensured the lifelong silence required in these matters. They had not counted on the woman's howls, awakening even the deep sleep of small children, embedding themselves in white folks' brains, turning up in the strangest places decades later, becoming the stuff of myth and story. All would wear masks.

All day the ordinary goings-on of Hamilton life seemed to float along on a nervous undercurrent. As little knots of stern men conferred outside his office window, Judge Williams went about the ordinary business of adjudicating human travail, ruling on estate matters, divorces, and adoptions, and signing marriage licenses. Across the square, cotton was being ginned at Hudson's and new plows purchased at Mobley's. Down the way, the blacksmith pounded hot iron into horseshoes while a crowd of women gathered at the window of Janie Prichard's millinery shop to admire winter bonnets. Around the village, women and their servants beat rugs, pruned rosebushes, and purchased grits and black-eyed peas at Cook's Mercantile.

In Washington, D.C., the black leader Ralph Tyler prepared for his meeting to discuss lynching the next day with President William Howard Taft, who was caught up in seating arrangements for a state dinner with Ireland's Lord and Lady Asquith. The party, held that evening, would be one of the most elaborate the three-hundred-pound president had ever hosted, and he was taking a personal hand in the details.

As dusk fell, only men dared venture outdoors. They wore broad-brimmed hats pulled tight over their ears and stood about in edgy clumps, gloved hands jammed deep in their pockets, rifles propped in wait behind the stores.

Toward evening, Fanny Graddick's water broke. She lived a short way from Friendship Baptist. She was expecting twins.

When the men and women and children drifted home for supper, homework, darning, and reading, the village seemed to settle into an ordinary evening. A smaller klatch of men, twenty-five or thirty, would take command at the appointed hour.

At precisely 11:20, after the last train had made its run, after most lights were out and folks had fallen into slumber, a larger crowd moved slowly westward down Blue Springs Road toward Friendship Baptist while their leaders marched resolutely over to Dr. Bruce's house, where the jailer and his family boarded. There they called out Zeke Robinson, who, though more addled than usual, went docilely, as they knew he would. Zeke's previous job was clerking at the drugstore. In addition to being a husband and new father, he'd lost his brother Will, the town marshal, to gunfire a decade earlier and was now helping to raise Will's orphan boy. He understood Harris County men and their temperament and Zeke was not made of hero material.

Inside the jail, Dusky Crutchfield and her cell mates huddled in wait. Throughout the day they'd have heard the stronger rush of business outside the stone walls, soaked up the tension, noticed

Alfred Williams's or his wife Ealy's drawn face, downcast eyes, or slower-than-usual shuffle as one or the other brought food and removed slop jars. If they were given a Bible it was not recorded, but they were churchgoing people and their pastor and one of his deacons was with them. Bible or not, they'd have girded themselves with scripture and song.

The men who yanked open the bars wore masks and brandished ropes, hunting rifles and pistols. They bound the prisoners' arms and shoved them outside, where more armed and masked men awaited, holding kerosene torches against the night air. Zeke Robinson, sworn to protect the prisoners, followed along as he'd been told to do.

The death march extended diagonally through the square, past the Confederate shrine. From her house on the southeast corner, Miss Lula Mobley was likely reminded of the Yankees' torches beneath her window that April day in 1865. Next door her nephew Brit Williams may have comforted his wife and young daughters, assuring them that everything was under control. The procession passed the Confederate soldier, gleaming like a god of war in the gaslight, under a radiant moon, a sign unto them of the righteousness of their mission.

Leaving the square and crossing the road, they continued past the bedroom window of little Edna and Mary Fort, who were startled from sleep by Dusky Crutchfield's shrieks. They lay there trembling, clutching their dolls, afraid to move. Nearby their little friends from the Juvenile Missionary Society also lay abed trembling. Francis, the daughter of former sheriff Joe Hadley, lived next door. Along with Brit Williams's daughters, they'd all read from the Bible's book of 1 Samuel at the Juvenile Missionary Society meeting the day before.

On the opposite corner lived Arthur and Irene Hardy. Next to them lived the young mulatta girl who had inspired his novel.

Past Hardy's window they marched, past the desk where he composed his recently published, wildly popular poem "The Demagogue."

A guessing game had been played around the county as to whom Hardy referred, and now some perhaps believed they'd guessed correctly, had him in hand and on his way to a permanent silence and held the rope that would shut this troublemaker's mouth for good. The poem had been printed in the *Journal* and in the *Golden Age* only a few months earlier. Could it be that Hardy, the writer and former newspaper editor, was now already at his desk composing the well-scripted lines he would submit to the Columbus and Atlanta papers in time for the morning news?

Only Hamilton Baptist and the Blue Springs Road sat between Arthur Hardy's house and the sheriff's. Magnificent in the moonlight, its windows dark, its occupants were quiet, though several pairs of eyes watched fearfully as the men shuffled past. The sheriff was away, hiding out in Columbus, and Emma was glad for that and glad that little Louise was deep in sleep, but worried for Douglas, whose whereabouts she would not know but must have suspected. She was unstrung that such a mess should mar her husband's first month in office. Perhaps she prayed hard, as had southern women for years, that the mob would not do their dirty work there on her sweeping back lawn. Mobs sometimes slaughtered and burned their prey at the white victim's homes or that of their kinfolk. Likely it had been arranged in advance that this should not happen, for everyone knew that Emma Hadley was a fragile woman. And the upper-crust residents in general would not want such a messy business performed under their very noses. It would be best to do it a few blocks down the way, at the Negro church, beside the Negro baptismal pool. Emma had worked hard to make the move from country farm wife to manse dweller, to hold her plain head high among the fancier townfolk. And now this. It was all so unnerving.

As the death squad neared its appointed place, terrified quarry in tow, people in the little Negro houses nearby sat silent, drawn into themselves as if trying to disappear. This included the house of Fannie Graddick, who was now deep into childbirth, slightly west of the church and within easy earshot of the hollering, then the gunfire.

Friendship Baptist deacons and a pastor lived close by and would know immediately what was going on. They also likely knew where the mob was headed, since it had been near their church that the mob made its first attempt when the three were brought to jail. Perhaps a great moan rose in the pastor's throat after all the sweat and the prayer and the tears and the love that had gone into the recent rebuilding of this, their only communal home, this place the freedmen had first called home and named Friendship for the fact the white men had given so generously of their money and time in the building of the first church and with the short-lived hope of an eternal amity between the races.

This was hard to understand, especially since, so recently, good white men like Brother Alex Copeland and his mother and Preacher Upshaw had come with olive boughs and prayed and sung with them and Preacher Upshaw had told them "never be discouraged" and "never give up." Now it seemed that all this rebuilding of both brick and friendship would be washed away by this devil-seized flood roaring past his door and headed for the heart of Hamilton's black community. Might he have been reminded of another radical preacher despised and crucified for his honesty? And rather than curse the darkness, did this good man bend over his Bible and pray for four souls, with that screaming woman so close he could almost reach out and touch her, with one of the men, like him, a preacher of the Word? What could he do when he saw where those torch lights stopped beside the sacred pool, except hold tight to his Bible and pray loudly to shut out the woman's screams as they reached a pinnacle of terror and desperation. He would look for fire and smell for smoke because every black man knew that white men seized so demonically would almost inevitably set their victims ablaze, along with anything "Negro" in sight—church, school, or person.

As the mob's high command and their captives neared the massive live oak beside the baptismal font, they were awaited by dozens more men, masked and armed.

Four ropes were pitched over the lowest branches of the magnificent tree, a tree they'd later say looked like those in the paintings of the Old Masters, an ancient, massive tree, one hundred years old or more. As each bound prisoner was moved into place, a noose was dropped over his or her head, and left slack about the neck. The three men loudly and frantically protested their innocence. Reports later claimed that, to the bitter end, John Moore blamed Gene Harrington and Harrington blamed Moore.

As for Dusky Crutchfield, the mob had a plan, which was revealed when one of its leaders slipped the noose around her neck and said, "This is war. You tell us who done it and we'll put you on the next train out of here." Or words to that effect. Some say he said, "This is war." Others say it was, "You're a woman," a way of explaining that they preferred not to kill her. With not so much as a word, with only a pointed finger, she could save her life.

She'd have known that no matter what she did or said her life wasn't worth spit anymore. All she had left was her word and what she took to God. The preacher had possibly talked with her about that.

She did not pause to think about it. What she had witnessed throughout her hard life she would not participate in. So many black women like herself had been forced to do the dirty work of white men. This one would not go to God with the blood of black men on her hands.

"Pull the rope, white man," she said.

At that, four nooses were yanked tightly, four bodies snatched brutally upward. Within seconds hell opened its mouth and rained forth hundreds of bullets and buckshot, and four human beings—Johnie Moore, Dusky Crutchfield, Eugene Harrington, and Burrell Hardaway—were cut to ribbons.

∿

At the sound of gunfire, some of the adults in the Williams families and the wife of Zeke Robinson slipped out onto their porches and later told their grandchildren they'd never heard such a racket.

From his elegant Victorian on the hill, the sensitive young Alex Copeland gazed through a large window, through the trees, down toward the sheriff's house, where dozens of torch lights twinkled like stars around the baptismal font, and wept as the gunfire began. Two years earlier he had returned from the conservatory in Atlanta, a new graduate and already an honored musician, and performed a recital at the library. He was, along with Hardy, Hamilton's genius. But neither his fierce Christianity nor his beloved Beethoven would comfort him in this hour. A regular guest and occasional speaker at Friendship, this was his church, too. Many in its congregation shared his blood; he knew that as well as anyone and in his dotage would not hesitate to acknowledge it.

Across College Street from where Copeland watched, Judge Williams was coming down with *la grippe,* but that did not deafen him to the familiar sounds coming through his window that night, the sounds of Gettysburg or Monocacy, reminding the old sharpshooter of just what such fire could do to human flesh. His influenza could not ward off old memories of men's brains tossed about on the ground, nor prevent his nostrils from recalling that coppery stench that comes when a body is savaged by bullets and buckshot. His near death as a mere boy on the banks of Monocacy Creek had taught him a thing or two. He knew what men were capable of. He knew as well the uselessness of individual heroics, like that of Major W. W. Thomas in nearby Coweta County, who'd served with the judge's late brother Ben in the Senate. Thomas had risked his life to save the life of that preacher they tried to hang after they were done with Sam Hose. To no avail. He thought he'd won when the mob promised to take their man to jail, but soon as his back was turned they savaged him. No, there would be no heroics tonight by Hamilton's most respected man nor by any of his network. Most of them considered this to be mainly Hadley family business anyhow; the Mobley aspect was a mere footnote in the minds of many. Williamses took care of their own Negroes, the good ones anyhow, and whether they approved of others' handling of "their Negroes," they generally kept their mouths shut about it.

Still, these men and this woman now being massacred were no strangers to the judge. Each had presented himself or herself at his office for marriage certificates or other civil matters at one time or another. Possibly he remembered many years ago when a newly freed woman named Jane appeared at his door with her former master, James B. Moore, to sign over to him her children, their children. Depending on the detail of conversation about kinship backgrounds of black men, he might have known the youngest man being shredded by bullets was Jane Moore's great-nephew, thus a cousin to both the sheriff and his son, the deputy. Perhaps he wondered if the young man's cousin the deputy had any such thoughts as he stood somewhere on the edges of this killing field, sworn by the majestic law the judge was also sworn to, sworn by the judge himself to protect all prisoners in his charge. But he knew well that the law in these days was mostly guided by politics and public opinion and he didn't think there'd be any inclination to haul in this sheriff, his deputy, or his jailer for turning their heads at this particular moment.

The author at age eleven, around the time her father confessed his "killing" of a young black woman.

The author and her sister, Barbara, at ages three and four, just before their parents divorced.

Edna Allen Armstead, the author's "black mamma" who cared for her and her sister from kindergarten until adulthood and remained close to them until her death in 2013 at age ninety-one.

The author's mother, Betty Hadley, as a young teenager, sometime before she discovered her mother's drug addiction.

Betty Hadley Williams, around the time of her marriage to Ben in 1934.

Betty Hadley Williams in her late seventies.

The author's father, Ben Williams, and
his little brother, Snooks, around 1913.

Ben Williams as a medical
student, just before he married
a Native American woman in a
drunken blackout.

Dr. Ben Williams near the time he
told his daughters he'd accidentally
killed a young black woman.

Ben Williams as a
counselor at Hazelden
Drug Treatment Center,
shortly before his death.

Sheriff Buddie Hadley, the author's maternal great-grandfather, with Ben Williams, Jr., the author's paternal great-uncle, cutting up in New Orleans. Date unknown.

Sheriff Douglas Hadley and his wife, Berta, on their farm near Hamilton in the late 1940s or early 1950s.

Will Williams, the author's grandfather, as a young college student circa 1890.

The author's "Big Mamma," Ethel Harris Williams, wife of Will Williams. Date unknown.

Will Williams around the time of the 1912 lynching.

Will Williams sometime after the murder of his brother, Dock, and shortly before his election to the Georgia State Legislature.

"Miss Lula" Mobley, leader of the Missionary Society Ladies, organized her fellow church women in their protests against the unjust murders. Date unknown. *Permission from John Bunn*

Members of the Moore family at Mountain Hill. From left to right: Lige Pierce, Foundland Moore Pierce, Bose Moore (first cousins of Sheriff Buddie, Douglas, and Norman Hadley).

Moore family picnic at Mountain Hill. Date unknown.

Georgia Ann Hudson Williams, born in slavery to Hamilton's Hudson family.
Courtesy of Deborah Daniels

Isaac Williams, born in slavery to the author's third great-uncle Britain Williams.
Courtesy of Deborah Daniels

Judge Stirling Price Gilbert, the vociferous foe of lynching who decided not to protect the four prisoners in January 1912. Gilbert went on to become a Georgia Supreme Court Justice.
Photo courtesy of Georgia Department of Archives and History

The Harris County Courthouse, built in 1908 at the strong urging of Judge Gilbert. This is where Louis "Sugar Bear" Murray and Albert Curry were sentenced to death.
Photo courtesy of Cholly Minton

Anna Julia Cooper, the author's distant cousin. Cooper was one of the most prominent African Americans of her era, but members of her white family burned her highly acclaimed book *A Voice from the South*.
Courtesy of Scurlock Studio Records, Archives Center, National Museum of American History

Leading African American intellectual and activist W. E. B. Du Bois. Residents of Harris County feared Du Bois and the NAACP would send investigators to uncover the truth behind the 1912 lynching.
Courtesy of the Department of Special Collections & University Archives, W. E. B. Du Bois Library, University of Massachusetts, Amherst

Confederate statue on Hamilton's Monument Square. Judge Cooper Williams, Miss Lula Mobley, and Governor Hoke Smith presided over its historic unveiling on November 29, 1910.
Photo by Cholly Minton

It was beside the outdoor baptismal font at Friendship Baptist Church that a woman and three men were lynched in 1912. *Photo courtesy of Deborah Dawson*

Hamilton residence of the Beall, Mobley, and Williams families from the 1850s until the 1990s.

This was, however, the Judge's sweet village and he would be fearful for it now, concerned for the family's old "darkeys" and their offspring. Would they pack themselves off north as some already had? Many still lived in town, worked in homes as servants. Others had their own land, out where the trouble began. They'd be worried sick. Word would have been sent quickly, if it hadn't already been. This and no more. He would be trusting the sheriff or his deputy to issue these orders and see that they were carried out. Perhaps he slept soundly, being in his elder years, and knowing things had been worked out in advance.

In the center of town, closest to the gunfire, but for two men who decided it was a good time to rob the post office, none dared venture beyond their front porch.

No Hamiltonians, neither white nor black, would rise up as heroes that night. As though scripted, everyone stayed put, cowering under their covers, ears stuffed, praying to God, reading their Bibles, weeping, breathing sighs of relief, praying their sons were not there, and if there, safe from apprehension and Hell's damnation. Some of my relatives, others recalled, simply sat on their porches and listened to the gunfire. Doubtless there were those who quietly clapped their hands and murmured "Hallelujah," imagining the scourge of drink and miscegenation and gambling and interracial troubles of every ilk magically washed away in that hail of hellfire. Perhaps they imagined themselves better than the mob and slept more soundly for that. They would have little reason at that point to know how these things lodge themselves in the cells and sit there, reverberating far into the future.

The air reeked of gunpowder, tobacco, adrenaline, of bullet and blood, horse and dog. A few hounds bayed as the four ravaged bodies swayed and more than one hundred sated white men—newly baptized and bonded beside the Friendship font in one of the oldest rituals of the Lost Cause—made their way home to families, gunpowder in the wool of their jackets, the creases of their necks, some carrying bits of skin and hair beneath their nails.

A small group escorted the jailer back home to his family, wishing him a good night's sleep. Next morning they'd arise, wash, and avoid the mirror and the eyes of wives and children at the breakfast table, though some told what happened and told it proudly. Said something had to be done. It was hard but it was right. Some said their only regret was the woman. But she could have saved her life. Over time, a fantastical story about the woman emerged out by the river. She ran from us at the tree. Ran screaming like a banshee. We chased her, but she was too fast. She's out there somewhere still. Others claimed they went to prevent the men from running roughshod over innocent Negroes in the neighborhood.

If the young deputy was there—and several say he was—that was certainly his reason. It was his duty to protect the town, since his father was, as the papers would say, "away in Columbus"; it was also his family duty to see that his mother and sisters were safe in their house just yards across the meadow. Some later told their black field hands they went to keep the mob from rampaging through Negro neighborhoods, from inciting an exodus of black people, the sort of thing that happened in other towns. They'd tell them, This has nothing to do with you. This is a private matter. Though no one dared call it what it was: a family matter.

CHAPTER SEVENTEEN

"So Quietly Was the Work Done"

Around 12:30 a.m. either Zeke Robinson or someone else picked up the phone and called the *Columbus Daily Enquirer* to tell the story. By sunrise its headlines would blanket the Chattahoochee Valley. The caller must have used the word *excitement* several times or appeared excited himself, for both Columbus papers that day spoke of the night's "excitement," as if a midnight carnival had pulled into town.

Word quickly spread that the four bodies yet dangled from the tree. Great banks of thick black clouds massed in the sky, but temperatures again were warm and no rain fell, so there was nothing to stanch the flow of men, women, and children as they poured into town on foot, by mule, buggy, and car. They came from over the mountain, up from Columbus, in from the riverbank to gawk at the shredded bodies and the pools of blood beside the baptismal font and to step into the shadows cast by the dead and seize the few souvenirs left lying about. The masks, shell casings, and cigarette butts were soon gone, so the crowds milled about under the tree and just stared. "A perfect quietude prevailed," according to the *Daily Enquirer*. In a morning interview with a reporter, the sheriff had used the word *quiet* numerous times. Elsewhere the article mentioned how "quietly was the work done."

Perhaps the morning onlookers posed smiling and pointing together with their children, as happened in countless other southern towns. Many owned Kodaks; the *Harris County Journal* had a special one for group shots. Likely, the "better people" had determined to prohibit them. After a time, when more was learned, a great shame seized even those who had been glad or simply caught up in the excitement. If photos were taken, they were destroyed or lost or lay tucked away in trunks, long forgotten. They were not, as elsewhere, made up as drugstore advertisements or postcards to be mailed to family and friends. None has ever emerged for public view—even today with good money being offered.

By phone the sheriff told a Columbus reporter that since "he had not been able to get any negroes to touch them, to take them down," he did not know when they'd be removed. His toddler granddaughter, Louise, and his new daughter-in-law, Berta, had already viewed the sight, and each, as did many others, would carry its imprint for life.

Carefully avoiding the gruesome scene, Hamilton's black residents, both Baptist and Methodist, gathered for worship and communal sustenance at the black Methodist church that morning. Little two-year-old Louise, the sheriff's granddaughter, was taken there by her nurse, Dig. Decades later, when in her eighties, Louise claimed to remember the moaning and the hollering in that pain-filled place on that day. No one seemed to notice or care that the sheriff's grandbaby was there. On the way back to the sheriff's house, where she lived, they passed the tree. "Mamma told her not to show me, but she did," Louise later recounted. More than anything else, she remembered Dusky Crutchfield's bulging tongue, pierced by a bullet, a sight that engraved itself on her memory for life.

When they got home, the sheriff's house overflowed with family and guests, eating and talking. Baby Louise toddled around babbling "nigger in the tree, nigger in the tree." This unnerved everyone, especially her grandmother Emma, an easily unstrung woman, and her mother asked Dig to please take the child to her room.

One of the early curiosity-seekers that morning was seventeen-year-old Berta Hadley. Her husband, the deputy, had told her not to go. But she was awakened early by the steady rush of footsteps outside her window and at dawn slipped from bed, dressed, and climbed through her window like a child so as not to awaken her quick-tempered father, who'd likely have been there drunk and would now be sleeping it off.

Her new husband had been out for hours, or all night for all she knew, seeing to things. She'd go just to the edge of the field, grab a quick glimpse, and be home before anyone knew she was up, hoping Douglas wouldn't find out. She knew she shouldn't, but she went because, as she later told me, "everyone else was going."

Jailer Robinson's nephew followed him everywhere he went. So, when he saw him head out for that grim scene the next morning, he took off after him. He later told his grown children: "I went and I've always wished to God I hadn't. It was a horrible sight. It was the biggest mistake of my life." The four bodies, he told them, were so full of bullets and buckshot that they rattled like wind chimes in the breeze.

A little boy seated high atop a cotton bale on a wagon bed came so close to the four that the foot of Dusky Crutchfield tapped his shoulder.

Later that afternoon, a coroner's jury performed their duties by craning their necks upward at the still-dangling bodies. Coroner Burford, a Confederate vet who'd shrouded countless of his comrades' bodies at Gettysburg and Cold Harbor, and who was a Mobley kinsman as well, came down sick that day and was replaced by Judge Lynch, Hamilton's newly retired mayor. The jury included one Williams, one Mobley, one Moore, and one Robinson. The Mobley was Henry, who had shot and killed a white man in 1908 and was acquitted on grounds of self-defense. I was told he was the man involved with Dusky Crutchfield. Hewing to an old script, the men concluded that the victims "came to their death by being hung, by the neck and by gunshot wounds at the hands of unknown parties."

❧

Despite concerns that the lynching would stain Hamilton's reputation, life quickly resumed its normal pace. Many of the sightseers turned to shopping, and storekeepers noted they hadn't seen so many country folks in town on a weekday since the Jesse James Wild West Show in 1906. To everyone's relief, no frantic parents showed up at the college to gather up their daughters. Maids reported for work. Laborers resumed their plowing. Farmers hauled bales of cotton in to be ginned at Hudson & Company.

It was a busy day. Judge Williams shook off his grippe enough to show up in his office and sign marriage licenses for several couples, some black, some white.

That evening President Taft sat down to prepare for a meeting next morning in the White House library with four black men, all appointees to federal posts. Since 1910, when southern newspapers and leaders had lambasted the president for attending a celebration in honor of the black president of Wilberforce University at Metropolitan A.M.E. Church in Washington, D.C., because the man's wife was white, he'd been careful about his public contacts with black people. But the 1912 presidential elections lay ahead and the campaigns were already being called the most racist in history. Taft's meeting with the four men was aimed at swaying a black vote now leaning toward Wilson, who lacked the racist record of Taft and Roosevelt and whose doctorate and campaign promises indicated to some he'd be more worldly and intelligent in racial matters despite the fact that he was born and raised in the South.

By the end of the day in Hamilton the bodies were removed from the tree.

The following day, Zeke Robinson journeyed to Columbus, carrying a few "souvenirs," and held a small press conference. As an unwilling eyewitness, he wished to correct the record on two counts: 1) there were fewer men in the mob than the 100 being reported; and 2) far more bullets were fired, probably 500, not the 300 in most news stories.

Three "negroes," he said, had all been buried in one grave, near the place they died. The preacher's body was taken by relatives. No one asked about the well-being of the dead folks' families, if they had children, and how this might affect them. That was never done in any lynching. No big deal was made over the fact that a woman—the first in Georgia—had been lynched. Omitted from Robinson's reports was the most electric item: Dusky's heroic refusal. That would remain a secret among a handful of whites. Revealing it would only raise more questions about the innocence of the three men and would give local blacks, and some whites, a martyr.

The same day something happened to suggest that the mob had not only ordered my great-grandfather to leave town but was also responsible for keeping the victims' remains dangling ignominiously for half a night and an entire day. Message was a key ingredient in southern lynchings and they intended this one to be heard near and far. *Let black folks get a good look at what happens when they go afoul of white folks.* Perhaps the sheriff reasoned it might make his job easier in months and years to come, but was he conscious of how very impotent and even complicit this made him appear?

With the bodies gone and the crowds cleared, the blood now dry and mostly soaked into the ground, the white man who owned the magnificent water oak went out with friends and began to chop it down. On returning from lunch, they found a note: *Cut down this tree and you'll swing from the next.* And so the Hanging Tree would remain another decade, haunting the town until its owner, finally sensing safety, had it cut down into logs and sold to the Bronco Wood Products Company in Wilmington, Delaware.

Any fears of culpability the sheriff or judge might have had were resolved by Columbus newspapers the day after the lynching. Both stuck largely by the official story. They had performed their duties as required by law—the sheriff in asking for a special court and the judge in granting it. The papers, longtime fans of Gilbert, gave him extra accolades for being "always anxious . . . to prevent mob violence."

A subheadline proclaimed that Hadley, "fearing no lynching," had been in Columbus during the incident, despite the fact that Hamilton started filling up with country men at least three hours before anything happened. The jailer, the paper recounted, was home in bed and had had no choice but to hand over keys. Reporters were told he had no force with which to protect the prisoners. The jail had been unprotected. Reporters did not seem to think this strange. Nor did they question the sheriff when he told them members of the mob were not known to the people of Hamilton.

The whereabouts of the deputy sheriff went unmentioned. Hamilton's law enforcement establishment had done everything but put out a welcome mat, yet the paper reported their side of the story as if it were utter truth. They reported with the straightest of faces the town's awareness that something was building all day and the sheriff's statement that "no trouble was expected," just as they'd reported of the 1896 lynching in Columbus.

For the time being, it seemed the judge, the sheriff, and the jailer were home free. There'd be no Walton County–like carping about culpability. The "Hamilton Avengers" were depicted as a nameless, faceless force, almost militarily precise, quiet, and organized. But those who read beyond that first day's headlines found a smaller article on the *Daily Enquirer*'s front page that signaled a crack in the façade by hinting at the "innocence" of some of those lynched.

The next day the *Constitution* revealed a startling new fact. "The four negroes upon whom the mob wreaked its fury had been arrested and held merely as suspects. Proof to convict had not been secured." The paper went on to display either its ignorance of the lynching's cause or its long-held policy of refusing to speak of miscegeny by stating: "The crime that supplied the provocation was of such nature that testimony concerning it could have been presented in open court without embarrassment or censorship; beyond a doubt the accused would have been given fair trial, and their guilt even reasonably established, legal execution would quickly have followed."

At the same time, two northern newspapers were letting the miscegenation cat out of the bag. On January 24, Wilmington, Delaware's *Morning News* and the *New York Evening Post*—both white Republican newspapers, one with ties to the NAACP— exposed Norman Hadley as having forced his attentions on a black girl just before he was killed.

Incorrectly assuming that the woman hanged was the girl whom "the very popular and unmarried planter was infatuated with," the *Evening News* reported that Hadley had gone to her home that day "to persuade her to come out and meet him."

While there, he was shot by a man who "had sought to marry the girl . . . who was only twenty years old and comely." This, some feared, would make things worse in the eyes of whites: not only was Norman seeking to satisfy his lust, he was 'infatuated' with her. She was not simply a black girl to be used at will but "a comely woman." This was shaping up to be the sort of Hardyesque novel that had both titillated and horrified the local citizenry over the past two years. Some surely wondered whether Arthur Hardy would now write a sequel or would an even better-known writer step forward to scoop up this tantalizing tale.

In these papers Johnie Moore became not a black man with a rent dispute, but a black man "in love with the girl," defending his girlfriend from a white man; still, they deemed him guilty. This love-angle version of the story began showing up in Associated Press stories around the country; but while southern papers ran AP on the Hamilton lynching generally, this particular information was removed.

While AP got "the girl's" last name wrong, calling her Hathaway instead of Harrington, this confusing of the victims' names occurred throughout the press. Dusky Crutchfield was called Belle Hathaway. Burrell Hardaway was called Dusty Crutchfield. White newspapers preferred to characterize lynch victims as strangers or "sorry negroes." They tended to reveal nothing of their lives and loves, successes and failures, hopes and dreams, anything that would humanize them. Neither white nor black papers mentioned the fact Dusky's tongue was pierced by bullets.

I do not know who in the black community leaked the true story to the northern press. The young and "comely" Bertha Harrington—saddled no doubt, as women usually were, with a wrongheaded sense of culpability for the deaths of her fiancé, father, and preacher—made no recorded statements and left no public record. Most of the victims' families deserted the neighborhood sometime after that night. My years-long efforts to locate descendants have come up empty. The closest I came was an African American librarian living near me in Maryland whose Harris County Hardaway family oral history included the story of a relative who was lynched for "going with a white woman": her family left the county two years after the 1912 lynching. She is a genealogist and wanted proof of their connection to Burrell, the preacher, which I could not provide.

In early February, the miscegenation motive for Hadley's murder showed up in an unlikely place. Previously, the only white papers to reveal it were owned by progressives associated with the NAACP. Now the *Advance*, a summary of white religious weeklies from all over the country, revealed in an editorial that "[at least] two and probably four innocent persons were put to death." It told the tale of Hadley's "unwanted attentions" to the "negro girl." The story had seeped into the sort of papers that the "good people" of Hamilton read and hairs were standing up on countless necks.

What few black publications still existed in Georgia omitted any hint of white male predation at the heart of this lynching. The reason, perhaps, was that in November, the black editor of a fraternal newspaper in Georgia had reprinted an article from the *Chicago Defender* claiming a black man recently hanged in Washington, Georgia, had killed a white farmer because the man had sexually assaulted his wife. The article was blunter than blunt. The editor was arrested for libel and jailed. The local author of the "scurrilous article"—a black man, everyone assumed—was being actively sought by law officers.

The *Defender* was the black newspaper feared most by white Georgians. Its editor, Robert Abbott, was a native Georgian who campaigned furiously for blacks to leave the South, and filled his papers with white-on-black southern crime. Large bundles of *Defenders* were smuggled aboard southbound trains by black porters, who tossed them out at prearranged spots in the news-starved black countryside. Some states or local jurisdictions had made possession of the *Defender* a crime and at least one southern sheriff had traveled to Chicago to personally threaten the editor with arrest.

Inexplicably the *Defender* failed to note the sex angle in the lynching, instead sticking to the white party line that the victims' motive in killing Hadley was a rent dispute. Instead he lambasted Georgia's blacks. Likening them to "guinea pigs," he excoriated their desire for money and security over the safety of their women.

I can only imagine the ire among Hamilton's strong black church elite, men whose parents or who themselves were enslaved by the Williams-Mobley-Hudson-Copeland clan. They had worked hard to build the region-wide Calvary Baptist Association, which collected a dollar each year from its many members to maintain the Hamilton Academy, a school that trained young men for the pulpit and the classroom. Some of these same men had formed that 1889 posse to track down the prominent white planter who'd raped one of their own children. But they were old men now and the younger ones had not tasted the strong promise of Reconstruction. They had their own Hamilton Academy now to consider. Besides, these four had been—or so they were told—the very sort of moonshine folk they preached against, the woman "the concubine" they abjured in the pulpit. How would it look to risk life and limb and longtime gains for something like this? They'd seen what happened to blacks who even mumbled a word against these massacres.

No doubt, blacks and some whites of the region took comfort when the *Columbus Daily Enquirer* and even Governor Joseph M. Brown promised investigations.

By March, newspapers across the county had gone silent on the subject. Only the March issue of the *Crisis* and the *Twentieth Cen-*

tury, a Boston-based white literary magazine, continued the discussion of Hamilton's lynching and its causes, which they did with searing honesty, moral outrage, and calls for action. The *Twentieth Century* dealt a stinging rebuke in an editorial which stated, "The latest indictment of our despicable Caucasian cowardice comes from Hamilton, Ga., where the murder of Norman Hadley led to the lynching of three negroes and a mulatto girl . . ."

Next to that ran another editorial, titled "Limits of Negro Endurance," approvingly quoting black leader Reverdy Ransom, who'd spoken recently beside former Governor Northen at Boston's Faneuil Hall, where he declared: "The only way to win respect is to mete out the white man's measure." One way to solve the problem posed by the true facts of the Hamilton lynching, the editorial suggested, would be to adopt federal laws that would force white men to support their racially mixed children. "Nothing else," they stated, "will arouse the cowardly white woman to a revolt against the pusillanimity of the white ravisher of negresses, the thin-blooded degenerate of a once-proud race, an adulterous race which still boasts naively that every colored woman is susceptible." Words of this nature would sit and simmer in some region of the Ladies of Hamilton's brains for a decade before something would start to change.

Any fears that the NAACP would send down an investigator were dispelled with the March issue of the *Crisis*. An article titled "The Terrorists" contained snippets of the most trenchant statements about the Hamilton lynching from black and white newspapers nationwide. An editorial by Du Bois, "Divine Rights," spelled out Norman Hadley's predatory behavior toward Bertha Lee Harrington, condemning white men for their three-hundred-year-old "jealously guarded" right to seduce black women with impunity. Neither did he spare white southern women of the best families, who "helped maintain this . . . custom." However,

Du Bois, like many editors, black and white, stuck to the story of Johnie Moore's guilt. And because he and other leaders of the antilynching movement wanted black men to protect black women against white men's aggression, Moore and the other men lynched served this narrative as much-needed heroes and martyrs.

For some whites who followed the black press, these words caused alarm. But the nascent NAACP, swamped with more lynching, more crusades, and now with a black martyr story none cared to unravel, quickly turned away from Hamilton, and the powerful families of the hamlet breathed deep sighs of relief.

As for the *Columbus Daily Enquirer*'s promised investigation, it never materialized. Instead they published a blistering editorial accusing Harris County of endangering commerce and investment in Columbus and "the entire South" through its "barbarism" and "the massacre . . . permitted in the shadow of its courthouse." As for whether the new governor had put his attorney general on the case, that would have to wait for the April grand jury.

The florid rhetoric with which the *Harris County Journal* covered the lynching was recognizable as pure Arthur Hardy, but with a distinct difference from his novel. There he'd written of "men who became monsters before one another's eyes." Those characters were black. The flesh and blood monsters he spoke of in his understated, philosophical front-page article three days later were men he knew well, men he'd represented in court or who were potential clients, whose goodwill he relied upon on many levels. So his tone was lofty—regretful but understanding. Countless articles had now appeared exposing true motives and victim innocence, yet Hardy omitted any mention of that. He described the quiet and orderly way the mob conducted itself. In his article as elsewhere, Dusky Crutchfield's screams were silenced. So also were her final words.

"While we do not seek justification for the terrible act," he wrote, "yet we ask that the cold arbiter, public opinion, in making up a verdict, take into consideration the fact of the killing of two white men, kinsmen from the same community, in close succession, by negroes—the race feeling with some in the section having been more or less estranged for a much longer period—take into account the proneness of the human heart to quickly gratify the element of revenge that will not down. Yet law, and law only, must e'er be the standard for which to strive."

Neither he nor any other editor would mention the fact that the judge, the sheriff, and the jailer had, by leaving the prisoners unprotected, made way for the lynching and broken the law. Nor did he mention that this law, at least, could be upheld, along with the potential for charges of murder against mob leaders.

❧

I began this journey believing myself to be an unflinching investigative reporter and a nonracist. Just as I'd "overlooked" the fact that one of the lynching victims was a Moore, I clung way beyond reason, and despite mounting evidence to the contrary, to the possibility that Buddie Hadley had done everything in his power to save those four people he held in his jail. I told myself I was just trying to be fair, but in hindsight I realize that I was simply unable to face the fact that he, Judge Gilbert and others had set the whole thing up in a way that would leave him largely unscathed.

All my life I'd heard, even from black Hamiltonians, that my grandfather Douglas Hadley was "one of the better sheriffs." And given Buddie's initial attempt to hold off the mob, I wanted to think that he, too, belonged in that category. A new book had come out in 2007, mentioning this lynching and relying upon old press reports that let Buddie Hadley off the hook. That book occupied a prominent place in the homes of some of my relatives, who found solace, even pride, in that version. When I learned the truth, knowing what happened to bearers of bad news I dreaded to tell it.

Facing the fact that both my grandfather and his father were an essential part of this "massacre," whether on the scene or not, has been an intense experience for me. Beyond forcing me to acknowledge the darkness in family history, this process has also pushed me to confront my own inherited prejudices. You don't spend your first twenty years of life in a system defined by racial segregation and white supremacist ideas without damage. That stuff lodges inside you and it's hard to get out. While I have spent the past fifty years working for racial justice, I still found myself making biased assumptions about African Americans, judging them as a race more than I judged white people as a race.

I have had to make a conscious effort to learn the many ways our system is still rigged against African Americans. I can't say how this happened, but not until I forced myself to confront the evil done by many of my ancestors to black people (and Native Americans), to sit with that harsh knowledge and the pain it caused and still causes, could I look clearly at my own racism. One aspect of that is a tendency to make quick judgments without prior investigation of the facts, something I believe us whites do to blacks far more often than to other whites. "I don't want to know about them," my mother said, referring to black people, and, knowing what I now know about our family history, I definitely see why. It's just that fear of knowing, however, that continues to keep blacks and whites divided. In the early years of my visits to Harris County, I would become so overwhelmed by what I encountered during my research in dark basements and on sunny front porches that—almost in a blackout state—I would find myself on the road speeding north toward my sister's house in Atlanta, unable to bear more. Slowly I learned I would not only have to stay put and do the work, but I would have to face that torment, look it in the face, and accept it as a part of my family's, my region's, and my country's past.

~

In mid-March 1912 the steady rains turned torrential, flooding houses, stores, and farmland, and unleashing landslides along the Chattahoochee. Cyclones tore up parts of the county, barely missing Hamilton. The multitude of preachers along the banks of the raging river spoke of God's fury and the sinful ways of His people and pleaded with parishioners to come to Christ.

On March 22, exactly two months after the lynching, Josie Gordon Beers, Norman Hadley's fifty-five-year-old mother, died. She was buried beside Norman in the Gordon cemetery.

Here in Hamilton, none of the most basic measures were being taken to determine and apprehend the killers behind the lynching. The sheriff could have asked the governor to post a reward for information on the mob members, but he didn't. The governor could have done so on his own, but he didn't. Perhaps, knowing how another governor's reward had led to Edgar Stripling's murder of Billy Cornett, they decided to forgo that option. Hadley would know well that anyone who tried to collect a reward wouldn't live long enough to spend it. Besides, he wasn't a man given to pretense. He knew who did it and everyone else knew he knew who did it. No investigations were made. No detectives were hired.

Black or white, everyone knew that no man would come to trial for what happened that night. As far as could be recalled, Edgar Stripling was the only white man to have ever been found guilty of murder in Harris County. Besides, just recently Yankees up in Coatesville, Pennsylvania, had refused to punish a group of white men for lynching. Why would it be any different in Hamilton?

CHAPTER EIGHTEEN

Parties Unknown

But for the fact that farmers to the west of Hamilton were slower than ever to plant their fields this year, life mostly went on as usual. Six weeks after the lynching, Deputy Sheriff Hadley and his wife, Berta, conceived their first child, my mother-to-be.

On the fourth day of April, Judge Price Gilbert settled himself onto the Hamilton bench. Facing the grand jurors—several of my relatives and his friends among them—he told them the January lynching "overshadows all other burdens of the court this session."

Launching briefly into one of his cherished themes, the citizen's responsibility for the prevalence of crime, he hinted at the social status of mob members, saying, "The indictment of a Negro or a friendless white man is easy, but it takes backbone to comply with the law when the offender is an old friend or the only fellow who is any good in his community." Though he didn't dodge the issue, his normally icy mien under such circumstance seemed to have melted. Perhaps he was tired or simply resigned. The white primary was four weeks away and his opponent was putting up a good fight.

Meanwhile the region was in the grip of an unseasonable cold spell and the grand jury was shivering in its unheated meeting room. An oil stove dragged in for the occasion didn't bring much comfort. Faced with an unusually heavy schedule—four murders, one rape, two white vagrancies, and a stubbornly fought land case, in addition to the lynching—and eager to get the entire mess behind them, the grand jury plowed through without delay.

While they deliberated, black newspapers nationwide were broadcasting a call from the NAACP for churches to hold Easter mass for the souls of lynching victims. The *Chicago Defender*'s front page on Easter morning bore a grim drawing of three men, wearing crowns of thorns, hanging from the branch of a tree.

On Easter morning, President William Howard Taft stood at the pulpit of the Metropolitan A.M.E. Church near the White House and spoke out against lynching, but failed to call a federal law against it. This did not surprise NAACP leaders who'd met with the president a year earlier and were told this matter rested with the states and they should lobby at that level.

On that same day in Hamilton, the young musician Alex Copeland and his mother held their annual Easter egg hunt. This year the fete was different: instead of the usual Sunbeam Band church group, "every child in town" was invited, according to the *Journal*. Either this referred to every white child in town, or this was an interracial event. These were not atypical during the slavery period when blacks and whites attended church together, but they were highly unusual in this era. A short time later, black and white young people in Mountain Hill would—even more uncharacteristically—participate in a joint baptismal ceremony.

Four days after Easter, on April 11, the grand jurors in the Hamilton courthouse brought forth eight true bills on the criminal matters. Their remarks on the lynching, typed on onion-skin, read: "We regret and condemn the Lynching that took place in our county, and have used our best efforts to find the perpetrators but have been unable to find out anything about it." These notes appear at the end of the page of presentments. Far more space was allotted to the sad state of bathrooms in the courthouse, the filthy and unsanitary condition of the jail, and the need to pay the sheriff fifty cents per diem to take proper care of it.

Once again in Georgia, no white man would be tried for a lynching.

On April 14, the anniversary of the assassination of Abraham Lincoln, the *Titanic* struck an iceberg and sunk, carrying with it over 1,500 people. It was an occasion tailored to the tastes of Arthur Hardy. Aching for heroes in these days of beastly behavior, he sat down and wrote a poem for *The Golden Age*, which also ran in the *Journal*.

> They conquered self and died to save the weak—
> would Christ have called upon them to do more!
> And though above them now the waters break
> There's added music in the Ocean's roar."

Meanwhile, later that week, Douglas Hadley led Johnie Moore's mother, Lula, to the filthy jail and locked her in the place her son had recently occupied. She had been hauled before Harris County grand juries twice in the past two years. First she was accused of attempted murder of a white man; then she was accused of manslaughter of a black woman. Both of her victims were neighbors. Each time she had pleaded "not guilty" and the grand jury had failed to indict her. This time, however, the manslaughter charge was changed to murder and she pleaded guilty.

Her jury of "twelve good and lawful men" was composed entirely of white men from the western district where she lived, including two white Moores, a Huling, and a Land. These were men all tightly tangled in relations among black and white in that benighted place, men likely to have been a part of the January mob.

This time she was convicted and sentenced by Judge Gilbert to twelve years at hard labor on the state prison farm at Milledgeville. She was known to be a volatile woman and now, with her only son dead at the hands of a lynch mob, she'd have surely spelled trouble. I suspect some just wanted to get her out of the way. Her guilty plea at this point suggests to me that she was somehow "encouraged" to submit. Or perhaps her white neighbors' recent macabre demonstration of their ability to eliminate enemies and the searing fact of her innocent son's fate was enough to win her cooperation. She'd not be the only relative of a lynching victim to be imprisoned that year. In the upcoming October court session, Dusky Crutchfield's husband, Jim, would be sentenced to ten years for burglary.

On April 19, the day Lula Moore was found guilty, Buddie Hadley announced another run for sheriff. The January election had been a special one because so many officeholders had retired, died, or simply quit; empty spaces needed filling. On May 1, the white primary was scheduled. Most contenders for other offices had long since announced. Perhaps Hadley was waiting to see how the grand jury would rule. If there was an uproar over his failure to produce suspects, or if the prosecutor did indeed find culprits and they turned out to be a passel of his kinfolk, he needn't bother to run.

❧

Many contradictory things had begun to happen in the county after that cursed night. More black men killed black women than ever in the past. More white men killed other white men. More black men were sentenced to die, while at the same time, more white men launched costly campaigns to free black men from prison or to see sentences reduced.

In the wake of the lynching, many Mountain Hill residents also took it upon themselves to write letters on prisoners' behalf.

The continued killing of black women would not be confined to black men or even to Harris County. No sooner had Dusky Crutchfield gone into the record as the first black woman lynched in Georgia when, in June 1912, sixty-year-old Anne Bostwick, a hundred miles away in Pinehurst, became the second. Longtime housemaid to a prominent white family, she'd been diagnosed as mentally ill, but the state asylum was overcrowded and would not admit her. She continued to work. One day she and her employer had an argument and she waited outside for her, behind a column on the veranda. When the woman came outside, Bostwick lunged at her with a knife, nearly severing her head. She then went and found the woman's husband and told him what she had done.

Newspapers reported that great crowds watched Bostwick seated in a convertible, a rope hanging from a tree placed around her neck. The car was then accelerated at high speed and as she was hanged her body was riddled with so many bullets it was cut in two.

An Ohio paper reported that despite the usual "parties unknown" ruling of the coroner's jury, the car used in the lynching was known to belong to "prominent citizens." This was unusual in that the ruling ideology of the day was that prominent whites were black folks' benevolent guardians, and that only "rednecks" resorted to lynching. Some papers also defied precedent by detailing the sterling reputation of Bostwick's family.

In the matter of Anne Bostwick, President William Henry Taft spoke out for the first time against a specific lynching. Taft was under pressure from lynching opponents, spearheaded by the NAACP, to support federal antilynching laws. This he refused to do, and in 1911 he had told black leaders asking for help that "federal authorities are not authorized to intervene unless it be for the purpose of protecting a citizen in the exercise of rights which he possesses by virtue of the Constitution and laws of the United States."

To Taft's proclamation, the May *Crisis* responded: "Well, in the name of justice, what rights does an American possess 'by virtue of the Constitution and laws of the United States,' if it is not the right not to be deprived of life, liberty, or property without due process of law as the Fifth Amendment guarantees?"

In the same issue, the *Crisis* revisited the Hamilton lynching and wondered who would be next, predicting that it would be children. Sadly, the prediction came true. More Georgia lynchings would occur that summer, though none more savage than that of a fourteen-year-old black boy in Columbus named T. Z. McElheney, in August.

In August, McElheney accidentally shot his friend Cleo Land, son of Brewster Land's brother Will. Such accidents were, unfortunately, not uncommon. No charges were even contemplated and papers extended sympathy to both families. But when the shooter was black and the victim the white son of the powerful Land family, with its ties to past lynchings, there would be no mutual sympathy.

In the days preceding the trial, lynch threats hung about the Columbus courthouse like flies in the thick heat of August. The dead boy's father visited Sheriff Jessie Beard and told him that if the verdict was less than murder, there might be trouble.

The boy was tried and found guilty of unlawful manslaughter. Barefoot and wearing shorts, he pleaded for leniency, weeping, "I am just a little black nigger." Gilbert sentenced him to three years in prison.

Despite the January lynching and the current lynch threats, Judge Gilbert ordered no extra guard and the sheriff appeared in court without his pistol. When Gilbert issued the sentence, he scurried quickly from the courtroom, heading up Broadway toward home for lunch. "Look out for the music!" someone shouted, a signal to the mob to make their move. When men began to converge on the boy with pistols drawn, the sheriff slipped into his office, where he remained until the prisoner was out of the building. He later claimed he went to get his gun. A bailiff managed to disappear as well. Another was kicked in the stomach. Before it was over, forty men—none wearing masks—had amassed to drag the boy, begging and screaming, onto a streetcar.

When the car crossed the city line into Sheriff Beard's county territory, the mob took its prey into a wooded lot on the edge of an upper-class neighborhood and pumped the fourteen-year-old full of lead. Hundreds came to stare at the mutilated body, which lay unclaimed on the ground until midnight, when a black undertaker found the courage to collect it. It was the boy's accidental shot to an eye that had killed his friend, and so T. Z. McElheney's killers had fired bullets through both the young boy's eyes.

Reactions to this new lynching in Columbus were mixed. The Lands were well-known. They had many friends who believed the boy deserved the death penalty and that a lynching was justified. But, for the first time in Georgia history, another crowd vociferously and publicly disagreed. Preachers spoke out from the pulpit and Columbus clubwomen circulated cards declaring their opposition to mob law. Newspapers published the names. Among the signatories was my great-uncle Tom Williams's wife, Erie, a proud member of the United Daughters of the Confederacy, and two of Dr. Charles Williams's daughters; the *Daily Enquirer* published their statement and their names. The signing of such a petition by these women might seem a simple act, but in that era of ironclad silence on the subject, it would set a new standard, one that would bear fruit in Hamilton in another two decades.

❧

Judge Gilbert had now seen fourteen occasions of lynching on his watch. He had lectured repeatedly on the need to bring mob members to justice but had never seen any brought to trial. This time he got his wish.

Having won the white primary but still facing general election, he reminded the grand jury that trials are at the foundation of our system of government and that the safety of both person and property is dependent upon enforcement of the law "without fear or favor." Wishing to remove matters from the torrid arena of race, he told them "the negro is an incident in the circumstances."

This time things took a different course. For the first time in the history of the Chattahoochee Valley Judicial Circuit, the grand jury returned three true bills in lynching against white men Brewster Land, his cousin Ed Land, the dead boy's uncle, and Lee Lynn, a mill worker, plus four bills against Will Land, the boy's father. They expressed regret that they'd not found evidence to indict more men.

Unlike the Harris County grand jury in April, which ignored law officers' roles in that lynching altogether, this one took the sheriff and his men to task. Still, the Land men were never actually arrested. Sheriff Beard claimed they could not be found. Arrogant men, they sent word they had a long train trip they wanted to take and would show up in November for trial. "It was summer and too hot in the jail," one later said.

They arrived as promised, backed by a team of the best lawyers Columbus had to offer. Brewster Land, a stern bull of a man, was asked where they'd been. "That is another matter, but a regiment of soldiers could not have brought me to town had I not wanted to come," he replied.

Leading the defense team was Judge Gilbert's recent opponent, Eugene Wynn. Assisting him was fellow native Harris County resident and Williams brother-in-law Henry C. Cameron. Not so long before that, Cameron had been willing to reveal publicly the identity of mob leader, Edgar Stripling, to help another client. Now, representing mob leaders, he and his colleagues used a loophole in the law to allow their clients to offer only unsworn testimony, which could not be cross-examined.

By the rules agreed upon in advance by all parties, the jury was required to find the men guilty of conspiracy to commit murder, or nothing; and the sheriff had presented no evidence to that effect. As for witness testimony that the defendants used violence against law officers in the courtroom and had even warned the sheriff beforehand of possible trouble, the defense used it as evidence of their clients' efforts to protect the officers from the real culprits.

The jury adjourned for exactly twenty-nine minutes and returned to pronounce the four men "not guilty" on all counts. Shortly thereafter, one of the bailiffs admitted that he and other officers were warned in unsigned letters, before the trial, that it would be wise for them to be careful about discussing the lynching. At that point Prosecutor George Palmer had a clear case for appealing the verdicts on grounds of witness tampering. Aware of the minuscule chances of any white jury convicting any white man for any crime against a black man, he chose not to.

CHAPTER NINETEEN

"... Died with Their Boots On"

Several things happened in Harris County as a result of the 1912 lynching. For one thing, whites in their county became sensitive about its reputation. Toward the end of January, an *Atlanta Journal* columnist rubbed salt into the wounds by revisiting a series of nefarious 1906 white-on-white, all-in-the-family murders, and comparing the county to Kentucky's Breathitt County, home of the Hatfields and McCoys. The local elites discussed a lawsuit for libel and the *Columbus Daily Enquirer*, which had reprinted the story, apologized. The sheriff, also sensitive to the stain on his own honor, set about to polish his image. His determination to mend his tattered reputation would be sorely tested. After the "Hamilton Avengers"—or murderers, as some took to calling them—were let off the hook, a crime wave unlike any other washed over the county. By the time the April 1913 court session rolled around, Buddie Hadley—who, with Judge Gilbert and Solicitor General Palmer, had won reelection—would present one hundred criminal cases to the grand jury.

Throughout the year and into the next and the next, Harris County lynch mobs—emboldened by the Avengers' escape from justice—would again form or threaten. Each time, the sheriff, backed by the judge and a grand jury, moved the defendant to the safety of Columbus or Atlanta. Twice the trials were held in Atlanta. In one of these, a mob of Mountain Hill area moonshine men packed the courtroom to glower at the jury.

Meanwhile, in Columbus, powerful white men continued to mount black church podiums to instruct blacks on how to live. In 1913, a superior court judge told St. James A.M.E. members they were to look to the church and to white men, not to the courts for their salvation. Negroes, as he called them, were simply unable to uphold oaths.

On a national level, President Woodrow Wilson was quickly disappointing any hopes that black Americans had for him as he set about to accelerate the segregation of federal jobs, removing blacks from decent employment unavailable to them elsewhere in the country.

❧

But it wasn't black men the white citizens of Harris County were worried about these days so much as their own fellow whites.

The Bible verse from 1 Samuel that Miss Lula's little Juvenile Missionary Society girls had read the afternoon of the lynching carried this ominous message: "and I tell him that I am about to punish his house for ever, for the iniquity which he knew, because his sons were blaspheming God, and he did not restrain them. Therefore I swear to the house of Eli that the iniquity of Eli's house shall not be expiated by sacrifice or offering forever."

Some would swear this was happening to them, but it would become harder and harder to tell just whose house was Eli's, given the large numbers of houses being punished, though close examination would reveal familial connections among them all. In 1914, several men from prominent families fell dead or met with serious accidents. John B. Mobley, son of James Monroe Mobley, brother of Miss Lula, and most prominent of all the Mobley men, dropped dead on a sidewalk just before Christmas. "Acute indigestion" was cited as the cause. One minute he was laughing and chatting on the sidewalk with the postmaster and another friend; the next he was gone.

The sheriff's brother Joe, himself a former sheriff who lived along the "Avengers'" line of march, spent months in an Atlanta sanatorium that year. Dr. Charles Williams died without warning. The judge suffered a stroke that paralyzed one leg. His brother Will's son Henry suffered life-threatening gunshot wounds in a hunting accident. In addition, four Hargett men died in 1914, including H.V., who suffered severe burns when a church furnace blew up in his face right after the lynching, then died of Bright's disease two years later. At the same time, Judge Williams's son would suddenly drop dead on his front porch. In 1918 Bessie Hadley, Buddie and Emma's youngest, beloved daughter, would be cut down by typhoid fever, leaving her two-year-old daughter Helen to be raised by her grandparents. And over the next decade, more Hargetts, Mobleys, and Williamses would meet untimely deaths, including Gamble Mobley, Miss Lula's nephew, stomped to death by a mule in 1920 when his buggy overturned. Will Williams's beautiful sister Mattie Florrie Kirven, married to the Kirven's department store heir, died in Will's Big House, recuperating from an illness in 1921; just a few years later, Will's eldest son, Worth, a musician with a new wife and baby, hit a large hog on the road and died instantly.

If this wasn't enough, there was also the long wave of white-on-white killings. In Harris County, as in most of the South, white men had always murdered other white men more freely than they murdered black ones, and with just as much impunity. But, after January 22, 1912, whatever floodgates still stood split wide open.

By 1915, five white men had been murdered by other white men. All the dead and some of the killers were believed to have been "Hamilton Avengers."

When I returned to the county for research, this is what I'd hear again and again: "Every man in the mob died with his boots on."

⤫

I took my cousin Louise with me to visit the Fort sisters. The three had played dolls together as children and talked about it as if it were yesterday, though all were in their late eighties and early nineties. They even remembered the dolls' names. Edna Fort, still living with her sister Mary, recalled how, at five and eight years old, they were awakened by the bloodcurdling cries of Dusky Crutchfield. "There was a country road over there. They marched them down beside Sheriff Hadley's house, down to [the Askew Creek] to an old tree that hung out over the road and they hung them there. It was just terrible, just terrible."

"And not a one of them was guilty," her sister added. It was Mary Fort, former American history teacher at Columbus High School, who told me, with some sense of satisfaction, that "every man in the mob died with his boots on." Edna, a former elementary school teacher, added for clarification: "Unnatural deaths, you understand." I asked them for names of these men, but they declined. Mary would later send me a note. She wanted me to know that "we were not stained." I believe she was referring to the curse many felt had fallen on the mob, and perhaps the town, and wanted me to know that she and her sister remained untouched by it. Possibly she also wanted me to know that no one from her family had been involved.

The boots-on killings began in 1913 and looked on the surface like white moonshine guys mad about getting ratted out or having something stolen or a fight over a woman. It hit the Hamilton

Irvins first, then the Mountain Hill Teels, and by the time the long spate of murders among families all tightly connected to Norman Hadley and the lynching ended in 1922, fifteen were dead, six had been tried for murder, and two imprisoned.

Nineteen fifteen was a year of enormous racial hatred in Georgia. The movie *The Birth of a Nation* had played steadily to huge Columbus crowds for most of the year. Audience estimates for that city alone were at a hundred thousand, with folks coming elsewhere by train to see it.

In a sensational case that same year, Leo Frank, a Jewish businessman, was convicted of murdering a young girl who worked in his Atlanta-area pencil factory. He was taken from the state prison and lynched by powerful men after Hoke Smith called for a retrial. Smith's old enemy Tom Watson returned from obscurity to rouse men to vengeance. Galvanized by the lynching, a new Ku Klux Klan had been resurrected outside Atlanta on Stone Mountain and a new conservative populist spirit was in the Georgia air.

Governor Nat Harris, who had been arranging Frank's retrial, visited him in prison just before he was lynched. There he bumped into Edgar Stripling's six-year-old daughter. Christmas was just weeks away and the winsome lass implored the governor to free her daddy. He promised that he would and he did.

~

Among the many killings, it would be those dubbed "the River Killings" that finally spelled doom for Buddie Hadley's short, stumbling career as sheriff.

The year 1913 had ended with a Christmas murder in Mountain Hill. A white moonshiner named Mack Melton shot a son of the powerful Teel moonshine family in front of his wife. Melton was rushed to safety in Atlanta by Sheriff Hadley and tried there. A Mountain Hill mob showed up to scare the jury into not making a decision. In his second trial he was acquitted and vowed never to return to Harris County, but in 1915 he and his brother and another man were pulled out of the Chattahoochee River (hence the name "River Killings") by a fisherman and a ferryman. They had last been seen in the company of their old enemies, the Teels, as well as Hargetts and Lands.

Again Columbus papers jumped on a juicy Harris County story, one with legs that would run for months. "One of the bodies was strung on a trot line like a fish. An incision had been made in his neck and the line passed through the mouth," the *Columbus Ledger* informed its readers. Their heads had been shot through, then crushed with a thirty-five-pound stone.

If ever there was a time for Sheriff Buddie Hadley to stand tall, this was it. But an early news item signaled that would not happen. This case, even more than the 1912 lynching, demonstrated to any and all that it was the Moonshine Mafia of Harris County that ran things and that, for the time being, Buddie Hadley did their bidding. By now, Mitch Huling, having roundly lost his race for Muscogee County sheriff, was justice of the peace in the Mountain Hill district. Confidently, he told a reporter that he was quite sure the men under suspicion would be cleared. Two of those men, Charlie and Shaffer Hargett, were his relatives. From the beginning, Buddie Hadley's efforts appeared sadly ludicrous. These were his people—relatives by marriage, old friends and neighbors, and political backers. Most important, however, they were the men who'd engineered and carried out the 1912 lynching, proven killers, firm in the belief they could do anything and get away with it.

Hadley would know as well as anyone the sophisticated ways these little moonshine fiefdoms had long organized themselves to fight the feds and to punish those who went against them. The newly formed Klan had nothing on these men, who for decades had polished their networks of information, informers, and executioners. They didn't yet go around in robes, or give themselves comical titles, but they could strike fear like none other. Because they were about the only people making any money in those rough times, they could easily buy protection from local law officers. Also, like the modern Mafia, they had many house lawyers, men of their own families. The mere fact that there were so many of them, most intermarried, provided considerable protection.

By October, Sheriff Hadley had issued at least a dozen subpoenas to people to appear before the grand jury to testify in the River Killings. When the day came, however, the blacks among them had mysteriously disappeared and the whites refused to talk. At this point, both Judge Gilbert and Prosecutor Palmer publicly blamed the sheriff for the county's high murder rate.

It was on the heels of this mammoth failure to obtain justice that Buddie Hadley went to Columbus to crow to reporters about the upcoming triple execution of three black men, who had been tried and found guilty at the court session in which the "River Killers" were supposed to be produced. Seeking to burnish his tattered reputation he announced the three would die in one month and described a hangman's stand rigged to handle three hangings at once. But, once again, he'd have egg on his face when two of the men escaped and later appealed. One's sentence was reduced to life. The next year, in separate executions, Hadley got to "pull the trap" on the other two.

Late in 1915, a Mountain Hill woman broke ranks. In an anonymous letter, she detailed firsthand reports about Shaffer Hargett, one of the River Killing suspects, and the white men's bodies, telling the sheriff just where to go to find eyewitnesses. It did no good. Rumors circulated that more dead black bodies had turned up in the Chattahoochee near where the white ones were found. Nothing happened, despite the fact the October grand jury had strongly recommended the case be continued.

In 1916, Sheriff Buddie Hadley was severely defeated in the white Democratic primary by Homer Williams, a man unrelated to my family but backed by the Williams-Mobley clique, in an effort to put moonshiners out of business and stop the killings. Knowing Hadley would likely lose, the moonshine district of the county had backed another of their own, a Gordon uncle of Norman Hadley.

The River Killings were never brought before another grand jury. Shaffer Hargett and his wife, both of them young, died of pneumonia in 1918. Stories of his violent, racist cruelty were still being told in Harris County in the 1990s.

In the fall of 1916, Buddie Hadley removed his badge, donned an apron, and became a grocer on the square. His son Douglas worked alongside him. He and Berta now had two daughters, ages one and five. The eldest, Marion Elizabeth, loved to play Hangman with seven-year-old Arthur Hardy, Jr. She'd climb into a gunny sack tied to a rope tossed over a low-hanging tree branch and he'd pull her up, screaming with excitement, then begging to come down. Her mother didn't like the game and told her so, but Elizabeth, who would one day be my mother, was a headstrong child.

CHAPTER TWENTY

Roaring Twenties

The curse many felt had been cast upon the county after the lynching continued to wreak havoc into the new decade. On a bright April morning in 1920, my great-uncle Dock Williams, my grandfather's youngest and most rapscallion brother, was found in a puddle of blood, his head "beat to jelly," alongside the bodies of two Irvin men. All of the men were believed by black folks to have been there at the tree beside the baptismal font that fateful midnight in 1912. Some descendants of former Williams slaves shook their heads and said things like "Vengeance is mine, said the Lord," and, given the extraordinarily high number of deaths dealt out to men known or believed to have been behind those masks, perhaps they knew whereof they spoke.

During the time I spent researching these stories, people talked about what came to be known as the Tip Top murders as if they'd happened yesterday. Much like the 1912 lynching, a black man had been executed for a white man's crime, but this time things took a somewhat different turn. This black man, Louis "Sugar Bear" Murray, had been in the service of the Irvin men since childhood and was deeply loyal to them. On that fateful night, a fight broke out over a twenty-dollar bill in a gambling den called Tip Top, at the top of Pine Mountain. Four drunk white men started shooting and knifing and wrestling, splattering blood all over the cabin. By the end, one Irvin lay dead and another Irvin and Dock Williams lay dying. It was revealed in various ways that the white Cook ordered the black Murray to "finish him," referring to Dock. Murray confessed to killing Dock Williams with a rock. He was sentenced to die but Dock's wife and two of his brothers—my grandfather Will and his brother Brit, a state legislator—decided they wanted Cecil Cook, a former close friend, to pay for killing Dock. So for the first time in Harris County history, a white man was indicted on the word of a black man.

This would not end well for Murray or the Williams family. Murray was represented by Arthur Hardy and his partner Joe Peavy, who was Cecil Cook's brother-in-law. In Murray's trial, his lawyers had failed to present the "ordered to kill" defense, instead claiming that Murray's loyalty to the Irvins and a desire to protect them led him to bludgeon Williams. To the amazement of most of the courtroom and despite his promise to the prosecutor to tell the truth, once on the stand Murray refused to speak. Cecil Cook went back to his work that day a free man.

Days later, as Murray stood on the gallows with the noose around his neck, he was confronted by Will Williams, who demanded he recount his story so he could tell it to the press waiting outside. He also demanded to know what happened to the money Dock had on him when he was killed. Murray had just spoken with Dock's widow, Kate, and told her he had nothing against "Mr. Dock," that he liked him, and only did what he did under orders from Cecil Cook. He also told her that five men, including his lawyers, Cook, and an Irvin brother, had told him before Cook's trial that "a Negro's statement wasn't anything next to a white man's," and that if he remained silent they would go to the governor and get him off.

All of this appeared on the front page of the next morning's Columbus newspaper. Also detailed was my grandfather's shameless attempt to pressure the wrongly convicted man to spend his last seconds on earth restating what he had already said. Perhaps it was because Williams showed Murray no remorse, perhaps because neither he nor his powerful legislator brother Brit had lifted a hand to obtain for him a new trial that he remained silent. Perhaps like Dusky Crutchfield, he'd simply had it with white folks and their schemes and was ready to be done with it all. As on the stand, he said nothing, simply gazing into the hard gray eyes of the man who would become my grandfather.

Louis "Sugar Bear" Murray would be the last convict to die by hanging in Hamilton. He would not, however, be the last black man executed for the crime of a white man. In 1923, the Georgia legislature voted to move all criminal executions to the state farm at Milledgeville. Within five years Kate Mobley Williams would be dead and Will Williams, in the grip of alcoholism, would be a regular patient at a sanatorium in Rome, Georgia, known for shock treatments.

Late in August 1921, just as the tension from all the trials was loosening its grip on Hamilton, yet another tragedy struck. This one involved a white man and a black woman and signaled that the 1912 lynching's message against miscegenation had gone unheard or unheeded in the heart of the village.

W. T. Whitehead, a bachelor, had been a close friend of Norman Hadley and shared his preference for black women. Descended from old families of large slaveholders, long known for their black or mulatto mistresses and large numbers of "outside children," Whitehead ran a small grocery on the square. Now forty-three, he'd had several black mistresses and produced numerous children with them. Currently living with him above the store was a twenty-three-year-old black woman named Adeline Mann. The census listed her as his "cook." The Manns were an old black Hamilton family. Her grandfather, a former slave, was a blacksmith living next door to Emma and Buddie Hadley. On the other side of the Hadley cottage was Whitehead's grocery.

The superintendent of the town's new lumber mill, a man named Comer Chancellor, was a newcomer, and while most old Hamiltonians had grown resigned to Whitehead's lifestyle or simply learned to ignore it, Chancellor was outraged by it. Perhaps he was a Klansman; perhaps he was just inspired by the Klan's now-regular whippings of women, black and white. One sizzling day in late August, he and some other men put Adeline Mann on the train and told her in no uncertain terms never to return. When Whitehead ordered her home and she returned, the men grabbed her again and took her out somewhere and flogged her, or so they told Whitehead, who grabbed his shotgun and headed down the block to Chancellor's house, aiming it straight ahead as he approached. Chancellor greeted him at the door with gunfire, leaving him dead in the street. It was midnight, close to the time of the 1912 lynching.

During this time, Douglas and Berta Hadley were living with their four young daughters close by the square. As Mitch Huling's assistant county police chief, Doug had been among the first on the scene at the Tip Top murders. His family had been startled from sleep at the midnight murder of W. T. Whitehead, an old friend. Miss Berta was becoming more and more like his hypochondriacal mother by the day, and she and the girls were eager for new vistas, so when Mitch Huling was appointed chief of county police in Columbus and invited Douglas to be his assistant, he did not hesitate to accept. This had to seem like the chance of a lifetime to him.

At first the twosome gained a modicum of fame by busting still after still, taking down bootleggers, including some of their own cousins. Newspapers boasted of Huling's prowess, one calling him a "a miniature Bat Masterson with a girlish smile." But when Huling riddled a bootlegger with bullets in his back on Broadway in the middle of the day, his heroic image darkened. As with the lynching, my grandfather was once again the man who wasn't there. Someone suggested he was, but that claim never took hold, and though Huling was ultimately found innocent and returned to his job, he was soon asked to leave and was replaced for a short time by my grandfather.

By the time Doug was in office, the Ku Klux Klan was in full flourish. With close connections to the city police and headquarters above their offices, as well as the full backing of the *Columbus Ledger,* they staged showy parades down Broadway and kept the city on edge. At one point, furious over the hiring of a "Yankee" city manager, they billy-clubbed the man senseless on a downtown sidewalk and dynamited the mayor's house.

An extraordinary journalist couple named Julian and Julia Harris had bought the *Daily Enquirer* and used it to take on the Klan. "These night riders must be run to earth," wrote Julian Harris in a call for a federal antilynching law. His exposés appeared in the New York *World.* In 1922 and 1926 the *Daily Enquirer* won Pulitzer Prizes for Harris's crusade and, by 1926, the Klan in Georgia would be still alive, but limping, ranking only ninth in the country in membership, with six northern states boasting more members.

In 1926, the Columbus Klan disbanded. Every Klan-backed candidate was defeated at the polls that year. Julian Harris was credited for not only driving them out of Columbus, but driving down their numbers throughout the South. Some would note, prematurely, that the state that spawned the Klan was the first to crush it, and Julian Harris would get the lion's share of credit. By 1930 its numbers had shrunk from an estimated five million to some 30,000 nationally and from 156,000 in Georgia to 1,400.

It was sometime during this raucous decade that Miss Lula Mobley and her Methodist Missionary Society women said, *Enough*.

CHAPTER TWENTY-ONE

The Ladies' Ultimatum

When I first returned to Harris County to research this story in the early 1990s, I had no idea where to begin. On a sunny Sunday afternoon I took a drive out toward Mountain Hill, looking for old folks. It was there that I first encountered C. D. Marshall hoeing his tiny cornfield. He wore a pair of faded overalls over a crisp white shirt emblazoned with large black musical notes. Off to his left was the neat L-shaped log cabin in which he lived. He told me it had once housed slaves and that his family had always lived on that land. "It's the last one left," he said.

He was born in 1926. I asked him if he knew about the lynching of the woman and the three men.

"Lynching was the law back then," he said. "They wuh always stealin' somebody outa his bed. . . ." He went on about this and that and then he stopped abruptly, dramatically. He bent down close to my face and said with a huge bright smile, "But they stopped it! Sho did, stopped it just like that. Uh-huh." His face glowed with pride.

"Who stopped it?" I asked. He looked at me like I was born yesterday. Shook his head. "You don't know?!" he said, and then he hollered triumphantly, like it happened yesterday: "The ladies! The ladies! The ladies done stopped it!" And in case I still didn't understand, he added, even louder: "The church ladies up in Hamilton! Them white ladies!" Nowhere is this recorded. Not in Louise Barfield's *History of Harris County, Georgia.* Not in the book of oral histories the Hamilton High students produced back in the 1970s, which I found in the Library of Congress. Not in any newspaper accounts. Not in any church histories I have been able to find. But I believe C. D. Marshall's oral history, passed down through generations of black, not white, Harris County folk. After some historical research, it all began to make great sense.

"How did they stop it?" I asked him.

"They called they mens into the church and they says 'Y'all better stop spinnin' all these haints or we gone move to Columbus.' Yes'm, that's what they said. And they meant it. And they mens knowed they meant it. That's when the ladies got their Voice. We got our Voice, too, but that took a while. So they said, 'Stop the killin', stop stealin' folks out'n their beds.' "

He had to be talking about "the Ladies" of the Ladies Memorial Association, of the Women's Christian Temperance Union, of the Methodist Women's Missionary Society. In short, he was referring to Miss Lula and her large following of strong white women, most of them relatives.

What these women did took a lot of guts. They knew they couldn't bluff. They had to mean it. And that was hard because they loved that little village. There'd been six generations of Williamses, Henrys, Mobleys, and Hudsons living there by now. Their family money—blood money, some would later say—had helped build the courthouse and many of the stores, schools, and churches, had bought the Confederate statue and the courthouse clock. And they were proud of the result. Their ancestors rested beneath this ground. They liked a small town where everyone knew everybody and everyone watched over everyone else. Or so it had seemed, until the women began to wake up.

At some point in the 1920s they could no longer continue to ignore the clash between their Christian beliefs and their kinsmen's social practices—the slaughter of innocents and the untimely deaths of loved ones, what some still believed was Dusky's ghost tormenting her killers and others knew was the lifestyle that had brought them such disgrace. Making matters worse was their daily witnessing of friends and family in the grips of drug addictions. Many of these had been deeply affected by that lynching—people like Arthur Hardy's wife, Irene, Berta Hadley, and the jailer's wife, and more lately the beloved Rev. Alex Copeland.

Through their church missionary work, Miss Lula and her "Ladies" had been subject to antilynching messages during the decade following the 1912 lynching. In 1913, a vast majority of the twenty thousand white southern women at a conference in Birmingham, Alabama, had voted for a resolution against lynching.

In that same year, Lily Hammond, head of the Georgia Methodist Women's Missionary Society, published a book titled *In Black and White,* in which she decried both lynchers and "we who could prevent it." She told of an unnamed town disgraced by mob violence that held a public assembly to confess its shame and pledge to see the law uphold henceforth. It's conceivable that Miss Lula's "Ladies" convened that public assembly in 1913, though I find no record of it but wherever it occurred, it could have inspired what C. D. Marshall described as an amazing convocation that stopped the killing "sometime in the 20s." It was in the early 1920s that the killings peaked, then stopped dramatically.

Given the deep religious feelings of Lula Mobley and her large following, coupled with their longtime political struggles in the temperance wars, where rough men blew smoke in their faces and sang bawdy songs, it would have come naturally—though not without great difficulty—for them to make this brave move. Long ago they'd learned to say to their men: *You won't protect us from the liquor evils; we'll protect ourselves, thank you.* They knew they were joined by thousands of white southern women elsewhere who had finally awakened to the ruse of the "black rapist" defense, saying *Not in our names, mister. This doesn't make us safer.*

Over the next decade, the southern white women of the Methodist church would stiffen their spines, inspired by the antilynching movement of black church and club women and perhaps by the whispered-about heroism of Dusky Crutchfield.

Miss Lula and her now-grown Juvenile Missionary Society girls may not have known it but it was, in part, their distant cousin Anna Julia Cooper's early and ongoing efforts at consciousness-raising and organizing among black women that was having this effect. As early as 1895, Cooper had begun urging church women to organize themselves at every level for the protection and improvement of their race and gender. While Miss Lula had been influencing her nieces and cousins, Anna Julia had been influencing a generation of young black women writers eager to fight lynching and other racial violence with the weapon of literature.

Angelina Weld Grimké, the niece of Cooper's close friends Rev. Francis and Charlotte Grimké, was among the first. In 1913 she wrote *Rachel,* a lynching play, which was circulated and produced in 1920. Grimké taught English at Washington, D.C.'s M Street School during the period that she was writing her plays. Anna Julia Cooper, former principal of M Street, had been fired in 1906 for trivialities. The real reason, everyone agreed, was that she refused to dumb down a curriculum that was sending an impressive number of graduates to Ivy League colleges at a time when whites and large numbers of Booker T. Washington–oriented blacks wanted black schools to emphasize the industrial and manual arts. The ousted Cooper, ever determined to uplift her people, then went on to found a night college for working black adults. For a time it operated out of her elegant home on T Street.

In 1910 she returned to M Street to teach Latin, becoming a colleague of the younger Grimké. Grimké's lynching dramas influenced a number of other black women and, in this way, the nation was introduced through literature to the inner lives of those faceless victims hanging from trees all over the South, as well as their nameless friends and families. Grimké wrote in 1920 that she sought a way to reach white southern women through the heart, through motherhood. She wrote of black women so traumatized by the lynching of their men and of pregnant women—their fetuses cut from the womb—that they refused to bear children.

Throughout the 1910s and 1920s, black antilynching activism mushroomed and bonds starting forming between black women's clubs and church groups and the white southern women of the Methodist Church South, especially those of the Women's Missionary Society. No one was more active in that organization than Miss Lula Mobley. Women she knew well were writing of the sinfulness of white southern men and the need for women to step in and stamp out violence against blacks and white women. The little Juvenile Missionary Society girls she'd tutored as children were now young women as active as she in the church. Louise Williams, Brit's daughter, a nine-year-old when Dusky Crutchfield's screams shattered her sleep that night, now traveled far and wide with Miss Lula to Women's Missionary Society conventions. The 1918 convention held in Tennessee made history when it voted to align itself with "colored women."

Miss Lula had been her father's daughter until his death in 1903. By now, however, she was a strong, independent businesswoman, selling and buying mules in Columbus, overseeing a large farm, and acting as matriarch, hostess, counselor, and inspiration for dozens of relatives and neighbors. By now women had shortened their hems and bobbed their hair. Her own nieces and cousins were rolling cigarettes, driving flivvers, and dancing a fancy buckwing at the Field Rock Club. They'd never formed a suffragist club in Hamilton, but Columbusites Augusta Howard and her sisters had brought the first chapter to Georgia in 1895 and the second convention of the National Woman Suffrage Association (featuring Susan B. Anthony and Carrie Chapman Catt) to Atlanta. Columbus papers were filled with feminist news for them to read and contemplate.

Through the WCTU and the church, through Hamilton Female College and its successor, West Georgia Agricultural and Mechanical, women learned to "point an argument," how to twist arms and argue principles as well as, if not better than, any man. At Methodist conferences they met black women much like themselves—middle class, educated, deeply Christian, with strong social consciences. While their notions of white supremacy were still largely intact, some began to question old notions about blacks' innate inferiority.

I do not know whether the Hamilton foremothers knew that Anna Julia Cooper had cofounded the National Association of Colored Women's Clubs, though that news had appeared in Atlanta papers, or that ideas from those groups were shaping their own. Anna Julia and Lula, each one a devout and active Christian, were both in their early sixties. Both had graduated from college at very young ages. By this time Cooper was defending her doctoral dissertation on slavery and the French Revolutionists at the Sorbonne in Paris. It was written in French. How the Hamilton "Ladies" would have negotiated a conversation with this sophisticated, worldly cousin is hard to imagine. It is equally hard to imagine Cooper relating to the Dusky Crutchfields of the day, poor and powerless, the kind of women she advocated for but rarely associated with. It was these women who represented the battle under way between the sexes, and who exemplified the deep class and cultural divisions that so weakened their cause. Working together without the debilitating divisions of race and class, the Miss Lulas, the Dr. Coopers, and the Duskys would doubtless have accomplished more change more quickly.

In 1920 a group of black women had started the Anti-Lynching Crusaders through the NAACP. To publicize their cause, they'd produced a pamphlet in which Dusky Crutchfield was highlighted as the first woman lynched in Georgia. They invited thousands of prominent white southern women to join. Few replied. They preferred their own organizations. Yet increasingly, white women of the South were opening their eyes to the fact that what they'd so long called "the Negro problem" was, instead, "the Anglo-Saxon problem."

Emboldened no doubt by the Nineteenth Amendment, which gave them the vote, in the early 1920s Methodist Women's Missionary Society groups were sending speakers out to country towns in mountains, swamps, and the Black Belt, in fervid attempts to prevent lynching. They passed out pamphlets created by the Commission on Interracial Cooperation, describing the mistakes mobs made and the "framed up" lies that had caused the deaths of innocent men and women. In 1921, amid the battles over who killed Dock Williams, Dock's brother Brit was elected to represent the county in the Georgia House of Representatives. There Brit sat in the august chambers listening to Governor Hugh Dorsey's astounding Inaugural Address.

Of all the pressing issues before them, the new governor said, the immediate passage of stringent antilynching laws was the most important, and without it no progress could be made. He read the names of more than one hundred Negroes lynched in the past two years—including the four from Hamilton—and noted those who were innocent. Despite the fact that many newspapers had by now decided they were innocent, Crutchfield, Harrington, Hardaway, and Moore were not among those names. It would not be until the 1930s that the white man who killed Norman Hadley made his deathbed confession, so it's likely few knew the truth at this juncture. Speaking angrily of innocent Negro blood on the hands of white Georgians and Georgia's "black eye" in the northern press, the new governor also called for one thousand dollars in compensation to lynching victims' families.

But the centerpiece of his proposal was the creation of a state police force. Local jurisdictions, he declared, had long since proved that they would not or could not mete out justice to mob members. He emphasized, in addition, that until a bill was passed that would give governors the right to discharge local law officers who did not act fearlessly and responsibly to protect prisoners from mobs, there'd be no end to lynching. Dorsey had earlier traveled around the state telling the press that lynchings were caused by white men and women who "got down on the same level with black people," then, when things went wrong, rose up and equated themselves with the law.

Thereafter, Dorsey did nothing of substance to end lynching or ameliorate race relations and accomplished none of the measures he'd called for in his address. But the fact that he took a stand may have made a difference. During his term, five white Georgia men received prison sentences—albeit, short ones—for lynching in the years 1922 and 1926. The number of people lynched in Georgia between 1923 and 1927 dropped to ten. From 1927 through 1929, there were no lynchings at all.

CHAPTER TWENTY-TWO

The Curse Continues

Nineteen twenty-nine would be a grueling year for the nation as a whole. It was the year the banks collapsed. The Great Depression was just around the corner. It was also the year that sixteen-year-old Elizabeth Hadley, called Betty, would discover her mother's drug habit. The girl who would later become my mother came home from school early one day to find her mother and her friends giving one another needle injections. These were the wives of highly placed men who held jobs in law enforcement or were lawyers. My grandfather was not yet sheriff, but soon would be. I envision half-filled glasses of iced tea, half-eaten tomatoes stuffed with tuna salad, nervous, girlish laughter, and my mother's frozen face. Before the women noticed young Betty, she turned silently and left, her face burning with shame. It was never discussed, but Betty thought differently about her mother after that. She held her back ramrod straight, her head a full inch higher, and determined that nothing, not even this shameful thing, would bow it.

It was also in 1929 that the last of the "boots on" killings occurred. Verna Green, in her pink wraparound and Nikes, told me she knew who did the 1912 lynching. "It was a Mobley," she said.

"He was the Klansman. He lived down there, ran a sawmill right down the road there down 27 on the Mulberry Creek."

Verna took me down the Hamilton Road to the Mulberry Creek, near the Big House, where my grandfather Will Williams had lived with his family, a short walk from where as children on our Sunday outings to Hamilton we stopped in Nana's DeSoto to pick up her laundry, and where we children had sneaked sips of old Mamie's muscadine wine. Verna showed me where John B. "Bud" Mobley was living back then, when she was "just starting to date." Bud Mobley's father, Henry, was said to have been involved with Dusky Crutchfield, but he'd also been the one who'd presided over the coroner's jury that peered up at the four shredded bodies and pronounced they had died at "the hands of parties unknown."

By now he had moved to Florida, perhaps to escape the eerie howls he'd sworn he heard at every full moon since January 22, 1912. Verna thought it was Henry who'd heard a ghostly howling at his window that night, but it was his son, Bud, who picked up his pistol and went after a black neighbor he suspected of tricking him. The black man—Ernest Farley—grabbed Mobley's weapon and shot him dead. Farley's brothers helped him escape. They were later found and, with their wives, jailed for questioning. Nothing ever came of it, no threats of lynching, no arrests, no claims of beatings, no convictions. The motive provided by newspapers was the same false one provided for Norman Hadley's: a dispute over money. Ernest Farley was never again seen. "I know his brother," Verna told me. "He's a good friend of mine. We don't never talk about it. He ain't never said a word about it all these years."

❧

The following year, 1930, my future mother graduated from high school. Betty Hadley had been named valedictorian of her tiny class but felt "too shy" to make the commencement address, so she passed it along to the salutatorian, a young man desperate to marry the pretty young flapper with bedroom eyes. His chances, however, were nil. Her heart and life were promised to the soon-to-be Dr. Ben Williams, off at medical school. Like her, he had already been deeply wounded by life. He was but an impressionable twelve when his father's harassment of Louis "Sugar Bear" Murray on the gallows made front-page news. Much later he'd tell me his father was a "sadist." He never explained this and would redden with instant anger each time I mentioned Papa Will. He told me a story of how he and his brother, as children, had put a cat in the well to see if it would swim and the cat had drowned. That night Papa Will stood outside their bedroom, scratching at the door and making cat howls as they trembled beneath their sheets.

Was my Williams grandfather at the 1912 lynching? I do not know for sure, but there were many reasons he might have had for going. Norman's mother, Josie, was the postmaster at Cataula, where he lived; he was the postal deliveryman. His brothers Dock and Ben were close friends with Norman. Dusky Crutchfield was his cousin Henry Mobley's concubine. Until shortly before the lynching, she'd lived on his place a half mile away from my grandfather's, a piece of backwoods grandly called Kingsboro. His brother Dock was Mitch Huling's best friend. If for no other reason, he'd have gone to make sure Dock didn't go wild with his gun after the lynching. And it was not only Dusky and her "Miz Mobley" outrage he had to worry about but another black woman, also one just a stone's throw away, who had recently borne the child of one of his brothers. He'd have perhaps relished the idea of sending a loud message to both silence blacks on the subject and warn white men away from these liaisons. My educated guess is that he was there and that his drinking escalated after that. When in 1974 I told Big Mamma, his widow, that I was divorced, she shook her head slowly, a pained look gathered on her sad old face, and she said, "I should have done that. There was too much pain in that marriage."

Sometime during adolescence, Ben had come to believe that he himself had killed a young black woman. This was the "secret" my father revealed to my sister and me on Clubview Drive when I was eleven and asked him to stop drinking. I do not know how that connects to the enmity between him and his father, but it happened at roughly the same time that my father got that dread notion in his head and that hostility forced him to leave home. He moved in to the Beall-Mobley-Williams house on the square with his uncle Brit and aunt Matilda. Soon after that he was shipped off to Georgia Military Academy. Upon graduation he left for Kirksville College of Osteopathy in Missouri. Before leaving, he placed a ring upon Betty Hadley's finger (the one I wear today) and she waited impatiently for his return.

In 1934, newly minted Dr. Ben Williams returned home from Missouri by bus with more than a degree in osteopathy. On one arm he was holding a much older Native American wife, Rose, and on the other, her ten-year-old daughter. This was Ben, great-great-grandson of General Elias Beall, who drove hundreds of Creek Indians from their Chattahoochee lands. This was the man whose engagement ring Betty Hadley wore, the man who'd give her a fine house, a country club membership, beautiful children, and fancy cars. Ben claimed he'd married Rose in a drunken blackout and asked his mother by mail to inform his fiancée of the situation before his return. My mother-to-be removed her engagement ring, picked up the family Bible, and took to her room for three days, where she cried and prayed.

After that, she and my father's mother hatched a plot to break up this unholy arrangement and send yet two more Indians packing west. It seemed the family was finding more civilized ways of ridding itself of inconvenient women. Apparently, as my father later recounted, Rose had hastened the process by throwing knives at him across the dining room table one night. Soon after the bus pulled out, and a quick divorce was procured, my parents were wed. Still, my father never forgot the little girl. He'd apparently promised her birth father back in Missouri that should the union collapse, he'd return the child to him directly, so he put her on a bus alone to a distant place. He never knew what happened to her and into his old age expressed remorse.

By the time they were married, Ben and Betty Williams had each been pretty badly damaged by the tiny, tumultuous world that spawned them. As children they'd heard endless stories of murder and melee. Betty had watched her mother slip into a needle addiction and knew her revered grandfather, the former sheriff, had turned to bootlegging in his retirement. Her mother was a talker and talked all the more when morphine was calming her nerves. Did she tell Betty that her cousin John Cash walked into a Negro church one Sunday morning, raised a ruckus, and was fatally wounded? Did she tell her that a great-uncle had shot and killed his father, her great grandfather?

While she would spend much of her adult life convincing herself that the heinous 1912 lynching never occurred, her new groom would spend the rest of his life convinced he had killed a young black woman who did not die. What chance did these two ever have—the sheriff's daughter wearing her own little shiny, invisible badge, and the "sadist's" son, condemned in his own mind to live a life of self-flagellation?

Perhaps they thought a new brick ranch house across from the Columbus Country Club and a shiny black Packard would wash away both the bloodstained stories they'd heard and the firsthand cruelties they'd witnessed.

Buddie Hadley had died of a heart attack in 1931. He was in his buggy on the way to the Columbus Farmers' Market with a load of collards and yams and, likely buried beneath them, moonshine, my mother told me. He'd gone into the business himself after he lost the sheriff's race. Years later, a great-granddaughter opened Buddie's Bible to discover a news clipping by a farmer who wrote of the need for cooperation among poor farmers, black and white.

Two years later, my grandfather Douglas Hadley was elected high sheriff of Harris County, a post he'd hold for the next twenty-four years. There'd be no public lynchings on his watch and fewer murders. Black and white alike would tell me that he was, more or less, a good sheriff. However, the dip in violence was not entirely his handiwork. Beginning in the 1930s, societal shifts and political change wielded a strong influence. Since the turn of the century, two hundred antilynching bills had been introduced in Congress and failed. While ongoing efforts by the NAACP continued to meet defeat, in 1939 a Civil Rights Section was created within the Justice Department in order to bring civil charges against law officers who surrendered prisoners to mobs.

Even before that, small changes were cropping up in Georgia. In 1930, two white men had been sentenced to prison for lynching two black men who were about to testify against a white rapist. Throughout the 1930s, thousands of Association of Southern Women for the Prevention of Lynching (ASWPL) members, aided by local Methodist Missionary Society women, began making regular calls on sheriffs to remind them of their oaths and laws regarding lynch mobs. They would call on ministers and other prominent citizens to help them prevent lynching.

Into the 1940s, they strong-armed sheriffs into signing pledges and publicized the names of those who refused. Law officers were being warned by these uppity but respected women of the adverse publicity that would result from any mob violence in their jurisdictions.

CHAPTER TWENTY-THREE

Dad Doug

On June 5, 1941, I was born into a world engulfed by chaos. A madman named Adolf Hitler and his deluded countrymen were destroying democracies across Europe while millions of people, including Jews, Gypsies, homosexuals, political dissidents, and blacks, were being herded into concentration camps and incinerated. Six months and one day after my birth, Japan bombed Pearl Harbor and the United States entered World War II. In the background of my formative years occurred cataclysmic events I would only later have words for: *Holocaust, Hiroshima, Atom Bomb, Nazi.*

The war brought indescribable upheaval to the world, the nation, and the South. A massive base of black veterans were returning home and expecting to share equally in a democracy they'd risked their lives to defend. This dissonance laid the groundwork for a new American Revolution that would be known as the civil rights movement.

At home in Columbus, Georgia, two black men found their own way to fight white supremacy and created a tool that would enable the upcoming civil rights movement to succeed. In 1943, when I was two years old, a black Columbus barber and his phy-

sician friend, Dr. Thomas Brewer, head of the local NAACP, cou-
rageously took the state's white primary system to court and won.
Along with a Supreme Court decision the following year that ruled
that the U.S. Constitution guaranteed the right to vote in primary
elections, regardless of race, this created a radical shift for blacks
throughout the United States and set the stage for the emergence of
the civil rights movement.

In the meantime, however, most white Georgians were not
about to surrender their cherished notions of superiority and the
right to mistreat black people, even black soldiers in uniform. In
Harris County, some of the old die-hards, newly returned from
"whuppin' Hitler's butt," found themselves identifying with his
white supremacy ideology and expressed reservations that they'd
fought him. There were vile rumors of black men, home from a
taste of French wine and women, who were now in hot pursuit of
white girlfriends. More, however, seemed inclined to pursue the
precious right to vote.

It was in this atmosphere that Sheriff Marion Douglas Hadley
began his second decade as chief law enforcement officer of Harris
County. By now my grandfather had been sheriff for ten years.
He was elected in 1933, a year in which lynchings spiked in the
South; they continued into the decade. Not so in my grandfather's
jurisdiction. But for a murder by law officers within the jail, Harris County saw no more. In addition, the murder rate decreased
and no one was sentenced to death. My grandfather was a man
congenitally averse to conflict. His experience as a new deputy in
1912 and during the years that saw the mob members murdering
one another—including several of his cousins—had no doubt
strengthened that aversion.

More recently, he'd seen his friend Mitch die a disgraced and
broken man, the result of his blazing-pistols approach to law enforcement. An ongoing factor would also be Berta's frail condition,

and her addiction to drugs, which may or may not have been the result of the traumas she suffered as a witness to the lynched bodies and from the bomb threats, the murder trial, and the spate of bad publicity she and her husband had endured while he worked for Mitch in Columbus.

The work begun by the ASWPL continued to reap local rewards. In 1941, a group of Harris County white women, schooled in the ideas and tactics of the ASWPL and possibly including some of Miss Lula's "Enough" club, physically intervened to stop a lynching in progress. The newspapers, long enamored of reporting successful lynchings, decided to keep mum on this particular success. By the 1940s the Georgia press had chosen to turn down the thermometer on "race" stories.

I do not know how my Hadley grandfather felt about black rights or white supremacy, but I do know that he was a politician through and through, acutely aware of which way the wind was blowing. In 1943, Herman Talmadge was defeated by a moderate Ellis Arnall. Though Arnall didn't subscribe to social equality, he did abolish the poll tax and chain gangs, revoke the KKK charter, and support the prosecution of thirty-eight Atlanta police officers for Klan membership.

Another moderating influence on my grandfather and Harris County came in the form of two rich and powerful white men: President Franklin D. Roosevelt and Cason J. Callaway. In the early 1930s Roosevelt began regular sojourns in nearby Warm Springs to seek relief from the effects of polio. During the Depression, Callaway scooped up thousands of acres of rolling woodland, including that of my Hadley family, at rock-bottom prices, and over the next twenty years developed experimental farms and a paradise for nature lovers and sportsmen. This area was referred to by locals as "the Gardens." In the 1935, Roosevelt created the Pine Mountain Valley Community, one of several experiments in communal farming that brought poor urban whites to rural areas to build their own houses and farm their own crops. With such largesse under way in this long-benighted land, it behooved the sheriff to keep a close eye on county affairs.

In 1946, black voter rights efforts were at a peak, spurred on by President Roosevelt's New Deal projects to support black professionals, who would in turn serve poor blacks. These programs drew thousands of African Americans from rural Georgia to Atlanta. Seven thousand black voters were registered during this time, and reports of senseless murders of black men began once again to fill front pages.

In July 1946, the last lynching in Georgia was carried out, in Walton County. In broad daylight, two dozen white men executed two young black men, one just home from war, and their wives. As with Hamilton's 1912 lynching and so many others, miscegenation was a major factor, though most papers remained silent on the subject.

For the first time in Georgia, large numbers of prominent whites stood up and spoke out. One was my grandfather Will Williams's son-in-law Dr. Hoyt Trimble, who served on the board of an anti-Klan organization outside Atlanta. In 1946 the group publicly protested the Walton County lynching. They used Bible verses and newspaper ads to try to persuade nearby Monroe's "best people" to reveal the lynchers' names, but to no avail.

There would be no justice for the families of the two men and two women lynched in Walton County. Because they'd been in the sheriff's custody just prior to the killings, the FBI had grounds to investigate, but Director J. Edgar Hoover's men got nowhere. Federal efforts to track down and convict the Walton County lynchers had come up empty. Hoover grumbled that he'd never seen such arrogance as he encountered among the whites in that county, nor so much fear of "negroes."

That summer, my father's alcoholism and womanizing cul-
minated in my parents' divorce, and my sister and I were tucked
away safely in the harbor of G'mamma and Dad Doug's home. I
believe it was that year when I sat on the grassy bank along Railroad Street in front of my grandparents' house and watched a ragtag Klan parade shuffle past their house and turn into the pasture
behind John Ivey Mobley's house, on the other side of my aunt
Evelyn's. I'd later learn that John Ivey Mobley, grandson of James
Monroe Mobley, was a Klan leader. He was also my grandfather's
chief backer, as his father had been my grandfather's chief backer.
I did not know at the time that, on my father's side, he was also
a cousin.

We returned to my grandparents the next summer, blessedly
oblivious to the fact that bloodlust over "biggity niggers" had
arrived in Hamilton before we did. In May of that year, a well-off
black farmer and Most Worshipful Master of a black Masonic
chapter, Henry "Peg" Gilbert, was locked in the Hamilton jail on
charges of harboring a fugitive. In a land where black cooperation with the law was crucial to social control, the appearance of
refusal was sheer heresy. Nothing so enraged most white men in
those days as the mere suggestion of blacks helping blacks against
whites, the way Dusky Crutchfield did, her story now legend, at
least among whites. Gilbert's other heresy was his success, affirm-
ing Ida Wells-Barnett's investigations decades earlier that identified black success as a common motive for lynching.

The cause of this new scandal was that a black man had killed a
white farmer from the same county and then fled, allegedly hiding
out at Peg Gilbert's farm. Because the murder had taken place in
Harris County, Gilbert and his entire family were arrested in their
own Troup County by an unnamed Harris County justice of the
peace, with a warrant that was honored by Troup's sheriff. The
children were reportedly whipped in front of their father. When

this failed to produce the desired confession, they were released with their mother.

Practical and politically astute as Grandpa Hadley was, he couldn't, or at least didn't, prevent what happened next. On May 23, 1947, Henry Gilbert was reported dead by the Hamilton police chief, who claimed he'd fired in self-defense when the prisoner came at him with a chair and "tried to gouge [his] eyes out." No charges were brought, but a black newspaper in Atlanta protested so loudly that the U.S. Justice Department launched its own investigation. According to C. D. Marshall, the black man I discovered in his corn patch, the "Ladies" had stepped in before the black people got their voice. This would be the first time that the voice of the oppressed was being heard.

The NAACP had been pressuring the FBI to investigate Hamilton, but the bureau's experience in Walton County had left it fearful of on-the-ground investigations. It did not help that Hoover was a racist who considered blacks to be easy dupes of the hated commies. So when Hamilton turned up on his radar and he smelled left-leaning activists behind the bullhorn, he was in no mood to nail this case. He would not send agents to town to sniff out trouble and return empty-handed, to be laughed at in restaurants and taunted on sidewalks. This time Hoover would handle matters over the telephone.

At the time, the NAACP was leading a strong national charge for a federal antilynching law and prospects looked good. In addition, Dan Duke, a Klan-busting former assistant state district attorney, was representing Gilbert's wife, Caroline. The *Pittsburgh Courier* and other black newspapers used the Gilbert case to underscore the need for "immediate passage" of antilynching legislation. Others warned it would do no good so long as local sheriffs, judges, and juries controlled prosecutions. President Roosevelt refused to support it on the grounds that it would lose him his southern support in Congress, which was vital to his New Deal programs.

❧

Cornelius Bugg was seventy-three when I first met him. He had lived through a lot and his memory was sharp. The first time we spoke, he asked to remain anonymous. He told me about how hard it had been for black men to buy farmland in the county and that he had as much as he did because his wife's family had inherited it from their slave owner. He still lived in the old plantation house that once belonged to his wife's white grandfather. A beautiful portrait of her grandmother graced the wide entry hall.

Bugg told me about the shooting of his friend Peg Gilbert. Word had come down at the time from the black undertakers who embalmed Gilbert's body that several of his wounds had occurred days before he died, and that he appeared to have been systematically beaten over a period of time. His friends and family came to the conclusion that he had finally snapped and lunged at the police chief. That's when he was shot.

The police chief was Willie Buchanan, the man with pasty calves, a Jesus fan, and a Coke whom I remember seated peacefully on the bench across from the square. Again and again throughout my research, these findings cast my halcyon childhood summers in an entirely different light, amounting to a belated and harrowing coming-of-age experience. A few years earlier I'd remembered Dad Doug as the adored grandfather who opened up the courtroom for his children's Sunday play, then suddenly I see him hiding a jailhouse murder from the FBI.

None of the massive damage to Peg Gilbert's body was reported in the FBI finding, nor was it commented upon by Hoover. The federal investigators did not bother to explain why Gilbert's leg was broken, nor why his face was pulverized, nor why it took six bullets to subdue an unarmed man with a broken leg.

When an FBI agent asked my grandfather why the entire family was incarcerated, he responded that "they seemed glad to be here rather than at home where they were in danger." He also stated that they had considered releasing Gilbert after a week, but "when this was mentioned to him, he stated he did not want to go back home because he was scared of what might happen to him." I can imagine that same line of reasoning being used by him and his father thirty-five years earlier, in 1912.

The FBI chose to exonerate everyone, including my grandfather, who told the investigators that his wife had been seriously ill the afternoon of the killing that led to Gilbert's arrest. That day, she was taken to the hospital, where she stayed for three weeks. He claimed he had taken no part in the investigation of the murder during that time. Though his name was on the warrant used to arrest Gilbert, he had not signed it; it was common practice, he said, for others to sign his name in such matters. No bond had been set because the prisoner never asked for one. No commitment hearing was held, since, again, none had been requested. That, my grandfather told the FBI man, was common practice in the county. If he was asked about his whereabouts in the days leading up to Gilbert's death, as common sense would dictate, his answer was not made a part of the record.

Director Hoover closed the case, concluding that Chief Buchanan alone had killed Peg Gilbert in self-defense.

Eventually, the Communist Party got involved in the case of Peg Gilbert's murder. In 1951, Peg's wife and daughters, along with a number of other black Georgians victimized by police brutality, flew to New York and joined entertainer-activist Paul Robeson to present a petition to the secretary-general of the United Nations. At the same time, a copy was being presented to the fifth session of the UN General Assembly at the Palais de Chaillot in Paris. The report detailed the depth of racist violence in the United States, calling it "genocide," and describing Henry "Peg" Gilbert's vicious murder in the Hamilton jail.

As his own father had done in 1912, my grandfather had talked his way out of prosecution even though it was the sheriff's duty under the law to ensure the protection of prisoners in the jail. I can say confidently that this man—whom I considered infallible—did not sit beside my grandmother's sickbed during that entire time. I was with her many times while growing up when she was infirm, at home or in the hospital. It was her daughters and her ever-present maid, Hopie, who tended her, not her husband. I do not believe he'd have taken part in the attack on Gilbert, but I do think that he would have known about the abuse taking place in his jail prior to his wife's illness, if indeed there was an illness. He was not the sort of sheriff who'd turn his back on the jail regardless of family circumstances (unless, of course, he was warned away, as his father had been warned away on that fateful night in 1912). But I expect he was the sort of man who'd lie to J. Edgar Hoover about matters that might send his friend the police chief and his staff to prison. Yet, as Cornelius Bugg told me, "It happened on his watch. He bears some responsibility." I concur and add: "more than just 'some' responsibility." I would learn from a descendant of the white man allegedly killed by the black man Peg Gilbert allegedly sheltered that even that suspect was not guilty.

Racial troubles confronted Bugg into the 1960s. He and others had tried to build a black farmers' cooperative. It had failed, he said, because white farmers didn't want it to succeed. On our first visit, he requested anonymity. The second time, eight years later, he said, "Go ahead and use my name. I'm eighty-one years old. What can they do to me now?"

The shooting of Peg Gilbert by Chief Buchanan was one of the very few times in my grandfather's twenty-three years as sheriff that racial violence in Harris County was made public, and even then, not by Columbus or Hamilton newspapers. But I do not doubt there were numerous instances of unrecorded police brutality. Cornelius Bugg spoke of many black men driving alone at night who were stopped by "deputies" and beaten for no reason. A Williams cousin who grew up in Hamilton and still lived there at the time of my research in the county told me that his own father, an abusive, tormented man in later life, "did the sheriff's dirty work." He said that Sheriff Hadley never wanted to make anyone mad, so that when "someone had to be locked up," he'd call on deputies, county policemen, or his father to do it. Sheriff Sam Jones, who succeeded Hadley, called him "the best politician this county has ever seen."

Whether these "deputies" did their deviltry with my grandfather's blessing is a mystery and flies in the face of how I saw him up until the day he died, when I was sixteen years old. Based on what I now know about Harris County during those Jim Crow years when Sheriff Hadley ruled, I must admit it's a strong possibility.

Accepting all of this is difficult for me, because as a child, Dad Doug was the only adult male figure in my family I felt I could look up to and trust. I have very few actual memories of him—I do remember being at the farm with my cousins, at Mr. Shorty's getting ice cream, playing in the courtroom on a Sunday while he worked. I also remember him teaching me and my sister how to take our thumbs to an ear of feed corn for the cows. And my sister remembers how he explained to her that when our horse kicked back and almost hit her that she was most likely flicking at a fly, not aiming deliberately at her. We did not spend a lot of time together, but the times we did were peaceful and mostly without incident. I suppose that in a family characterized by anxiety and outburst, it was his quiet that drew me to him.

In the late 1940s and early 1950s—during my storybook summers when I splashed in the Mulberry Creek and picked blackberries across the railroad tracks, oblivious to what the grown-ups were doing—two potentially inflammatory situations would put Dad Doug's political acumen to the test. Both involved "race-mixing," still a felony in Georgia at that time. It was a matter the 1912 mob had hoped to put to rest, but one that—human nature being what it is—would not even play dead. Long after it occurred, the "two-family families" my mother mentioned would abound throughout the county. Each of these new cases involved a Williams, one black, one white. And because they came to public attention, he could not ignore them.

May Brit Cramer was the daughter of Louise, the daughter of my great uncle Brit. Louise was one of the little Juvenile Missionary Society girls living along the line of march of the lynch mob. Louise grew to adulthood in a time of great ferment over race, and especially lynching, within the Methodist Women's Missionary Society. She had married Charles Cramer, a Pennsylvania-born educator who was superintendent of the Mountain Hill elementary school. Their daughter May Brit had been an impressionable child growing up on Hamilton square when her cousin Curtis Dixon was publicly pilloried by Governor Eugene Talmadge, who fired Dixon and other University of Georgia chancellors for being "integrationists." For many years Dixon, a white man, served as southeast director of the Rosenwald Fund, as well as Superintendent of Negro Schools.

In the mid 1940s, the Cramers moved to Baltimore. At Eastern High, a girls' public high school attended by May Brit and her sister, the principal told students about the dangers to society that the newly created atom bomb posed and the concurrent need for racial equality. While there, the Cramer girls would likely have heard news of both the Peg Gilbert killing and the Walton County lynching. When May Brit, a beautiful, petite blonde with blue eyes, graduated from college, she returned to Hamilton and took a teaching position at a black school. Today, a cousin still living in Hamilton refers to May Brit as "the first white person to teach in black schools."

A few also refer to her affair with a black man, a man with whom she openly consorted in his home, her car "shamelessly" parked outside. I remember, as a child, hearing the whispers on my grandmother's porch: "ran her out of town," "shot him in the knees." May Brit left town, never to return, taking with her a Bible that once belonged to Uncle Brit, the bachelor slave owner. She had become every white Hamilton family's worst nightmare. Her lover was Square Copeland, a member of one of the oldest, most respected black families, related to the white Rev. Alex Copeland. Square was reportedly beaten up by "thugs," but he stayed on to live a long and respected life in the county.

I spoke with several of the black man's cousins, one of whom told me that his wife, still living, did not like to talk about this old history. In 2013, my cousin Doug McLaughlin, who grew up in Hamilton and knew Square Copeland, urged my sister to tell me not to use his name, fearing he might still be alive. "He was a good man," my cousin, also a good man, said. "I wouldn't want any harm to come to him."

It was during the 1930s and 1940s that an audacious and brilliant white Georgia writer named Lillian Smith began publishing books and articles that articulated the thoughts of women like May Brit, and likely even her mother. An integrationist, Smith wrote boldly of the ways white men used race and sex to instill fear and maintain power. Her novel *Strange Fruit* depicted the lynching of a black man involved in a dispute with a prominent white man having an affair with a black woman. The book made its controversial appearance in 1944 and enjoyed wide circulation, often in brown paper bags, throughout small towns in Georgia.

I do not know if May Brit's mother ever crossed paths with Smith or her partner, Paula Snelling, but both Louise and Snelling graduated from Georgia State College for Women and taught in high schools around Georgia. Smith and Snelling ran a girls camp in north Georgia, which many Columbus girls attended. Both Louise Williams and Paula Snelling were girls in 1912, when black women were lynched in their respective hometowns. Like both Snelling and Smith, Louise Williams, and later her daughter, chafed against the puritanical demands that white southern men placed upon white women. Louise and Charles's wedding took place in the Hamilton mayor's office. His family attended; hers did not. I do not know why, but I figure the bride's obvious pregnancy had something to do with their desire to turn away from trouble, an old Williams trait as well as an old white southerner trait.

My grandfather's role in May Brit's exile and her lover's beating is unknown. Given that both May Brit's powerful grandfather and her great-aunt Lula Mobley still lived on the square, combined with Douglas Hadley's recent brush with the FBI, I doubt he needed counsel as to the quiet methods required. No news reports of the scandal were ever filed in Columbus papers.

In 1952, Sheriff Hadley encountered more miscegeny. This time a married descendant of formerly enslaved Williamses was involved with a married white woman. She'd had several children with him. The fiancé of the woman's white daughter decided to call in the law on them and one afternoon Sheriff Hadley pulled up at the black man's house with a convoy of "friends." He told the man's wife that he'd be back that evening, a clear signal that the man should hightail it out of Harris County. I don't know what else he told her, but I later learned that some white "Masons" drove him to a bus and bought him a ticket to Birmingham. The woman's husband, who was Hispanic, sued for divorce and custody of their children. The judge granted him that and ordered the "illegitimate" children by the black Williams man put up for adoption. About a decade ago, one of them showed up a reunion of her African American half-siblings, looking for some answers.

I want to see this story as a tale of rescue. I see Dad Doug cannily satisfying his Klan friends with the threat at the black man's house, hoping to head off another lynching. But I was not there and cannot know. And I have to wonder if I'm not just, once again, hoping for a hero. In all my years of visiting Hamilton on Sundays and in summers, I cannot recall hearing Dad Doug use racially offensive language or behave meanly toward anyone, black or white. My cousin Doug McLaughlin, who grew up next door to him and followed him everywhere, agreed. This was not, however, true of my own father, a polished, educated physician.

In 1954, when I was thirteen, my father took my sister and me on a ferry to Hilton Head Island, South Carolina. He was living near Savannah at the time and his medical practice consisted partially of black patients, many of whom paid him in wild game and greens. A new black church had recently been built and named Williams Memorial in his honor. The still-pristine Hilton Head was about to be developed, and he had a chance to buy cheap land. We were the only white people on a ferry filled with black workmen. My father, a heavy smoker, was coughing and a black man started coughing. For some reason I'll never understand, I said, "That nigrah is mocking you, Daddy." And from his pocket my father drew a switchblade, which he snapped open, held against his leg, and said, "Tell me which one." I knew he had been drinking. I froze on the spot and refused to answer. Years later, learning of young Emmett Till, so swiftly executed on the careless word of a white woman at about the time of my ferry experience, I realized with a chill what landmines we were all navigating in those days.

Caught up in being a teenager—dating, dancing, dressing up, hanging out with my girlfriends at Dinglewood Pharmacy—I was barely aware that a revolution called the civil rights movement was churning around me. I did, however, know that a black doctor named Dr. Thomas Brewer was killed by a dime store owner whose son was a classmate of mine. I knew that the minister at First Presbyterian was sent away for suggesting it was time for blacks and whites to work on race issues together. I knew that my mother was antsier than ever on the subject of race, and that she stopped shopping at the downtown open-air market because the black vendors were now refusing to be bartered down.

Dr. Brewer, head of the local NAACP, had joined a black Columbus barber named Primus King in a lawsuit that ended with Georgia's white primary system being declared unconstitutional and laid the groundwork for the civil rights movement. At the time of his murder, Brewer was challenging segregated schools, and the KKK had threatened his life. Solicitor John H. Land, the son of Brewster Land, who stood trial in 1912 for the lynching of fourteen-year-old T. Z. McElheney, declined to bring charges.

There was no black uprising over Brewer's murder. While bus boycotts and lunch counter sit-ins spread throughout the South, they never came to Columbus. Over the years, a sizable black middle class had emerged. Its leadership, schooled in the old Booker T. Washington ways by the city's white leaders, didn't relish conflict. Unlike nearby Albany, there was no black student body to be organized. The YMCA, built to keep blacks in their place, still stood at the center of "Negro life." As in Columbus, the more activist element of the civil rights movement never set foot in Harris County, a relief to all my white relatives and many of the older blacks.

In 1961, as other southern cities were erupting in violence over black students' attempts to integrate bus stations, Rev. J. W. Hurley, the pastor of Columbus's St. James A.M.E. Church, which had refused Martin Luther King's request to speak in the late 1950s, announced that he and his Columbus Youth Movement had accomplished a speedy and peaceful desegregation of city buses. Meanwhile, Rev. Hurley explained to city officials how they could avoid a city-wide boycott. All this happened after local NAACP officials refused to support black students arrested earlier for attempts to desegregate buses. NAACP leaders from elsewhere attempted to step in, but were rebuffed by the local leaders, long accustomed to accommodating whites in exchange for privileges. This history, plus the assassination of Dr. Brewer, had clearly left its mark.

On April 30, 1957, a few weeks after my grandfather won his seventh election, he pulled into our driveway in a brand-new Ford, a gift for my mother. All his life he'd lived in a small country house, always driving old cars. Throughout his entire marriage, he and his wife had taken but one vacation. Now here he was with this brand-new car. It was so out of character that I think we all feared something was amiss. We were right. He died the next day of a heart attack at the age of sixty-seven. The church filled up with weeping people, most of them white, while Rev. Alex Copeland sang "The Old Rugged Cross" in a quavering contralto and played the organ as if his heart would burst from his tiny body.

There was no more lynching in Harris County, but Georgia's criminal justice system was still badly broken. Just as Georgia had for many years led the South in lynching, it has often led the nation in death sentences, and the Chattahoochee Valley Judicial Circuit has led the state. In 1972, the U.S. Supreme court invalidated state death penalty statutes nationwide for a time. Georgia was at the top of the list for executions—with 80 percent of those executed being black, and the vast majority of whom had allegedly murdered whites—and played a strong role in the justices' decision.

CHAPTER TWENTY-FOUR

Guilt and Innocence

Ever since I was a child, I wanted to be a writer. More specifically, I wanted to write a book about a small town in the South. I believed it was meant to be, but I wasn't sure what exactly the story would look like. Early in my writing career, I wrote an embarrassingly nostalgic piece for the Sunday magazine of the *Hartford Courant* about playing as a child in a jail cell in Hamilton. I knew nothing then of the tortured week that Dusky Crutchfield and her comrades had suffered there or the countless other falsely imprisoned men and women who would eke out their last days in that dark space. Later I tried my hand at a screenplay about a young girl discovering her sheriff grandfather's Klan robes in the attic. During those years I had no reason to suspect my grandfather of anything dire. He was Daddy Doug and I had loved him. I was merely a writer dabbling in fiction.

I became a journalist, and by the time I began this book, I had spent the past three decades writing magazine and newspaper articles about childrearing, education, labor and the women's movement, death squads, corporate and government corruption, sexual harassment and discrimination, and medical malpractice.

But the book was a whole other matter. I began my visits back to Hamilton with trepidation. All of the years I spent writing had not prepared me emotionally for this new assignment.

Figuring no one would believe me or know about the lynching, I took copies of the newspaper articles with me as proof. I went down in 1995 fearing that elderly black folks would be scared to talk about it and that old white folks would be defiant and convinced it had been necessary. Or perhaps they would say what my mother had that day when G'mamma, from her sleigh bed, told me the story of her most unforgettable memory—"the hanging." *"Don't believe everything she tells you. She embroiders, you know."* When I went back to Hamilton a decade later, my mother insisted it never happened. I showed her the article and she said: "Do you believe everything you read in the newspaper?" Some years later, she let herself slip a couple of times, claiming that "some men from Columbus came up to Hamilton and did that," and, most important, revealing to me the existence of the "two-family families."

But the old folks who'd remained in Harris County neither denied it nor sought to shift the blame. It was as if they'd been waiting for me. Twenty-two elders, black and white, detailed the event as it had been told to them. I didn't even have to ask about their guilt or innocence—the answer often came before anything else, at times stated matter-of-factly, at times with regret. In so many words, most of them told me that "they got the wrong folks" or that "those people had nothing to do with Norman Hadley's murder."

Clyde Slayton still lived in the bare-bones cabin of his youth in Mountain Hill, close to the scene of much of the mayhem. He turned out to be a cousin on the Cash side of my family and was one of the many I call "Ancient Mariners." Like the bearded character with the "glittering eye" of Coleridge's poem, they told their terrible tales with a bold urgency born of the knowledge that they'd soon be gone and that these truths might serve some good in the world they were leaving behind. Indeed, many of them, including Slayton, died shortly afterward.

Carefully removing a plug of Red Man from his jaw, Slayton placed it gingerly on the piece of cheesecloth stretched across a McDonald's paper cup. "A white man done it," he growled out of that fierce and forthright face, fixing me with a milky stare. "But I can't remember his name for the life of me."

He combed through cobwebbed memory to no avail. "I just thought of it the other night," he said. "Now it's gone." He wasn't the sort of man to cover up for anyone and in any event was too old for such foolishness. It had been a deathbed confession, he told me. Sometime in the 1930s, but he could be wrong about that. "Everybody pretty much figured that to be the case all along," he added, "that it was a white man who killed Norman Hadley." He didn't want to discuss the details. He reckoned the man was jealous. Everybody was jealous of Norman because he was so popular, he told me. I slowly ticked off a list of names, all the white folks living around there in 1912. Nope. Nope. That ain't it, either. "Something like Sizemore," he said, but what records exist show nothing similar to that name.

"We had a lot of bad people around here," Slayton kept repeating as if to make the point: what real difference does naming one of them make any more?

Slayton was one of only two white men I met who were willing to talk about the lynching. The others either said they never heard of it or denied it had happened. He wasn't the only person I interviewed to tell me he had just been thinking about the incident the other night. I had called no one in advance.

C. D. Marshall, leaning on his hoe, was one of only two black people to bring up the victims' innocence. "They hung 'em just for nothin'. They just talkin'. They done hung 'em and they wudn't guilty. They hung a lady and they hung three mo." He said this cleanly and matter-of-factly, gazing straight into my eyes.

Iva Hodge, a white woman still living near the Gordon place in Mountain Hill, insisted on taking me to where the tree had stood. It was Iva's brother, sitting atop a cotton bale on a wagon bed, whose shoulder was brushed by Dusky Crutchfield's foot that next morning. "Papa said they arrested the wrong people," Hodge confided. "He saw them do it and said they got the wrong people."

Edna Fort, still living with her sister Mary in their childhood home, both unmarried and childless, pointed toward the back window of her spacious parlor, toward the old Mobley place, where Sheriff Hadley and his family had lived at the time. She recalled how, at five and eight years old, they were awakened by the bloodcurdling cries of Dusky Crutchfield. "There was a country road over there. They marched them down beside Sheriff Hadley's house, down to a branch—it was Askew Branch on the Askew farm—to an old tree that hung out over the road and they hung them there. It was just terrible, just terrible."

Her sister added, "And not a one of them was guilty." It was Mary Fort, former American history teacher at Columbus High School, who told me, with some sense of satisfaction, that "every man in the mob died with his boots on." And it was Edna, a former elementary school teacher, who added for clarification, "Unnatural deaths, you understand." I asked them for names of these men, but they declined. Two of the people I interviewed, both of them black, told me that "the woman" was pregnant. "They hung a woman and she was pregnant, they say, with a white man's baby," Verna Hudson told me, looking down.

A. J. Murphy, a senior deacon at Friendship Baptist, was tending to church business at his kitchen table when I stopped by his house, just steps from the fork in the Blue Springs roads where the lynch mob made its first attempt. He graciously invited me in and told me I resembled Sheriff Hadley. Like Verna, he told me Crutchfield was pregnant by a white man and that the mob "cut the baby right out of her belly." These were the only two with that story and I have found no news accounts to back this up, so am not able to verify it. I admit I may not be psychologically able to face this last intolerable, but possible, fact. While I have, more or less, come to terms with the rest of this Greek tragedy I found in my family tree, this possibility still stops my breath and congeals my blood. I like to think it got mixed in later, with reports that two other Georgia black women, who were lynched—Dorothy Malcolm in Walton County in 1946 and Mary Turner in Valdosta in 1918—were pregnant.

Iva Hodge and I could not find the tree. Later I learned it had been chopped down before I was born. It dawned on me that the white women most obsessed by the lynching were Iva and my cousin Louise, each with intimate connections to several men named through the years as mob members. This was somewhat the case with G'mamma. After all those years, the lynching remained her "most unforgettable memory," though in her version of the story, as in Louise's, the victims were guilty.

❧

Later on, I tracked down Horace Gordon, Norman Hadley's nephew. Life hadn't been easy for Gordon. His teeth were mostly gone, and his hand trembled as he cradled his morning bourbon. A silverfish skittered across the black and white checked linoleum in his seedy apartment. He'd worked in the mills and done construction on a big dam on the Chattahoochee. Gordon believed the lynching was wrong, he said, mainly because that "nigger woman wasn't guilty." "She was the one who told them who done it," he said. "My daddy always felt bad about her." He still believed the black men were guilty. He said his father was away in Milledgeville that day and didn't go, but he told me of some who did. "Mr. Lum Teel told me he was in it. John Whit Hargett was in it. I think Bud Cannon was in it. Truett. Old man John Land. They was all in on it. Mostly moonshiners, just a bunch of the neighbors trying to help out."

Clyde Slayton said he was almost sure that Mans and Walter Gordon, Norman's uncles, took part in the lynching. These were all Mountain Hill men. A. J. Murphy, a black man, added some Hamilton names: John Storey. Mobley. Osborn. Farley. Gordon's list included my cousin Louise's father, Gordon Murrah, who was the sheriff's son-in-law. "He showed me the notches on his pistol when I was a boy, said four were for those folks."

I took Horace over to visit Louise, an old friend he'd not seen in years. She told the story of her mother forbidding her father to join the mob. Horace gave me a secret knowing look, but held his tongue.

It didn't surprise me that those who willingly admitted that the victims were all innocent—people like the Fort sisters, C. D. Marshall, and Clyde Slayton—were not connected by blood to men central to the lynching. It was those connected to the killers—like Iva Hodge, G'mamma, and Louise—who clung to the illusion of the victims' guilt, people like Horace Gordon, who believed only "that old woman" was innocent. Another was Sambo Gordon's grandson Jimmy Kidd, who'd been told that the blacks had a plan to kill the whites. He said he was happy we don't live in that sort of world anymore. It was the same with Mitch Huling's nephew Woody Huling, who expressed regret about Dusky: "She was the star [witness]. She shouldn't have been killed."

My cousin Louise, who'd been so eager in the beginning of my search to learn what happened and kept telling me that "time is running out," showed little interest or even belief when I told her of the four people's innocence. By now she was losing her mental grip on the world and simply muttered, "Things had just got so bad. Something had to be done."

No one I talked to knew the victims' names. Some called Dusky Crutchfield "the woman," "that ol' woman," "the star witness," or "the concubine." Though nameless, she was the only one most people knew about. The men's existence had faded with memory. No one knew that one was a preacher. No one knew where they were buried. They were taken by friends, the press reported. Nameless friends to a nameless place.

I suspect the three buried together are in an unmarked grave a few yards from their death place, in the Friendship Baptist cemetery, where graves date back to the mid-nineteenth century and include many descendants of men and women enslaved by my family. Some still bear evidence of African customs: seashells and broken crockery.

Les Gore, an old black man who told me he worked for one of my grandfathers and even remembered the name of his ox, said that "back then if we heard something, saw something, we just walked away." The message black people received from the lynching was the message that was intended: don't mess with white people. It was a message they had heard a million times, but this time it scalded, seared, and scarred. If you see something, you just walk away, don't stop and look, don't say nothing about it. Avert the eyes, cloud the brain, zip the lip. Natural abilities to observe, analyze, criticize, or grow were nipped in the bud. And not only in black folks, but in all of us. The one thing, the most important thing, no black person seemed to know, a thing the whites would not have wanted them to know, was that Dusky Crutchfield had refused to be intimidated.

The "see no evil, hear no evil" injunction preached to black people was rife in my Hadley family as well. When I mentioned the lynching to my mother's sister, Lillian, whom I called Nana, she quickly pinched two fingers together and drew them quickly across her lips, her eyes shooting daggers into my very soul. She was standing in a closet filled with old photographs as she did this.

It wasn't just the lynching that people refused to discuss or even remember over time. Most difficult subjects became taboo and many subjects were difficult. Some simply turned their heads whenever something unpleasant happened.

Some of this fear doubtlessly arose from the "whuppins" they received as children. The grandfather who had never raised a voice or a hand to me was a harsh disciplinarian of his own daughters. That information slipped from my normally secretive mother's lips once on the phone when we were talking about all the accounts of child abuse coming out in the press. She said, "I never knew about things like that except a few times when Mama couldn't handle us and turned us over to Daddy." She paused a moment, took a sharp breath, and said in a tight voice, "I guess it would be called child abuse now." I could feel her pain coming through the phone lines. It was the first and only time I had heard her say anything negative about him. Some of the sisters' fear of facing and speaking truth came from their mother's increasing inability to cope. "Don't tell Mamma," I often heard them say to one another. "It would just kill her." Long after Daddy Doug died, however, G'mamma got down to her own "nitty-gritty" one Sunday afternoon in her living room. Her daughters had been sharing affectionate memories of a wonderful father. "He wasn't all that wonderful," their mother said.

CHAPTER TWENTY-FIVE

Enslaved by History

Throughout the 1990s and during my frequent returns to Georgia, Hamilton remained much as I remembered it as a child. While nearby Pine Mountain (formerly Chipley) modernized and flourished, drawing tourists from Callaway Gardens, Hamilton—aside from a renovated courthouse—remained a case of arrested development. The old jail still stood, as did the old hotel turned post office, now an insurance business with its iron balcony next to the courthouse and overlooking the square. A deputy sheriff showed me and my son the courtroom where the 1912 mob members were declared "unknown," where Louis "Sugar Bear" Murray was unjustly sentenced to hang, and, with no hint of irony, called it "our *To Kill a Mockingbird* courtroom." A block away, the old Mobley mansion where Buddie and Emma Hadley lived still stood. Janie Prichard's millinery, Henry's Confectionary, Hamilton Female College, General Elias Beall's mercantile, and Susan Robinson's hotel had long since burned or been replaced. In the middle of Monument Square the twenty-one-foot marble soldier, now darkened with grime, still kept a close eye on the North.

Within the Confederate soldier's gaze lay the former Cook's

Mercantile where Cecil Cook returned from Dock Williams's murder to sell calico and cornmeal, and where my father believed until his death he had killed a black girl. It was now owned by my brother-in-law, who hoped in vain for a high-end restaurant rental. In the 1960s, G'mamma, who seemed to blossom in widowhood, had put her considerable dramatic skills on display when she donned period dress and bonnet and regaled visitors at the store with old-timey tales. The dark green train depot with its white trim had long ago been razed, but down Railroad Street near G'mamma and Dad Doug's old house, elderly black women wearing cotton wraparounds and baseball caps still lived in asphalt shingle-sided shacks set high on stacks of rock, where they raked their dirt yards and tended the bright hollyhocks beside their wooden stoops.

A British couple resided next to the old Hudson house, while a Hudson descendant practiced optometry in the old cotton warehouse. The tiny building on the square's east side where a Williams pharmacy once flourished now sported a Christian bookstore with a tanning booth, owned by a Vietnamese woman and her African American husband, named Williams. Recently they'd offered the shop's upper quarters as a meeting place for the local Democrat Party, which claimed only 20 percent of the county's registered voters.

The old black men still gathered around the well at the edge of the square each morning, just as they did in my childhood. And the old white men gathered at the same time directly across the street inside the drugstore to swill coffee, complain, and stare out at the old black men chatting around the well.

It was beside the well that I found Jimmy Weaver. When I asked the men if any had known Sheriff Hadley, he jumped up quickly, looked me over, and asked, "Are you Karen?" Jimmy grew up on Dad Doug's farm. As kids we played together, but it had been at least fifty years since we'd seen each other. Jimmy had only good things to say about Dad Doug. "He was a good man. A good man. He used to bring Bobby and Buster over to our house to supper all the time." He insisted on taking me to visit his mother.

Across from the well still stood the Amoco station where Mr. Shorty gave Nehis and ice cream to us children on those long-ago summer days. But sad things had happened here, in 1958, just after Dad Doug died. Shorty Grant had been bludgeoned to death in the station with a tire iron. A young black man named Albert Curry was quickly tried and convicted, and six weeks later, electrocuted. Though forty years had passed, people both black and white still wanted to talk about the wrong that was done that day. Evidence points to yet another black man having been killed for the crime of a white man. A relative of the white man, Jimmy Jordan, a justice of the peace at the time and Shorty's son-in-law, had told folks Jordan did it. Some things, it seemed, just never settled down. My review of the trial transcript indicated this to be a case that bears reopening.

Just down the way from Shorty's Amoco, Rev. Alex Copeland's old manse was now a restaurant. Not so long ago, the eighty-two-year-old had been found on his parlor floor, beaten to death with chains, my mother told me, by a motorcycle gang that was black-mailing him over his homosexuality.

By now the county had become a hodgepodge of high-end developments inhabited by Columbus's upper middle class, drawn by low taxes; unemployed rednecks living in rusty trailers surrounded by pickups propped on cinder blocks; a handful of transplanted artists, writers, and musicians; black families still living in the houses their freed ancestors built with sweat-earned cotton wages or replaced by redbrick ranch houses built in the 1940s and 1950s; retired white corporate executive couples moving from all over the country to Callaway's idyllic new Longleaf subdivision;

and fifth- and sixth-generation survivors of founding families, black and white, returning from lives elsewhere to recapture sweet childhood memories or just live simpler lives on land inherited from ancestors.

Though the students at Harris County High no longer laid wisteria wreaths at the feet of the monument each April, the Sons of Confederate Veterans showed up from time to time to place small Confederate flags on the graves of Captain Cooper Williams and his Camp Williams comrades in Hamilton City Cemetery. Dusty and tattered, the flags remained in place each time I visited. An old, mostly black, cemetery next door had returned to nature, until a young white woman who had fought in Afghanistan discovered it and organized other veterans in a partial cleanup. A drawn-out dispute between city and county ensued as to who was responsible. In the meantime, a young member of the white Hudson family, the woman veteran, the Cataula VFW, and the black Men's Club have joined hands to provide several cleanups and raise money for larger repairs.

The NAACP had tried and failed to establish a Harris County branch, but the Columbus chapter held meetings there and every January a Martin Luther King Day parade passed by the Confederate memorial. The schools were better integrated than most in the country, and while students, as elsewhere, often self-segregated by race, several young black women had been named Homecoming Queen. Hamilton's old dream of becoming an "education center" was reality with a system that was academically impressive. Countless black students from these schools had gone on to colleges and careers.

But Edward DuBose, a member of the national NAACP board, had seen things in Harris County that weren't immediately apparent to me. As president of the Georgia NAACP, he visited counties throughout the state, organizing chapters. "There are four counties in Georgia that have not changed that much," he said. "All are in the Chattahoochee Valley Judicial Circuit and one is Harris." On the surface, he mused, things can look very peaceful. But beneath the façade, he sees that "things are very tense, but you don't experience it until an issue brings it back to life."

Though the county population (25,000 at the time) had not quite doubled since my grandfather's day, the current sheriff, Mike Jolley—who remarked, on meeting me at a catfish restaurant along the Chattahoochee, "I hope you're a conservative"—oversaw dozens of cars and deputies and a hefty annual budget. Moonshine was still being brewed in the county, but rolling meth labs claimed more of the law's attention. At the time of this writing, the crime rate, according to a recent *Columbus Ledger* interview with Sheriff Jolley, is the lowest per capita in Georgia.

During my visits I encountered some behaviors, especially from the older generation, that took me back to childhood. In Mary Fort's parlor, as she talked about the lynching, she caught a look from sister Edna and lowered her voice. I recognized the transaction. It meant, "Quiet. A maid who might overhear is nearby." While both black and white people spoke candidly with me about the lynching and other racial wrongs, they did so separately. A biracial conversation on these subjects—sensitively conducted and maintaining the same level of truth, if possible—could work wonders.

Rev. O. C. Stiggers at Friendship Baptist was the only person I interviewed who asked me to stay off the subject of lynching. "Our folks are just starting to make some progress here. A lot of us are getting hired at Callaway [Gardens] and we wouldn't want anything to hamper that," he said, adding, "This might upset things."

The Columbus head of the NAACP said Stiggers told him the same thing when he asked him to start a local chapter. I'd traveled to nearby West Point to find the pastor at home with his wife. A handsome couple, they showed me into a comfortable paneled den with thick red carpeting. They were watching television. I surprised myself by breaking down in tears as I told them my story. "Our people have gotten past all that," the pastor told me kindly. "We have forgiven and forgotten." In my rounds, I would find some forgiveness, but not much forgetfulness. I told him that whites needed to deal with this history, but given so much of the black community's dependence upon the goodwill of whites, and its unwillingness to upset them, I realized that much remained unchanged for them as well.

At breakfast with an African American couple whose great-grandfathers had been among Brit Williams's slaves, I asked whether they thought people in Hamilton would be willing to hold a memorial service for the four who were lynched. They agreed that it "needs to be done" and "would be a good thing," but feared that black people in the area would not want to make their white neigh-bors mad. Not long before our breakfast, Tea Party members had demonstrated in the square, carrying placards of President Obama's picture X'd out in red. "It gave me cold chills," the woman recalled. "It felt like old times."

❧

To southern whites and their descendants, the lesson of the lynch-ing and the system of segregation was that when blacks and whites get together on anything other than a master-servant level, explo-sions were likely to occur. I heard this sort of message many times as I came of age. In 1961, I was a sophomore at the University of Georgia when Charlayne Hunter and Hamilton Holmes were de-segregating the school. I went with friends to meet Charlayne and we offered to walk her to class the next day. We were confronted by Ku Klux Klansmen, who were joined by Kappa Alpha fraternity boys I knew well, shouting epithets, flashing switchblades, and throwing beer cans. I remember my father's voice over the phone that day: "Don't get involved. You never know what will happen with these things." His words angered me, but I paid him no mind. I now understand where that fear came from and also the way it stunted my own growth. Within weeks of my graduation from college, I married and moved to the North, only to encounter different versions of racism. There, however, it was easier to find opportunities, and the courage I needed, to advocate for racial justice.

Still, my mother and I continued to do battle. The subject of race, I now understand, was a kind of shorthand for all our many differences. The fears that she bore for me and for herself were based on her long-buried but never-forgotten knowledge of the lynching and other racial violence at the hands of her relatives. It stemmed from her sense of my being just like my father, which I took to mean "crazy," "dangerous," or "trouble." And it came from her knowledge of the several racially liberal men and women in his Williams family, especially May Brit. She knew I yearned to be a writer and that early on I admired the work of Carson McCullers, a Columbus-born novelist, whose sister-in-law was once my father's office nurse. She admonished me when I was in high school and devouring McCullers's books, saying, "I hope you won't grow up to embarrass Columbus the way she did." By this she meant showing the city's seamier side, depicting people in their full humanity.

This fear was often expressed in harsh bouts of anger and emerged most strongly in 1981, long after I'd grown up. During a seven-month period four years earlier, seven elderly white women, most known by my mother, were raped and strangled to death in their homes in neighborhoods near hers. She and every other white woman in Columbus lived in terror during that time. She slept in a girdle, a screwdriver in her hand, her bedroom door locked. Once or twice, her friend Jack, whom she always sent home by 10 p.m., was allowed to sleep in the guest room. In her mind, all the warnings and fears that she'd been raised with had come to pass; a black rapist was stalking her pristine neighborhood and she could be next. Only much later would a black man be convicted, but that fear had been drilled into her with the alphabet and would never be removed. It created a thicket of emotion that I had to traverse every time I tried to have a discussion with her about race. The issue came between us repeatedly throughout my life.

One night, many years into my adulthood, she got some kind of perverse payback when, home on Clubview Drive for a visit, I asked about the fate of the man sentenced to death for two of those crimes. "I blame you somewhat for that," she told me, meaning the murders. Nothing had ever cut so deeply. She reminded me that a black man had knocked on our door one night when I was home from college and asked to come in and talk with us about civil rights. I had invited him in, agreed with his ideas, and encouraged his work. She'd eavesdropped in the hallway. From there, she'd made this leap. At the time this struck me as, quite simply, insane. Now, after almost two decades unearthing this history, I understand how my mother's twisted thinking came about. I remember G'mamma's words of long ago, when Mamma told her I liked black people, and she spat, "Won't like 'em so much once one of 'em rapes her." "Treat a black man like a man and you end up dead," was the bottom line of white southerners' teachings in my mother's day.

"The Stocking Strangler," as he came to be known, was determined by a jury to be a black man named Carlton Gary. Sentenced to die in 1986, his case drags on. His original judge was John H. Land, the man who sent young Albert Curry to the electric chair and was called "the hanging judge" in a magazine long before Gary's case. It was his decision not to pay for the lawyer Gary had chosen that set in motion a series of appeals. Land later recused himself because of prejudicial statements he made to another magazine. But the man who replaced him also ruled against paying Gary's lawyer, a policy that has persisted as the case goes on.

Throughout the 1990s and until very recently, the person responsible for making these and other decisions regarding Gary's appeals was federal judge Clay Land, the great-nephew of John H. Land. Due to the groundwork of journalist David Rose and his book *The Big Eddy Club,* so many chinks in the case have by now been exposed that, as I write, Gary's case is back in court. Since 2001, federal judge Clay Land made numerous decisions thwarting Gary's efforts to obtain a new trial. One recent decision by Land, however, changed that course, giving Gary another chance to escape execution.

John Land, a cousin of Clay Land, and the great-grandson of John H. Land, recently went public in Columbus to express remorse for his ancestors' role in the 1912 lynching of young T. Z. McElheney and to call upon the city and county officials to do the same. Though Clay Land publicly expressed his unwillingness to take responsibility for an act that occurred more than one hundred years ago and which he had no part in, he did give an address to the local bar association on the fine civil rights work done by the barber Primus King and Dr. Thomas Brewer, the man whose assassination his great-uncle, then-solicitor general John Land, chose not to investigate.

In 2007, I attended a large Columbus reunion of the Hudson-Williams family, descendants of my family's slaves, and shared with them some of our ancestral history that I had unearthed—the lists of slave names, their ages, their children, their prices. I could barely choke out this last part. Deborah Dawson, the family's genealogist, was glad to have the particular information, but for years she'd compiled books of family history which included white Williamses. "Don't be nervous that you'll be the only white person here," she'd told me. "We are a rainbow family." The room contained every shade of skin color, and everyone I spoke with was respectful of and interested in the past, but rooted firmly in the present and planning wisely toward the future.

A few years later, in 2012, I stood in a large circle of black and white descendants of enslaved people and slave owners, some of whom had ancestors who were lynched. These were members of Coming to the Table, an organization formed by Thomas Jefferson's black and white grandchildren, among others. We were in Richmond, Virginia, capital of the Confederacy, standing in the shadow of the largest Confederate memorial in the South. There we linked arms, spoke our harsh truths, and offered forgiveness.

❦

My own father, finally sober, found his way back to Harris County sometime in the early 1970s. He'd fallen far, landing in a federal drug treatment center, from which he escaped in order to give me away at my First Baptist wedding in Columbus. In a suit two sizes too large and with eyes that swam like goldfish in his emaciated face, he was a pathetic sight. Soon after that he stopped drinking. Early in his recovery, he completed a Fourth Step, "a searching and fearless moral inventory," but hadn't found the courage to take the next step, in which he'd admit his wrongs to another human being. With this unfinished business burning inside him, he pulled off the road near Hamilton one afternoon, walked into a farmer's field, and asked a black man with a hoe to sit down on the ground beside him while he confessed his many sins.

Fourteen years later, he'd return to Hamilton in a casket. He'd spent fourteen years sober, a counselor at the prestigious Hazelden Drug Treatment Center. He died, however, believing he had killed that young black woman across the street from the Hamilton square, something he confessed as his most shameful memory at his last AA meeting. From across the nation recovering alcoholics came to the Hamilton cemetery to see my father laid to rest and to testify to his contributions to their lives.

The grip of history, as I discovered, affects people in different ways. A few blocks from the Hamilton square, an African American funeral home director, Bobby Thomas, wept as he told me about white grandfathers who would not acknowledge him and whom he was forbidden to acknowledge.

I myself almost went down a path akin to that of my white ancestors who had rejected their own "taboo children."

Six years before I began the circuitous journey that took me back to Hamilton and face-to-face with the ghosts of my past, I had become the grandmother of a racially mixed child. When I first heard news of her impending birth from my son and his girlfriend, I was devastated. This was partially because I believed they were too young and immature to make good parents, but also because I did not want to face the racism of my mother and her generation still living in Georgia, and, as I would come to realize, the racism still existing within. For six long years I kept her existence a secret from my Georgia family.

Underlying my cowardice was a deep sense of impending doom. Since much of my adult life had been devoted to interracial work, I was dumbfounded by my reaction. At the time I had never heard of Norman Hadley or Dusky Crutchfield or Bertha Lee Harrington, nothing of all the killings that came in the wake of the lynching. I hadn't heard the story of W. T. Whitehead, the white man shot on the Hamilton square while defending his black mistress. I simply knew I was afraid for my son, his girlfriend, and their child, as well as for myself, an entirely unrealistic fear, a haunting dread that entered my heart and stayed there until the birth of this beautiful child and then a mysterious woman propelled me to go back home and find out the truth and walk a path of honesty and action.

Perhaps that ghost woman was an inner part of myself—an older, wiser Self (called "soul projection" by some psychologists), weary with conflict over my values versus the expectations of family and history. Perhaps it was distant cousin Dr. Anna Julia Cooper, who'd lived much of her 105-year life three miles from where I now live, looking for yet another student to inspire. Perhaps it was Dusky Crutchfield, calling for her story to be told, or old Jane Moore, who saw so many of her and my great uncle's boys ruined by a corrupt, racist community and legal system. No matter who the ghost woman was, I knew my time had come to stand up for what mattered. I now know that in order to become a loving grandmother to my granddaughter, and to break the family cycle of rejecting, even destroying, its own children, I had to make this journey. This most crucial of issues had been presented time and again to my ancestors, who had refused a humane response. Now it was my turn.

$\sim$

When I first read about the lynching, I felt at one with all its players—villains, bystanders, and victims. I now know why. Through my research I learned that I share genes with many of them. I discovered a murderous heritage, as well as a biracial heritage I had never known. As I sifted through boxes and filing cabinets, chatted with elders and trolled the Internet, I often felt as if I'd stumbled into Bluebeard's Castle. I never dreamed there had been so much violence and tragedy in my family's past, and yet, strangely, in making these discoveries I was finally able to acknowledge some of my forebears' characteristics within myself, both the good and the bad.

The "bad" includes alcoholism, emotional instability, poor parenting, unfaithful relationships, and self-condemnation. I was beset by my own demons, perhaps as a result of my father having told me that he killed that young woman, coupled with my mother telling me I was just like him and later blaming me for serial killings.

In the distant past I knew moments of anger, jealousy, fear, and the urge for revenge; emotions so overwhelming that, in a different culture and a different era, encouraged or joined by others, may well have resulted in dire and irreversible action. Somewhere along the way, I got the idea that I had actually done something evil, or, if not, was certainly capable of it. By the same token, like the "innocent bystanders" at the lynching, I have often stood passively by as others spoke or did racial harm.

The "good," I am happy to add, includes the capacity for recovery and positive relationships with family and friends. As a result of this difficult journey, I have achieved a greater sense of peace and wholeness, of being at home in the world, than I have ever known.

I now understand that the lynch mob was not made up of monsters (perhaps with the exception of one or two), but of ordinary men who had little or no awareness of the history they carried within themselves and who did a monstrous thing. Unable to deal with their own demons, they took everything out on those hapless four people who represented everything they hated in themselves. They had convinced themselves that the Negro was not fully human and, therefore, that killing him or her was not of great import. I realize the fact that they lived in a time and a place that reinforced and even encouraged these delusions made it much easier for those men to carry out the lynching.

AFTERWORD

August 1994

I am at the Jefferson Memorial with my granddaughter, who is eight years old. We have taken turns reading all of the magnificent Thomas Jefferson quotes inscribed upon the walls. She looks at me quizzically and says, "But didn't he own slaves?" This is the kind of question I have dreaded ever since she was born.

We sit down on the steps and I make some stumbling explanation about how sometimes people can do things that are very wrong while, at the same time, doing other things that are quite noble. But I also tell her that he was a hypocrite. This is hard stuff for an eight-year-old, even a very bright one like her, but I know I should use the opportunity as a teaching moment: "You know that you are descended from both slave-owners and slaves, don't you?" I say.

She sinks into thought, and when she emerges she looks into my eyes and says, "Yes, I know. But, if I ever have to choose, I'll choose the slaves." I tell her that I hope she never has to choose. And yet I realize that in writing this book, I have had to make that choice again and again. I have not relished revealing my forefathers' crimes, but in order to face history squarely—my nation's,

my family's, and my own—I have had not so much to "choose
the slaves," but to choose the truth, which in many ways is the
same thing. Most important, I have had to find my voice, and to
choose honesty and truth over the feelings and opinions of friends
and family. I have also chosen to break that ancient, ironclad rule
that women must keep the family secrets. This breaking of official
silences is still regarded as shameful, even monstrous, by many
people, something I learned at my fiftieth high school reunion.
At the dance, which was held on Confederate Memorial Day in
the Confederate Naval Museum in Columbus, the band played
Dixie and former classmates chided me for not standing with my
hand over my heart. There I told some old friends about my book.
"No!" some of them gasped. "Surely you wouldn't!"

Well, surely I have. I have done it not only for the descendants
of those enslaved and otherwise victimized by my ancestors, but
for men and women like me who want to know the truth of our
families' and our region's histories, with all of their treachery and
dishonor, as well as their occasional greatness. I believe it is only
with such knowledge that we and our own descendants can heal
and move forward to build a nation and a world where all humans
can be free.

Today, twenty years later, as I plan a retreat in the Cascade
Mountains with my beautiful twenty-seven-year-old granddaughter and friend, I shudder at how close I came to rejecting her,
the way so many beautiful mixed-race babies were rejected by
my family in times past. I now know well the riches I'd have cast
aside, including my mother's loving relationship with her only
great-grandchild, and my own with dozens of newfound "cousins"
(by blood or by choice), descendants of the people my people once
enslaved. Through their Williams-Hudson Family Association,
which welcomed me as one of their own, and through Coming
to the Table, I have found ways to rebuild and work for change.

I realize, as never before, how much the white South lost when it embarked, at its dawning, upon a wicked and brutal course of rejecting and repressing not only its own flesh and blood, but all its precious black citizens.

As I bring this book to a close, America is once again aflame with racial violence and discrimination. There is no question that, as a nation, we have yet to honestly face our history and to truly embrace African Americans as full-fledged citizens and members of our human family. I believe this is the only way we can heal, as individuals and as a nation.

ACKNOWLEDGMENTS

At the top of my gratitude list is my family—my sister Barbara, son Brad, granddaughter Fallon, nephew Ben, cousins Bill, Bobbie, Jennifer, Em, Cholly, Sallie, Diane, Peggy, Alex, Deborah, Betty, Tommy, Tommy, Jr., and Mack. They gave me family stories and photos, hugs, a hot meal, and a good bed at the end of a long day. They listened and often urged me on. More important, they provided psychological space to discover what I would and ears that listened quietly to my tales.

Special thanks for invaluable editing advice along the way from dear friends Barbara Mowat, Suzannah Lessard, and Vincent Virga.

There are more friends, who have stuck with me through these many years, cheered me on, and reminded me of my reasons for writing this book. These include Randy Gamble, Dorothy Sauber, Kaia Svien, Bob Lyman, Margaret Veerhoff, James McCourt, Carole Look, Pat Moore, Celia Morris, Elizabeth Hagerman, Patsy Sims, Bob Cashdollar, Deanna Marquart, Alec Dubro, Kim Fellner, Noel Brennan, Alison Day, Patricia Gray, Rae Bayer, Karyn Fair, Arlene Gottfried, my 10th Street neighbors, Kevin Flood, Jimmy McCourt, my Hill Lunch bunch, Bill Turnley and family, the Coming to the Table folks, and all you out there who "know who you are."

I am forever grateful to those who provided me with a peaceful "room of her own": Blue Mountain Center, Lillian E. Smith Center for Creative Arts, the Apple Farm Community, Sweetapple, the Turnley cottage at Good Harbor Bay, and the Library of Congress for its generous gift of an office for many years. Heartfelt thanks to the Sapelo Foundation, which supported me with a grant in the early stages of this work.

I could not have undertaken this investigation without the resources of many archives and their staffs, including the Library of Congress, Columbus State University Archives, the Georgia Department of Archives and History, the National Archives in Washington, D.C. and East Point, Georgia, and Stacy Haralson, clerk of court in Harris County.

Many thanks to researchers Barbara Stock and Gwen Lott, editors Carole Edwards and Alice Falk, graphic designer Sally Murray James. For excellent advice along the road: Steve Bright, Bernice Reagon, Joe Hendricks, John Egerton, Randy Loney, Fitz Brundage, Rose Gladney, Woody Beck, Carolyn Karcher, Diane McWhorter, and Laura Wexler. For more wise counsel, Pamela Wilson, Bobbie Holt, Jane Bishop, Kay Koch, Sandy Geller, Bruce Heustis, and Jim Hollis.

To my incredible agent Charlotte Sheedy goes my deepest appreciation and admiration for so graciously sharing her wisdom when mine ran out and for always being there; and to my Simon & Schuster editors Malaika Adero, Peter Borland, Daniella Wexler, and Carla Benton, my sincere appreciation for making it all come together.

I wish to pay profound tribute to the many Harris County elders, the "Ancient Mariners," who so graciously welcomed me onto their porches, into their parlors, and unflinchingly shared stories that had haunted them for years. To them and to my dear Edna, the "black mamma" who "raised me up right" and told me at the end that she was glad that I was "different," I dedicate this book.

NOTES

Epigraph
ix Ancient Negro folk curse quoted by Alice Walker in "Only Justice Can Stop a
Curse," *In Search of Our Mothers' Gardens: Womanist Prose* (Harvest Books,
1983), 1.

Prologue
6 "Four Negroes Lynched": *Atlanta Constitution*, January 23, 1912, 1.
6 "a Well-to-do Planter": *Atlanta Constitution*, January 23, 1912, 1.

Chapter One: My Sweet Village
10 "Red and yellow / Black and white": "Jesus Loves the Little Children," words
by Clare Herbert Woolston (1856–1927), sung to the 1864 Civil War tune
"Tramp, Tramp, Tramp" by George Fredrick Root.

Chapter Two: Plantation Politics
20 Georgia history information from James C. Cobb, *Georgia Odyssey: A Short
History of the State* (University of Georgia Press, 2008); Columbus history
from Nancy Telfair [Louise Jones Dubose], *A History of Columbus, Georgia,
1828–1928* (Historical Publishing, 1929).
21 Harris County and Hamilton history from the *Organ*, the *Enterprise*, and the
Hamilton Journal; Louise Calhoun Barfield, *History of Harris County, Georgia, 1827–1961* (Columbus Office Supply, 1961).
22 Williams family information from family charts prepared by Welda Williams
Shuford and Britain Williams Walton; Hadley genealogy from charts provided by Louise Murrah Teel and Clara Bailey Daniel.
22 "to point an argument": Hamilton Female College program dated July 4,
1858, Chipley Historical Center, Pine Mountain, GA.

22 "moral, intelligent, and refined citizens": recruitment brochure, Chipley Historical Society.

23 Slave information: 1840, 1850, 1860 U.S. Censuses, Slave Schedule, Harris County, Georgia; Last Will and Testament of Britain Williams, Inventory and Appraisement Sales, Returns of Vouchers, Book 53, 47–49, Harris County, Georgia, microcopy DDC-9L, Georgia Department of Archives and History, Morrow. Other estate matters: September Term of Ordinary Court of Harris County, 1863, Harris County Courthouse.

24 "1 negro man Dick": Estate Listing for Britain Williams, Inventory and Appraisement Sales, 1863.

24 "The man must be a prodigy": Thomas Jefferson, *Thomas Jefferson: Writings: Autobiography/Notes on the State of Virginia/Public and Private Papers/Addresses/Letters* (Library of America, 1984).

25 Slaves in Greene County: Jonathan M. Bryant, *How Curious a Land: Conflict and Change in Greene County, Georgia, 1850–1885,* 2nd ed. (University of North Carolina Press, 2004).

25 "In the buck": *Slave Narratives: A Folk History of Slavery in the United States,* vol. 4, *Georgia Narratives,* part 2 (Library of Congress, 1941), 25.

27 Dr. E. C. Hood strings freedman up by thumbs: National Archives, Freedmen's Bureau papers, A.C. 632 8 Mar 1866, M1903 Records of the Field Offices for the State of Georgia Bureau of Refugees, Freedmen and Abandoned Lands, 1865–1872, RG105.

28 "J. Curtis Beall, a mulatto": I surmise, given the heights he attained and the white protection he was afforded, that J. Curtis Beall was an offspring of a white Beall. He became active early in the Republican Party, twice ran unsuccessfully for the legislature in the 1880s, and served on the Georgia Republican state central committee for several decades. White newspapers, calling him "spirited," reported regularly on his efforts, mostly omitting the usual derisiveness accorded most black Republicans. Only in 1880 did Columbus papers seek to cast him as a "dangerous" character, who "works crowds into a frenzy," when reporting his support for a white Democrat for governor. In 1882, Georgia Republicans passed Beall's resolution to support no office seeker who did not favor the inclusion of blacks on juries. In that same year, President Chester Arthur appointed him postmaster in nearby Lagrange. A year later, however, Beall was replaced with no explanation. The next year he attended the Republican National Convention in Chicago as a Georgia delegate. His reputation in the Republican Party remained untarnished and his leadership in its ineffectual Georgia chapter remained steady into the 1890s. I found no information about his death.

28 George Ashburn information: *New York Times,* April 6, 1868; *Atlanta Constitution,* July 4, 1868.

29 First biracial vote: Returns of Qualified Voters under Reconstruction Act of 1867, vol. 84, District 25, microcopy RG4-360, Georgia Department of Archives and History, Morrow.

29 Camilla massacre: Eric Foner, *Reconstruction: America's Unfinished Revolution, 1863–1877* (Harper & Row, 1988), 342.

29 "state constitutional convention": *Journal of the Proceedings of the Constitu-*

tional Convention of the People of Georgia Held in the City of Atlanta in the Months of December, 1867, and January, February, and March, 1868. And Ordinances and Resolutions Adopted (E. H. Pughe Book and Job Printer, 1868).

31 "Sam Williams remained in office": A plaque on the grounds of the Georgia Capital in Atlanta memorializes those first African American legislators, including Samuel Williams.

32 "gang system": Susan Eva O'Donovan, *Becoming Free in the Cotton South* (Harvard University Press, 2010), details ways in which southwest Georgia planters drove their workers in freedom more viciously than most.

33 "at this trough": Another illicit source of family wealth, lawyers using their positions to cheat clients out of land, was described by Lewfay Mobley, speaking of his great-grandfather James Monroe Mobley, in an interview (Columbus State University Archives, 1972).

33 Convict lease system: Best described in Douglas A. Blackmon's *Slavery by Another Name: The Re-Enslavement of Black Americans from the Civil War to World War II* (Anchor Books, 2009); *Proceedings: Joint Committee of the Senate and House to Investigate the Convict Lease System of Georgia*, 2 vols., Georgia Department of Archives and History, Morrow.

34 "grievously wounded": Frederick Douglass, *The Life and Times of Frederick Douglass* (Dover Publications, 2003), 396.

35 "rich man's war and poor man's fight": David Williams, *Bitterly Divided: The South's Inner Civil War* (New Press, 2010).

35 "Many wealthy planters opposed Secession": Harris County was one of the few Georgia counties to vote no at the secession convention, and the Chattahoochee Valley as a whole was a strong force against secession. But Robert Toombs, a powerful Georgia politician and a hard-drinking firebrand if ever there was one, held sway and, with his mesmerizing rhetoric and political skullduggery, pulled Georgia into the secession camp. Many modern historians claim the final vote was rigged.

36 biracial political rallies in Harris County: *Columbus Enquirer Sun*, September 17, 1892.

Chapter Three: The Unveiling

38 Background on "Lost Cause" movement: David Blight, *Race and Reunion: The Civil War in American Memory* (Belknap Press, 2001).

40 Waddell referred to as "cousin": Letters in University of North Carolina, Wilson Library, Southern Historical Collection Number 01290, Ernest Haywood Collection of Haywood Family Papers, 1752–1967. The Haywoods were cousins of the Williams family. Waddell called on white men to rise up against black political incursions even if it meant choking "Cape Fear with carcasses" just before the Wilmington "riot" (designated a "coup" in 2006 by the 1898 Wilmington Race Riot Commission). He was declared mayor of the city in the wake of the riots. Chief fund-raiser for the coup was Preston Bridgers, husband of Eliza Haywood, granddaughter of author's great-uncle Alfred Williams. See Catherine W. Bishir, "Landmarks of Power: Building a Southern Past in Raleigh and Wilmington, North Carolina, 1885–1915," in W. Fitzhugh Brundage, ed., *Where These Memories Grow* (University of North Carolina Press, 2000), 161.

42 "above politics": *Hamilton Journal*, December 2, 1910.
43 "Alfred Williams, who accompanied Charles to battle": *Harris County Journal*, June 6, 1913.

Chapter Four: New Sheriff in Town
44 Information about Friendship Baptist: Louise Calhoun Barfield, *History of Harris County, Georgia, 1827–1961* (Columbus Office Supply, 1961); *Harris County Journal*, April 17 and July 27, 1911; Friendship Baptist's Facebook page, https://www.facebook.com/pages/Friendship-Baptist-Church-of-Hamilton-GA/231198386930141, accessed August 1, 2015.
44 "Dearly beloved": Romans 12:19 (King James Version).
45 "Convenient to church, near school, 2 wells, splendid water—all conveniences," *Harris County Journal* advertisement, January 1911.
48 Edgar Stripling: *Harris County Journal*, March 3, 1911; *Macon Telegraph*, April 5, 1911.

Chapter Five: Norman's Murder
50 "pleasant as May": *Harris County Journal*, December 8, 1911.
51 "There is no excuse": *Harris County Journal*, January 11, 1912.
53 "no business on this wagon": Georgene Holman, interview, Monmouth, IL, November 1999.
53 Norman's job as jail guard: *Harris County Journal*, March 8, 1907.
54 "Quit your meanness": *Harris County Journal*, July 27, 1911.
54 "the routing of gamblers and rowdies": *Harris County Journal*, June 9, 1911.
54 "fear of the hangman's rope": *Harris County Journal*, May 10, 1907.
55 "a negro named John Moore": *Columbus Ledger*, January 15, 1912.
55 "Sunday": *Columbus Daily Enquirer*, January 16, 1912.
55 "Saturday": *Columbus Daily Enquirer*, January 15, 1912.
55 "an existing feud": *Columbus Daily Enquirer*, January 16, 1912.

Chapter Six: Though Silent He Speaks
58 "the connections": Apr. 1880 letter from Lizzie Hadley, Lamar, AL, to Buck Hadley, Hamilton, GA.
58 "orderly" and "upright" people: *Columbus Daily Enquirer*, March 25, 1886.
59 "the whites forgot they were whites": Interview with Horace Gordon, Columbus, GA, October 7, 1997.
59 "prove it on me": *Atlanta Constitution*, March 7, 1911.
59 "I do not say he had no faults": *Atlanta Constitution*, September 1, 1911.
62 "If ever again we are threatened": *Atlanta Constitution*, April 28, 1911.
64 "the slave called Boy George": *Columbus Daily Enquirer*, February 2, March 3, and March 14, 1861.
68 "apple of discord": *Augusta Chronicle*, October 23, 1879.

Chapter Seven: Negro Desperadoes
69 "there was an Indenture of Servitude": Minutes of Harris Court of Ordinary October Term 1868, Harris County Courthouse.
71 "she signed herself over": For excellent information on this era and how women

like Jane Moore were affected, see Catherine Clinton's *Half Sisters of History: Southern Women and the American Past* (Duke University Press, 1994).

72 Sambo Gordon assaults officer: *Columbus Daily Enquirer,* October 5, 1896.

77 "Shaffer . . . one-man lynch mob": Interview with Frank Moye, Columbus, Georgia, April 2, 1998.

77 Information about Sog, Louis, and Milford Moore and Laney and Flynn Hargett: Inventory and Appraisement Sales, Returns of Vouchers, Estate of Edward (Sog) Moore, 1900, Harris County Courthouse; *State of Georgia vs. Louis Moore,* April Term of Superior Court, Harris, 1901; *State of Georgia vs. Milford Moore,* February Term of Superior Court, Muscogee, 1901; Governor—Convict and Fugitive Records—Applications for Clemency, 1858–1942, Moore, Milford, Muscogee, Georgia Department of Archives and History, Morrow; *Macon Telegraph,* December 27, 1900; *Columbus Daily Enquirer,* January 15 and February 20, 1901.

Chapter Eight: Nobody's Negroes

78 "worst in the state": *Atlanta Constitution,* December 8, 1889.

79 "turn wind or rain": "Grand Jury Presentments," *Harris County Journal,* October 12, 1912.

Chapter Nine: Vendettas

85 "Mary David": *Macon Telegraph,* December 10, 1885.

85 John Cash: "White Man Shot in Negro Church," *Columbus Daily Enquirer,* June 30, 1903, 2.

86 "sensational shooting affray": *Macon Telegraph,* June 11, 1908, 2.

87 Ransom Gordon assassination: *Macon Telegraph,* January 16, 1890.

87 Information on Edgar Stripling's role as mob leader: H. C. Cameron letter to Governor Joseph M. Brown, J. E. Chapman affidavit, Georgia Governor's Office, Convict and Fugitive Records, Applications for Clemency, Thomas Edgar Stripling, Harris County, Georgia Department of Archives and History, Morrow; W. Y. Atkinson, "Effects of Lynching," *American Lawyer,* February 1898, discussed Stripling without naming him: "Recently a man tried on the charge of murder and convicted of shooting a citizen through the window, as he sat by his own hearthstone at night, confessed also that it was he who tied the rope around the necks of the two men who were lynched in Columbus in 1896. I condemn it and will not apologize for such lawlessness. To exterminate the practice it must be made odious and dangerous. The penalty should be the scorn of the people and the punishment of the law."

87 "substitute policeman": City Directory, Columbus, GA, 1896.

88 "I'd do it again": *Columbus Daily Enquirer,* March 5, 1911.

88 Sambo Gordon–Josh Caldwell shootings: *Columbus Ledger,* August 20, 1911.

89 "I got you. I got you, Mr. Sambo." And Sambo said back, "I got you, too, Josh": Ibid.

89 In the matter of Jule Howard: *Columbus Daily Enquirer,* June 11 and 13, February 24, November 28, June 14, and March 12, 1907; Bryant's affidavit, *Savannah Tribune,* August 22, 1908; *Harris County Journal,* March 8, 1907. News accounts quoted Bryant as saying that Howard was upset that Huck-

aby was playing with a little "ginger colored baby" and ignored Howard's orders to leave it alone, saying these were "his" Negroes.

Chapter Ten: Brazen Iniquity

91 "Brazen Iniquity": Governor W. J. Northen, in a 1907 speech to the Evangelical Ministers Association in Atlanta on miscegeny between white men and black women, asked, "When did the ministers of our city ever denounce this brazen iniquity?"

93 Hutchinson obelisk: Georgene Holman, interview, Monmouth, IL, November 1999.

93 Joseph Edgar Biggs: Interview with Alfonso Biggs, Columbus, Georgia, December 1995.

93 "children of color": Bureau of the Census, Fifth Census of the United States, 1830, Greene County, Georgia.

94 "let our ladies alone": Crystal N. Feimster, *Southern Horrors: Women and the Politics of Rape and Lynching* (Harvard University Press, 2011), 53.

94 "Louisiana anti-miscegenation movement": *Columbus Daily Enquirer*, September 24, 1886.

94 "all on the other foot": Tera W. Hunter, *To 'Joy My Freedom: Southern Black Women's Lives and Labors After the Civil War* (Harvard University Press, 1998), 34.

Chapter Eleven: Heroines

96 Ida B. Wells speech: *Columbus Sunday Herald,* February 17, 1900.

97 "nasty-minded mulatress": W. Fitzhugh Brundage, ed., *Under Sentence of Death: Lynching in the South* (University of North Carolina Press, 1997), 305.

97 Wells's investigation of Hose lynching: David Levering Lewis, *W. E. B. Du Bois: Biography of a Race, 1868–1919* (Henry Holt, 1993).

98 "colored girls of the South": Anna Julia Cooper, *The Voice of Anna Julia Cooper: Including a Voice from the South and Other Important Essays, Papers, and Letters* (Rowman & Littlefield, 1998), 61.

98 "I knew he was a cousin": Brit Williams's brother Alfred, a successful Raleigh businessman, lived close to his Haywood cousins. It was to Alfred that the six Williams brothers turned for advice as young men.

99 "Without wealth": Cooper, *Voice*, 97. Copies of Cooper's book were sent to various white Haywood relatives, some of whom burned them. Interview with Betsy Haywood Foard, Raleigh, NC.

100 "the painful, patient": Cooper, *Voice*, 202.

102 "a Haywood cousin": Governor Charles Manly refers to Haywoods as "cousin" in letters in the Haywood Collection, University of North Carolina.

102 "Alex Manly . . . a descendant": Ray Stannard Baker, *Following the Color Line: American Negro Citizenship in the Progressive Era* (Harper, 1964), 160–61.

102 "a Big Burly Black Brute": Philip Dray, *At the Hands of Persons Unknown: The Lynching of Black America* (Random House, 2003), 125.

102 "a lot of carping hypocrites": Ibid.

104 "hyenas," "no federal aspects": Anna J. Cooper, "The Ethics of the Negro Question," delivered at the Friends' General Conference, Asbury Park, NJ, September 5, 1902.

104 "young colored girls" . . . their "rightful prey": "Lynching from a Negro's Point of View," *North American Review* 178 (June 1904): 865.

Chapter Twelve: Race Wars

105 Atlanta riot: Mark Bauerlein, *Negrophobia: A Race Riot in Atlanta, 1906* (Encounter Books, 2002).

105 "seeking European settlers": Efforts to replace black labor with Europeans were led by Columbusite Gunby Jordan. *Columbus Daily Enquirer,* August 21, 1910.

107 "Mob of 2,000 gathered": Bauerlein, *Negrophobia*; Crystal N. Feimster, *Southern Horrors: Women and the Politics of Rape and Lynching* (Harvard University Press, 2011), 99.

108 "calls for . . . castration": Bauerlein, *Negrophobia*, 100.

108 "Scripture Justifies Lynching": *Harris County Journal,* September 28, 1906, 1.

109 "touched on political matters": David Levering Lewis, *W. E. B. Du Bois: Biography of a Race, 1868–1919* (Henry Holt, 1993). 355. An article on the same subject by Du Bois on assignment for *McClure's Magazine* was, in the words of the publisher to the author, "destroyed." Ibid. 356.

110 Du Bois and George Foster Peabody: John Dittmer, *Black Georgia in the Progressive Era: 1900–1920* (University of Illinois Press, 1977), 157.

110 Information on Northen's crusade: David Fort Godschalk, *Veiled Visions: The 1906 Atlanta Race Riot and the Reshaping of American Race Relations* (University of North Carolina Press, 2005).

111 "the keeping of negro concubines by white men": *Macon Telegraph,* January 28, 1908.

114 "100 armed negroes": *Atlanta Constitution,* June 3, 1899.

117 "neat cottage": Ray Stannard Baker, *Following the Color Line: American Negro Citizenship in the Progressive Era* (Harper, 1964), 165.

117 "The hatred and fear of such relations": Ibid. 168.

Chapter Thirteen: Clutch of Circumstance

121 "fluffy little baby": *Harris County Journal,* August 6, 1909.

121 "to my wife": Dedication in Arthur L. Hardy, *The Clutch of Circumstance* (Mayhew Publishing, 1909).

122 "[T]he book of the decade": *Harris County Journal,* December 31, 1909.

Chapter Fourteen: Special Court

124 Judge Marcus Beck information: Obituary in *Columbus Enquirer,* January 22, 1943; Louise Calhoun Barfield, *History of Harris County, Georgia, 1827–1961* (Columbus Office Supply, 1961), 466.

125 "scalawags": *Macon Telegraph,* February 6, 1909, 3.

126 Rev. Ashby Jones: *Columbus Daily Enquirer,* October 2, 1906.

127 YMCA: *Columbus Daily Enquirer,* July 31, 1906.

128 "denounce a class of young men": *Columbus Daily Enquirer,* January 13, 1907.

130 "Georgia the number one lynching state": Between 1877 and 1950, 586 people were lynched in Georgia, more than any other state. *Lynching in*

America: Confronting the Legacy of Racial Terror. (Equal Justice Institute, 2015).

131 Judge Gilbert's belief that blacks were incapable of full citizenship: Gilbert's unpublished manuscript: Columbus State University Archives: S. Price Gilbert Collection.

131 "meet it with cold lead": *Columbus Daily Enquirer,* February 6, 1909, 3.

131 Shooting of Jailer Phelts: *Columbus Daily Enquirer,* December 13, 17, and 18, 1910; February 7 and 27, 1911.

132 "a man and not a pea-hen politician for a judge": *Columbus Ledger,* February 15, 1911, 5.

135 "I don't propose to be the engine": John Dittmer, *Black Georgia in the Progressive Era: 1900–1920* (University of Illinois Press, 1977), 139.

136 Columbus lynching: *Columbus Daily Enquirer,* May 30, 1896 (Howard appeals to mob) and June 2 and 7, 1896; *Atlanta Constitution,* June 2, 1896, 1; *Savannah Tribune,* June 6, 1896; *Columbus Daily Enquirer,* November 13 and December 5, 1890 (Bickerstaff trial).

142 Dynamite: *Atlanta Constitution,* June 3, 1896.

Chapter Fifteen: The Die Is Cast

146 "Negro conspiracy": In an August 20, 2004, e-mail, Jimmy Kidd, Sambo Gordon's great-grandson, wrote the author: "The community thought it was a planned killing so they retaliated with the hanging of many blacks in Harris county, at what was to become known as the hanging tree. Thank goodness that era is over with."

146 "Before Day Clubs": *Atlanta Constitution,* September 13, 1904.

146 "race war": "Harris County Scare," *Columbus Daily Enquirer,* February 20, 21, 1895.

146 lynching of blind preacher: *Columbus Daily Enquirer,* June 22 and 25, 1909; *Augusta Chronicle,* June 24, 1909; Will Campbell, *Forty Acres and a Goat* (Peachtree, 1986).

148 Jim Crutchfield's prison letters sent to Cataula: RG21, Prison Records, National Archives and Records Administration, East Point, GA.

151 "Deeper than physical fear must the blow be struck": *The Crisis,* January 1912.

152 Edgefield, South Carolina: Orville Vernon Burton, *In My Father's House Are Many Mansions: Family and Community in Edgefield, S.C.* (University of North Carolina Press, 1987); Joel Williamson, *New People: Miscegenation and Mulattoes in the New South* (Free Press, 1980).

155 "Georgia's own Rebecca Felton": Felton's *Atlanta Journal* columns made inroads in white women's consciousness about white men's predations and use of political power to protect themselves.

Chapter Sixteen: The Lynching

156 "best catch the afternoon train": told to the author by her father in 1953.

158 Taft and state dinner: Library of Congress, Manuscripts Division, William Howard Taft Papers, Reel 125, January 1, 1910– March 21, 1912.

159 Miss Lula and Yankee torches: Lula Mobley's memories are in Louise Cal-

houn Barfield, *History of Harris County, Georgia, 1827–1961* (Columbus Office Supply, 1961), 468.

161 "Fannie Graddick": interview with Lester Gore, Hamilton, GA, May 30, 1996.

161 "never be discouraged": "W. D. Upshaw Speaks," *Harris County Journal*, April 13, 1911. The paper added, "The problem will be solved when we come in closer touch with each other."

162 John Moore blamed Gene Harrington: "each of them putting the killing of Hadley off on the other," *Columbus Ledger*, January 23, 1912, 1.

162 "Pull the rope": Author's conversations with cousins Emily Williams, Hamilton, GA, May 30, 1996, and Mary Williams, Columbus, GA, May 18, 1996.

163 Alex Copeland's recital: *Harris County Journal*, March 18, 1910.

164 Major W. W. Thomas: Rebecca Burns and June Dobbs Butts, *Rage in the Gate City: The Story of the 1906 Atlanta Race Riot* (University of Georgia Press, 2009).

165 "rob the post office": *Harris County Journal*, February 1, 1912.

166 "like a banshee": Interview with Horace Gordon, Columbus, GA, October 7, 1997.

Chapter Seventeen: "So Quietly Was the Work Done"

167 "A perfect quietude prevailed": *Columbus Daily Enquirer*, January 24, 1912, 4.

168 "not been able to get any negroes to touch them": *Columbus Ledger*, January 23, 1912, 1.

170 "at the hands of unknown parties": Coroner's report, January 23, 1912, Harris County Courthouse.

171 Zeke Robinson press conference: *Columbus Ledger*, January 24, 1912.

172 "*Cut down this tree*": Interviews with Horace Gordon and Louise Teel, Columbus, GA, October 7, 1997.

172 "always anxious . . . to prevent mob violence": *Columbus Daily Enquirer*, January 23, 1912, 4.

172 "fearing no lynching": *Macon Telegraph*, January 23, 2012, 1.

173 "Proof to convict had not been secured": *Atlanta Constitution*, January 24, 1912.

174 "and comely": *New York Evening News*, January 23, 1912, 1.

175 "*Advance*": February 15, 1912.

175 "unwanted attentions" to the "negro girl": *The Crisis*, March 1912.

176 "guinea pigs": *Chicago Defender*, January 27, 1912, 1.

176 "promised investigations": Governor Joseph M. Brown letter to William Henry Fleming, March 13, 1912, Georgia Department of Archives and History, Morrow. An African American, E. D. Rosewood, wrote President Taft requesting an intervention in the Hamilton lynching. Assistant Attorney General Harr replied that the federal government was "without power" to intervene." Kidada Williams, *They Left Great Marks on Me: African American Testimonies of Racial Violence from Emancipation to World War I* (New York University Press, 2012), 153.

177 "Limits of Negro Endurance": *The Twentieth Century*, March 1912.

177 "only way to win respect": *The Twentieth Century*, March 1912.

177 "cowardly white woman": Ibid.

177 "Divine Rights": *The Crisis*, March 1912.

178 "heroes and martyrs": An editorial in the March 1912 issue of *The Crisis* called upon black men to "kill lecherous white invaders of their homes and then take their lynching gladly like men." The issue included an oath for black men to swear to defend black women against insults and injury by any man, black or white; the oath was reprinted in countless black publications.

178 "the massacre . . . permitted in the shadow of its courthouse": *Columbus Ledger,* January 26, 1912, 4.

179 "justification for the terrible act": *Harris County Journal*, January 25, 1912, 1.

179 "A new book": David Rose's *The Big Eddy Club: The Stocking Stranglings and Southern Justice* (New Press, 2007). His account was taken from William Winn's series on Columbus-area lynchings in the *Columbus Ledger-Enquirer*, January 25 through January 31, 1987.

Chapter Eighteen: Parties Unknown

182 "overshadows all other burdens of the court this session": *Harris County Journal*, April 4, 1913.

182 "indictment of a Negro": Ibid.

183 "every child in town": *Harris County Journal*, April 11, 1912.

183 "We regret and condemn the Lynching": Grand Jury Presentment to Superior Court, April Term 1912, Harris County Courthouse.

184 "They conquered self": *Harris County Journal*, July 10, 1912.

184 "Johnie Moore's mother, Lula": *The State vs. Lula Moore, Murder*, Minutes, Harris County Superior Court, April Term 1912, Harris County Courthouse.

186 "prominent citizens": *The Crisis*, July 1912.

186 Taft speaks out: *Springfield* (Mass.) *Daily News*, June 27, 1912, 12.

187 "just a little black nigger": *Columbus Daily Enquirer*, August 14, 1912, 1.

189 "the negro is an incident in the circumstances": *Macon Telegraph*, August 16, 1912.

Chapter Nineteen: ". . . Died with Their Boots On"

191 "Hatfields and McCoys": *Columbus Ledger*, January 28, 1912.

192 The Bible verse from 1 Samuel: "And I tell him that I am about to punish his house for ever, for the iniquity which he knew, because his sons were blaspheming God, and he did not restrain them. Therefore I swear to the house of Eli that the iniquity of Eli's house shall not be expiated by sacrifice or offering forever."

196 "strung on a trot line like a fish": *Columbus Ledger*, July 16, 1915.

196 "Moonshine Mafia": Interview with Horace Gordon, Columbus, GA, October 7, 1997.

197 triple hanging: *Columbus Daily Enquirer*, October 17, 1915.

197 "River Killing": *Columbus Ledger*, July 6 and 7, 1915; *Columbus Daily*

Enquirer, July 2 and 3, 1915. Anonymous letter courtesy of members of victims' family.

Chapter Twenty: Roaring Twenties
199 Tip Top: *State of Georgia vs. Louis Murray,* Governor—Convict and Fugitive Records—Applications for clemency, 1858–1942, Louis Murray, 1921, Georgia Department of Archives and History, Morrow; *State of Georgia vs. Cecil Cook,* Court Documents, Harris County Courthouse.
201 Whitehead information: "Tragedy over Negress," *Columbus Ledger,* August 24, 1921, 1; "White Man Loses Life over Negress," *Columbus Daily Enquirer,* August 25, 1921.
203 "miniature Bat Masterson": *Columbus Daily Enquirer,* May 8, 1921.
203 killing of bootlegger: *Columbus Ledger,* May 30, September 10, and November 22, 1922.
203 Information on Julian Harris: Gregory Lisby and William F. Mugleston, *Someone Had to Be Hated: Julian LaRose Harris: A Biography* (Carolina Academic Press, 2004); Papers of Julian LaRose Harris and Julia Harris, Manuscript, Archives, and Rare Book Library, Emory University, Atlanta, GA.
203 Information on Ku Klux Klan in Columbus: At the time of the Harrises' stint, there were about five hundred Klansmen in the city. The organization was endorsed by the chief of police and the mayor, and it was permitted the use of the armory at police headquarters for its meetings. "Defying the Klan," Thomas Boyd, *The Forum,* July 1926.

Chapter Twenty-One: The Ladies' Ultimatum
207 "we who could prevent it": Lily Hardy Hammond, *In Black and White: An Interpretation of the South* (University of Georgia Press, 2008). Hammond also wrote columns for the *Atlanta Journal* in 1913.
208 background on black and white women's political work: Crystal N. Feimster, *Southern Horrors: Women and the Politics of Rape and Lynching* (Harvard University Press, 2011).
211 Anti-Lynching Crusaders pamphlet: Library of Congress, Manuscripts Division, NAACP Papers.
211 "Governor Hugh Dorsey's Inaugural Address": *Columbus Daily Enquirer,* June 26, 1921, 5.

Chapter Twenty-Two: The Curse Continues
214 Ernest Farley kills Bud Mobley: "Mobley Slayer Still at Large," *Columbus Daily Enquirer,* February 5, 1929; *Macon Telegraph,* February 7, 1929.
216 "In 1934 . . . Native American wife": The year my mother and grandmother helped run off my father's Indian wife and stepchild, Anna Julia Cooper engaged a lawyer to obtain information about her paternity. Ernest Haywood, the nephew of Cooper's father, "Wash" Haywood, and the grandson of my great-uncle Albert Williams, replied candidly but curtly that "Wash had one child by his slave Hannah without benefit of Clergy," confirming what Cooper had long known. Among Cooper's papers at Howard University's Spingarn Library is a copy of the obituary for her grandmother Eliza Eagles Asaph

Williams Haywood. It was Eliza who wondered in her journal whether women and Negroes might not be as smart as men, given equal opportunity. Anna Julia Cooper Collection, Spingarn Library, Howard University.

216 Elias Beall in Alabama: John T. Ellisor, *The Second Creek War: Interethnic Conflict and Collusion on a Collapsing Frontier* (University of Nebraska Press, 2010), 215.

217 "Cousin John Cash": "A White Man Shot in a Negro Church," *Columbus Daily Enquirer*, June 30, 1903.

Chapter Twenty-Three: Dad Doug

222 ASWPL: Jacqueline Dowd Hall, *Revolt Against Chivalry: Jessie Daniel Ames and the Women's Campaign against Lynching* (Columbia University Press, 1993).

223 FBI in Walton County: Laura Wexler, *Fire in a Canebrake: The Last Mass Lynching in America* (Scribner, 2003).

231 "the first white person": It is likely that May Brit Cramer was inspired to teach in a black school by her cousin J. Curtis Dixon, who was superintendent of Negro schools in Georgia for many years. Dixon was a director of the Rosenwald Fund and the Rockefeller General Education Board, both of which funded much of black education in Georgia for the first half of the twentieth century. When Cramer was a young girl in Hamilton, Dixon made headlines when Governor Eugene Talmadge kicked him and others off the Board of Chancellors of the University of Georgia for allegedly supporting integration and intermarriage. "Reminiscences of J. Curtis Dixon," 1967, Oral History Collection, Columbia University.

Chapter Twenty-Four: Guilt and Innocence

240 "cut the baby right out of her belly": Interview with A. J. Murphy, Hamilton, GA, November 30, 2003.

Chapter Twenty-Five: Enslaved by History

246 Albert Curry execution: *State of Georgia vs. Albert Curry*, October Term, Superior Court, 1958; *Macon Telegraph*, July 20, 1958, 2.

250 Definitive account of Columbus serial murders: David Rose, *The Big Eddy Club: The Stocking Stranglings and Southern Justice* (New Press, 2007).

255 "Perhaps it was distant cousin Anna Julia": At the age of one hundred Cooper published a poem entitled "Grapes from Thorns," asking to be remembered as "somebody's teacher on vacation . . . resting for the Fall opening." She died six years later. Born into slavery, she lived to see Martin Luther King, Jr.'s March on Washington. Louise Daniel Hutchison, *Anna J. Cooper: A Voice from the South* (Smithsonian Institution Press, 1982).

SELECTED BIBLIOGRAPHY

Alexander, Adele Logan. *Ambiguous Lives: Free Women of Color in Rural Georgia, 1789–1879*. University of Arkansas Press, 2009.

Alexander, Michelle. *The New Jim Crow: Mass Incarceration in the Age of Colorblindness*. New Press, 2010.

Allen, James, and Hilton Als. *Without Sanctuary: Lynching Photography in America*. Twin Palms, 2000.

Ansley, Mrs. J. J. *History of the Georgia W.C.T.U., 1833–1907*. Gilbert Printing Co., 1914.

Baker, Ray Stannard. *Following the Color Line: American Negro Citizenship in the Progressive Era*. Harper Torchbooks, 1964.

Barfield, Louise Calhoun. *History of Harris County, Georgia, 1827–1961*. Columbus Office Supply, 1961.

Bauerlein, Mark. *Negrophobia: A Race Riot in Atlanta, 1906*. Encounter Books, 2002.

Blackmon, Douglas A. *Slavery by Another Name: The Re-Enslavement of Black Americans from the Civil War to World War II*. Anchor Books, 2009.

Blight, David. *Race and Reunion: The Civil War in American Memory*. Belknap Press, 2001.

Brawner, Darnell L. *Whither Thou Goest*. Vantage, 1991.

Brown, Mary Jane. *Eradicating This Evil: Women in the American Anti-Lynching Movement, 1892–1940*. Garland, 2000.

Brundage, W. Fitzhugh. *Lynching in the New South: Georgia and Virginia, 1880–1930*. University of Illinois Press, 1993.

Brundage, W. Fitzhugh, ed. *Under Sentence of Death: Lynching in the South*. University of North Carolina Press, 1997.

Brundage, W. Fitzhugh, ed. *Where These Memories Grow*. University of North Carolina Press, 2000.

Bryant, Jonathan M. *How Curious a Land: Conflict and Change in Greene County, Georgia, 1850–1885*. 2nd ed. University of North Carolina Press, 2004.

Burton, Orville Vernon. *In My Father's House Are Many Mansions: Family and Community in Edgefield, S.C.* University of North Carolina Press, 1987.

Cameron, James. *A Time of Terror: A Survivor's Story.* Black Classic Press, 1982.

Cash, W. J. *The Mind of the South.* Vintage Books, 1941.

Cecelski, David S., and Timothy B. Tyson. *Democracy Betrayed: The Wilmington Race Riot of 1898 and Its Legacy.* University of North Carolina Press, 1998.

Chesnutt, Charles W. *The Marrow of Tradition.* Houghton Mifflin, 1901.

Clinton, Catherine. *The Plantation Mistress: Woman's World in the Old South.* Random House, 1984.

Cobb, James C. *Georgia Odyssey: A Short History of the State.* University of Georgia Press, 2008.

Cooper, Anna Julia. *A Voice from the South.* Schomburg Library of Nineteenth-Century Black Women Writers. Oxford University Press, 1988.

Cooper, Anna Julia. *The Voice of Anna Julia Cooper: Including A Voice from the South and Other Important Essays, Papers and Letters.* Rowman & Littlefield, 2000.

Curtin, Mary Ellen. *Black Prisoners and their World, Alabama, 1865–1900.* University Press of Virginia, 2000.

Dailey, Jane, Glenda Elizabeth Gilmore, and Bryant Simon, eds. *Jumpin' Jim Crow: Southern Politics from Civil War to Civil Rights.* Princeton University Press, 2000.

DeWolf, Thomas Norman, and Sharon Leslie Morgan. *Gather at the Table: The Healing Journey of a Daughter of Slavery and a Son of the Slave Trade.* Beacon Press, 2013.

Dittmer, John. *Black Georgia in the Progressive Era: 1900–1920.* University of Illinois Press, 1977.

Dray, Philip. *At the Hands of Persons Unknown: The Lynching of Black America.* Random House, 2003.

Egerton, John. *Speak Now Against the Day: The Generation Before the Civil Rights Movement in the South.* Alfred A. Knopf, 1995.

Feimster, Crystal N. *Southern Horrors: Women and the Politics of Rape and Lynching.* Harvard University Press, 2011.

Foner, Eric. *Reconstruction: America's Unfinished Revolution, 1863–1877.* Harper & Row, 1988.

Fox-Genovese, Elizabeth. *Within the Plantation Household: Black and White Women of the Old South.* University of North Carolina Press, 1988.

Giddings, Paula J. *Ida: A Sword Among Lions: Ida B. Wells and the Campaign Against Lynching.* Harper, 2009.

Giddings, Paula J. *When and Where I Enter: The Impact of Black Women on Race and Sex in America.* William Morrow, 2007.

Gilmore, Glenda Elizabeth. *Gender and Jim Crow: Women and the Politics of White Supremacy in North Carolina, 1896–1920.* University of North Carolina Press, 1996.

Gladney, Margaret Rose, ed. *How Am I to Be Heard? Letters of Lillian Smith.* University of North Carolina Press, 1996.

Godshalk, David Fort. *Veiled Visions: The 1906 Atlanta Race Riot and the Reshaping of American Race Relations.* University of North Carolina Press, 2005.

Gordon-Reed, Annette. *The Hemingses of Monticello: An American Family.* W. W. Norton, 2009.

Grant, Donald L. *The Way It Was in the South: The Black Experience in Georgia.* Birch Lane Press, 2001.

Grantham, Dewey W. *Hoke Smith and the Politics of the New South.* Louisiana State University Press, 1967.

Hall, Jacqueline Dowd. *Revolt Against Chivalry: Jessie Daniel Ames and the Women's Campaign Against Lynching.* Columbia University Press, 1993.

Hammond, Lily Hardy. *In Black and White: An Interpretation of the South.* University of Georgia Press, 2008.

Hardy, Arthur L. *The Clutch of Circumstance.* Mayhew, 1909.

Herron, Carolivia, ed. *Selected Works of Angelina Weld Grimké.* Oxford University Press, 1991.

Hollis, James. *Hauntings: Dispelling the Ghosts Who Run Our Lives.* Chiron, 2013.

Hunter, Tera W. *To 'Joy My Freedom: Southern Black Women's Lives and Labors After the Civil War.* Harvard University Press, 1998.

Hutchinson, Louise Daniel. *Anna J. Cooper: A Voice from the South.* Smithsonian Institution Press, 1981.

Ifill, Sherilyn A. *On the Courthouse Lawn: Confronting the Legacy of Lynching in the Twenty-first Century.* Beacon Press, 2007.

Irving, Debbie. *Waking Up White and Finding Myself in the Story of Race.* Elephant Room Press, 2014.

Jones, Jacqueline. *Labor of Love, Labor of Sorrow: Black Women, Work and the Family from Slavery to the Present.* Basic Books, 2010.

Journal of the Proceedings of the Constitutional Convention of the People of Georgia Held in the City of Atlanta in the Months of December, 1867, and January, February and March, 1868. And Ordinances and Resolutions Adopted. E. H. Pughe Book and Job Printer, 1868.

Lewis, David Levering. *W. E. B. Du Bois: Biography of a Race, 1868–1919.* Henry Holt, 1993.

Lisby, Gregory, and William F. Mugleston. *Someone Had to Be Hated: Julian LaRose Harris: A Biography.* Carolina Academic Press, 2004.

Loney, Randolph. *Dreams of the Tattered Man: Stories from Georgia's Death Row.* Wm B. Eerdmans, 2001.

Mahan, Joseph B. *Columbus: Georgia's Fall Line "Trading Town."* Windsor Publications, 1986.

Majette, Vara A. *White Blood.* Stratford, 1924.

Martin, John H. *The History of Columbus, Georgia.* Thomas Gilbert, 1874.

May, Vivian M. *Anna Julia Cooper: Visionary Black Feminist.* Routledge, 2007.

McLean, William Hunger. *Alexander Beall—1649–1744—of Maryland: One Line of Descent in America.* Fort Worth Genealogical Society, 1977.

McWhorter, Diane. *Carry Me Home: Birmingham, Alabama: The Climactic Battle of the Civil Rights Revolution.* Simon & Schuster, 2013.

Mitchell, Koritha. *Living with Lynching: African American Lynching Plays, Performance, and Citizenship, 1890–1930.* University of Illinois Press, 2011.

Moore, Albert Burton. *Conscription and Conflict in the Confederacy.* University of South Carolina Press, 1996.

O'Donovan, Susan Eva. *Becoming Free in the Cotton South.* Harvard University Press, 2010.

Oney, Steve. *And the Dead Shall Rise: The Murder of Mary Phagen and the Lynching of Leo Frank*. Pantheon, 2004.

Painter, Nell Irvin. *Southern History Across the Color Line*. University of North Carolina Press, 2002.

Patterson, William L. *We Charge Genocide: The Crime of Government Against the Negro People*. International Publishers, 1970.

Read, Warren. *The Lyncher in Me: A Search for Redemption in the Face of History*. Borealis Books, 2008.

Reese, Albert L., Jr. *The Changing Years: A History of the Harris County Schools, 1955–1976*. Reese, 1978.

Reidy, Joseph P. *From Slavery to Agrarian Capitalism in the Cotton Plantation South: Central Georgia, 1800–1880*. University of North Carolina Press, 1992.

Rose, David. *The Big Eddy Club: The Stocking Stranglings and Southern Justice*. New Press, 2007.

Shaw, Barton. *The Wool-Hat Boys: Georgia's Populist Party, 1892–1910*. Louisiana State University Press, 1984.

Smith, Lillian. *Killers of the Dream*. W. W. Norton, 1994.

Smith, Lillian. *Strange Fruit*. Reynal & Hitchcock, 1944.

Stevenson, Bryan. *Just Mercy: A Story of Justice and Redemption*. Spiegel & Grau, 2014.

Telfair, Nancy [Louise Jones Dubose]. *A History of Columbus, Georgia, 1828–1928*. Historical Publishing, 1929.

Tolnay, Stewart E., and E. M. Beck. *A Festival of Violence: An Analysis of Southern Lynchings, 1882–1930*. University of Illinois Press, 1995.

Weingarten, Theodore. *All God's Dangers: The Life of Nate Shaw*. University of Chicago Press, 1974.

Wexler, Laura. *Fire in a Canebrake: The Last Mass Lynching in America*. Scribner, 2003.

White, Gregory C. *A History of the 31st Georgia Volunteer Infantry: This Most Bloody and Cruel Drama*. Butternut and Blue, 1977.

White, Helen, and Redding S. Sugg, Jr. *From the Mountain: An Anthology of the Magazine Successively Titled Pseudopodia, the North Georgia Review, and South Today*. Memphis State University Press, 1972.

Wiencek, Henry. *The Hairstons: An American Family in Black and White*. St. Martin's, 2000.

Williams, David. *Bitterly Divided: The South's Inner Civil War*. New Press, 2010.

Williams, Kidada. *They Left Great Marks on Me: African American Testimonies of Racial Violence from Emancipation to World War I*. New York University Press, 2012.

Williams, Sarah Stone. *The Man from London Town*. Neale, 1906.

Williamson, Joel. *A Rage for Order: Black-White Relations in the American South Since Emancipation*. Oxford University Press, 1986.

Williamson, Joel. *New People: Miscegenation and Mulattoes in the New South*. Free Press, 1980.

Willoughby, Lynn. *Flowing Through Time: A History of the Lower Chattahoochee River*. University of Alabama Press, 1999.

Wood, Amy Louise. *Lynching and Spectacle: Witnessing Racial Violence in America, 1890–1940*. University of North Carolina Press, 2011

Woodward, C. Vann. *The Burden of Southern History*. Vintage Books, 1968.

INDEX